THE INVESTIGATOR

THE INVESTIGATOR

Drugs, Guns, Gems and Porn:
Inside the Secretive World
of Customs Investigation

Michael Knox

Milo Books Ltd

Published in September 2016 by Milo Books

ISBN 978-1-908479-89-1

Typeset by Jayne Walsh

Printed in Great Britain by CPI Group (UK) Ltd, Croydon, CR0 4YY

MILO BOOKS LTD

www.milobooks.com

Contents

Introduction

WHEN MY GRANDDAUGHTER EMILY was fourteen years old, the subject of my past career came up for the first time. I was taken aback when she expressed genuine surprise that I had worked for HM Customs and Excise; she said she thought I was an artist. Well I've been many things in my time, and the word 'artist' may have been appended to some of them, but a professional fine artist? Hardly. The reason for her ignorance, apparently, was not only did my daughter Julie not talk to her children about me, but also because when they were young I had painted a watercolour of Treasure Island – which I renamed Teddy's Island – with my three children's toys on the beach, in the sea and on their toy boats. This had somehow been passed down the line and ended up on Emily's wall. It's still there to this day.

Her sudden curiosity allowed me to wax lyrical about a thirty-seven-year career that had given me so much pleasure and reward, especially in the investigation service. I regaled Emily with stories about how I was arrested by the police in Switzerland when collecting evidence against the biggest watch smuggler we had ever tackled; about travelling to a cannabis farm in Morocco only to be stopped and surrounded on the way back by a band of desperadoes; about my visit to Rolls-Royce where I thought I had discovered a fraud involving the despatch of aero engines to South Africa in breach of a government embargo at that time, leading to an interview with a Minister of Defence. And so on…

Needless to say her fourteen-year-old eyes glazed over and I realised why her mother had been so discreet. Emily was, however, tickled to hear about my address to the annual Association of Chief Police Officers (ACPO) conference in Manchester in which I mentioned the use of sniffer pigs by German police in the fight against drugs. All the UK police forces were there, as were all of the media. As soon as I had finished my talk, I was deluged with a posse of reporters anxious to find out all about this new revolutionary anti-drugs method. All I could do was fend them off, explaining that, although it was true, it was meant as something of a joke because I wanted to cap it by wondering where we were going to house all the pigs at Heathrow Airport. The story captured the headlines the following morning, eclipsing, to the profound annoyance of ACPO, many much more worthy and important matters. I was summoned to see my Chief, Douglas Jordan, to whom they had complained, and he asked me for an explanation. All I could tell him was that one of my team had read about it in a German newspaper. The story wouldn't go away, but fortunately some days later an intrepid *Daily Telegraph* reporter found the policeman and his pigs in Germany and ran the full story. My bacon, as it were, was saved.

Nevertheless, this incident with Emily led me to think seriously about writing an account of my work, initially for my present and future offspring. Emily has two of her own children now, bringing the number of my grandchildren to nine; who knows where all this will end? So here are some of the more interesting cases out of over one hundred I was involved in during sixteen years in investigation. I also hope that, for a wider readership, *The Investigator* provides an insight into some of the more unknown, arcane and clandestine practices in the world of Customs – without breaching the Official Secrets Act, of course. I also couldn't recount my time in HMCE without mentioning an even more intriguing period, for me, when I became head of the Single Market Unit in 1990. This led to a personal presentation to John Major in the Cabinet Room on our approach to the removal of frontiers at the end of 1992; and a lengthy paper on VAT policy for the Single European Market for one of the three Chancellors of the Exchequer I advised, Norman Lamont, giving me a front row seat on the workings of a senior government minister. I never thought at the time how, twenty-five years later, much of that work might be undone by the so-called 'Brexit' referendum vote.

This is a true story. A number of people or their names have not been included to respect their privacy. Some names – very few – have been changed to protect the guilty.

Michael Knox

1

False Friends

T HE SLEDGEHAMMER STRUCK THE door almost before I was able to shout the obligatory warning. I could see that Detective Constable Prichard was in no mood to observe the usual courtesies as he swung the hammer a second time, splintering the panel above the lock. I was furious with him. This was a Customs, not police, operation. We were supposed to be taking the lead, but Prichard was acting as if he was in charge. Six o'clock in the morning was not a time when the occupant was going to be at his liveliest, especially this type. We had the time to go through the normal drill of knocking on his door; we didn't have to smash it in.

At least we were in. As the door swung open and crashed against the wall, a dazed young man greeted the onrush of Customs and police officers charging into the small entrance hall of the flat. I confronted this pale, open-mouthed figure while the others pushed past into a large living room and dispersed into the two bedrooms and tiny kitchen. I held up a worn, burgundy-coloured wallet and shouted above the din: 'Customs! This is a Writ of Assistance. We have reason to believe …' But my words were drowned out by the noise coming from the other rooms. I ushered the man into the living room, where officers were stepping over bodies scattered about the floors in various postures and stages of undress. It looked like the London Underground during the Blitz; but it didn't smell like it. The sickly-sweet stench of vomit, intermingled with sweat, alcohol and cannabis, invaded our nostrils. The contrast with the icy-fresh air of the clear winter morning outside could not have been more acute.

The bodies began to take shape: to move, groan, curse.

'On your feet, sunshine.'

'Ahhh, shit, man.'

'Come on, rise and shine. We've got work to do.'

A stick insect of a girl, sixteen at most, wearing only a pair of torn knickers and two butterfly tattoos on her small breasts, stood up and began screaming at one of the policemen, who had just tipped the contents of her bag onto the wooden floor.

'What the fuck do you think you're doing? Who the hell are youse lot? Leave me things alone, you bastard!'

DC Prichard, still holding the sledgehammer loosely by his side and looking much like one of the motley crew we were facing in his scruffy jeans and crumpled shirt, stepped roughly over two comatose bundles in the centre of the room to reach the girl. One of the bundles groaned as his outstretched arm took the weight of the detective's boot. Prichard glanced at the officer holding the girl's bag. The officer winked. Prichard turned to the girl and said menacingly, 'Clean your mouth out, girlie. In my day young ladies were taught manners. Now just calm down and tell me your name.'

Her pale, pockmarked face stared defiantly up at the large frame of the policeman. They made an incongruous pairing. She was half his size but every bit his equal in aggression. 'Julie. What's it to you?' she spat out.

'Well, Julie,' said Prichard, lowering his face to look straight into her eyes, 'this is not your lucky day. You've been caught in possession. You're nicked.'

This was not going at all right. The information had been specific: two addresses in Streatham and Clapham used as stores, with only a caretaker to guard over £10,000-worth of cannabis resin in each place. The informant was reputed to be reliable. So what the devil were all these toerags doing here? Before I could get my head around the question, my senior colleague, Don Holmans, emerged from one of the bedrooms and announced that there were thirteen people in the flat – six men and seven women. By this time, judging by the noise level, they were all awake and most were alert, or as alert as they were ever going to be that day.

'Now listen, everybody.' I tried to raise my voice above the hubbub. 'We're going to search this place from top to bottom. If you've anything to tell us, do so now. It could save us all a lot of time and grief.'

'You could tell us who you are please?' The soft, cultured voice came from a tall, lean man with a drooping moustache, very much the latest Seventies' fashion accessory, standing by the window. 'We have the right to know.'

'Shut your face!' Prichard shouted across the room at him. 'You …'

'Customs and police,' I interjected, before Prichard could make our job even more difficult. I needed to get the search underway, and Prichard sidelined, to stand any chance of finding what we had come for. Prichard's colleague, DC 'Nobby' Pilcher, was leading the raid on the other house 'to avoid territorial disputes', my boss had said. I was annoyed that he had so untypically given way to the Metropolitan Police Drugs Squad on what was clearly an HM Customs job. The last thing I wanted now was to be upstaged by Pilcher and to come in with only a handful of petty possession charges to show for it. I didn't like working with the Flying Squad or the Drugs Squad, and with DC Prichard even less. Their methods were clearly not ours. Their priorities were different. They were not as thorough, especially with searches, a field where I knew Customs excelled. A few collars were enough to satisfy their appetite, it seemed, whatever the quantities involved. And in this crowded situation I had little control over their actions. Had he really caught the girl 'in possession'? I had to find the stash and quickly.

'If you're going to search, we want to be sure you don't stitch us up.' It was the cultured voice again. 'I've been here before and I don't want to end up in the slammer for something I didn't do.'

Prichard looked as though he was going to burst.

'Don, make sure that everyone sees everything that we do,' I said. 'Now let's go. Come on jump, to it!' Then I stepped over to the detective. 'Prichard, a word.'

As the officers began opening cupboards and drawers, I took an angry policeman into the hallway. 'Listen to me, Prichard, I don't want this to be a foul-up. We're not here for ounces. We've paid good money for this info. It's got to be right. There should be over ten kilos in this flat.' My reaction was instinctive. This was the first operation I had led since joining the Investigation Branch two years before; the first where I had any real say over proceedings. It was new to me, but I wasn't going to be pushed around by a scruffy copper.

'OK, OK, but what's the point of pussyfooting around?' said Prichard. 'You're all the same, you Customs people, soft as shit. It's not your job, anyway. This is police work.'

'It is the way you're going about it,' I retorted sarcastically, 'but import jobs are ours. Don't forget it.'

'And crime is ours. This is open and shut crime.'

'I'm not standing here arguing the finer points of the law with you. We've got a job to do.'

'So let's get on with it then,' snapped Prichard, making sure he had the last word before turning on his heel and trundling back into the living room in an even fouler mood than before. I stood for a moment as doors banged, people shouted and the swearing level reached new heights. Then I re-entered the room to see carpets and floorboards being lifted. 'It's got to be right, it's bloody well got to be right,' I intoned, swearing under my breath.

THE HEADLINE AND SUBHEADING in that day's London *Evening Standard* were unequivocal: 'Police Swoop: 14 people arrested and £10,000 of drugs seized in police raids.'

'Bastards!'

Several people in the pub turned to look at me.

'It's as if we weren't even there!' I howled.

'Are we not mentioned in the story below?' asked Don Holmans.

I read aloud from the late edition: 'In two coordinated raids on premises in Clapham and Streatham this morning, police arrested a total of fourteen people and took away a quantity of drugs, with an estimated street value of £10,000, from one of the premises.'

'Not our premises,' said Don ruefully.

I continued: 'A man alleged to have been in possession of over ten kilos of drugs at an address off Clapham High Street is helping police with their enquiries, while thirteen persons arrested at the Streatham address were later released on police bail. One of the thirteen told our reporter that he would be suing the police for wilful destruction of property. Chief Inspector Kelaher of the Drugs Squad praised the actions of his officers and said that the cannabis resin had been imported from Morocco but that it had been taken out of circulation before it could do any harm by the swift action of his force.'

Holmans and I looked at each other.

'We were just unlucky,' said Don, trying to mollify me. Although senior to me in service, and more experienced, Holmans – lean, medium height, with a shock of tousled fair hair to go with his rather direct manner – was not usually softer in temperament. But he could see how aroused I was.

'Unlucky? Unlucky, my arse!'

The noise in the pub died away as I pushed my chair back with a thud against the wall and stormed out. Holmans glared back at the curious early evening drinkers until they lost interest in proceedings, then shuffled out after me.

I stood fuming on the pavement outside.

'Tell me, Don, just tell me, why the team led by Pilcher finds a storeman and ten grand's worth of gear, and the team led by Her Majesty's Customs and Excise Investigation Branch finds a load of hopped-up junkies and only the gear the Old Bill brought in with them? Eh?'

Holmans, untypically, decided silence was the best option. I don't think he ever forgot the look on my face, nor the effect this early experience had on my future relations with, and attitudes towards, the Metropolitan Police. I found what came to light about 'Old Bill' over the next few years, my early and most impressionable time in investigation, simply astonishing. This was emphatically not *Dixon of Dock Green*.

2

Baccy, Betting and Booze

'I WANT TO BE a teacher.'

I stared back at the British Army major interviewing me in the recruitment centre in Newcastle without blinking.

'Have you always wanted to be a teacher?'

'For as long as I can remember.'

My memory was clearly faulty, as I had only wanted to be a teacher for a matter of days, since seeing that the highest rank it would be possible to achieve during my National Service was sergeant in the Education Corps. The next highest was as a corporal in the Pay Corps, which was not my cup of tea at all: the pay, yes, but not paying someone else. This was entirely about rank and money, not vocation, but the major swallowed it and put me forward. However, it would also give me an opportunity to see if I was, in fact, cut out to be a teacher.

The very highest rank would of course have come with a commission, but I didn't hold much hope of that. I was from a working class family. My father was an electrical engineer in a factory while my mother was a clerical assistant in the Civil Service, and you didn't get much lower than that in Her Majesty's Government. Commissions in the Army were not for the likes of me in those class-conscious days. My parents had aspirations for me though, pushing me to sit for the public school exams in Newcastle upon Tyne. I managed to pass the entrance tests and took up a place in Dame Allan's (founded 1705; motto Mens Agitat Molem – Mind Over Matter). Incredibly, Northumberland County Council picked up the fees for the next seven years, as I had passed the eleven-plus and wasn't taking up a place in Wallsend Grammar. I couldn't quite understand the economics of that, but we weren't complaining. It was only four years after the War and Clement Attlee was in charge of the country.

Then National Service intervened and I spent two superb, character-building years from 1956 to 1958 teaching in an Army HQ in Bielefeld, Germany. There were three levels of teaching: third-class for privates, second-class for corporals and first-class for sergeants. If someone wanted promotion they had to pass the appropriate exams, which consisted of English, maths, geography, history and current affairs. I also taught map-reading, as I had come top in the subject at the training centre in Beaconsfield. The most motivated classes were the first-class for sergeants wanting to become warrant officers. But while the experience was thoroughly stimulating, teaching didn't grab me as a possible future career.

What to do then? How does anyone know what to do when one is twenty years old with no particular enthusiasm for anything other than enjoying oneself? After my German experience I decided I liked travelling; so, join Thomas Cook, of course. However my parents wanted me to join the Civil Service. After a lifetime moving around the country following limited job opportunities, my father put security of tenure and a guaranteed pension at the top of his shopping list for his two sons. My brother Geoff had already succumbed, having rejected his university offer and chosen to apply to HM Customs and Excise nine years before. He passed the exam, coming fourth in the country, to become an Officer of Customs and Excise. It meant attaining the rank of higher executive officer without having to go through the lower ranks, or join the uniformed Preventive Service, for a career involved in all the 'edgy' things in life: beer, whisky, drugs, gambling, pornography, money (customs, tax and excise duties); and all the nefarious activities associated with them such as smuggling and duty evasion.

But that was not all. My sixth-form history master had a particular interest in money. Although my A-level history course was narrowly confined to the Tudors, he would often broaden the syllabus to include the finances of Henry VIII and Elizabeth I to show how they could pay for all those palaces, wars, courts, banquets, jewels and weddings. Nor did it prevent him from straying even further, into the funding of Ancient Rome's expansionism, the invasions, the creation of their huge empire through, for its time, a sophisticated if nepotistic taxation system of tax farming. And it didn't stop there. He would explain that the collection of taxes or tributes for the benefit of tribal leaders, kings and the state – or what was reckoned as the state – goes so far back in history that it is impossible to trace its true origins. He would wax lyrical about some of the most well-known people of our times who helped to shape our literary, economic and political history, men such as Geoffrey Chaucer, Robbie Burns, Adam Smith, Thomas Paine, and even Dick Whittington: all, at some point in their lives, revenue men. It was then I learnt for the first time that so many of these luminaries had direct associations with the Excise and Customs of their time.

Originally, the term customs meant customary payments or dues of any kind – for example, to the king, a bishop or the church – but later became restricted to duties payable to the king on the import or export of goods. The centralised English customs system can be traced to the Winchester Assize of 1203-4, in the reign of King John, from which time customs were to be collected and paid to the state treasury. Legislation concerning customs can be traced to King Edward I. Under the *nova custuma* in 1275, Collectors of Customs were appointed by Royal patent and, in 1298, *custodes custumae* were appointed in certain ports to collect customs for the Crown. The first Customs officers were appointed in 1294. Like the Roman model, the system was run by tax farming.

A Board of Customs was not created until 21 January 1643, under which the regulation of the collection of customs was entrusted, by ordinance, to a parliamentary committee. As soon as mediaeval taxes were charged on imports and exports, people began smuggling, shipping goods out of the sight of Customs officers. In the eighteenth century, custom duties were imposed on luxuries like silk and lace, tea, tobacco and brandy. At each port, staff from the Custom House searched cargoes and collected dues. At sea, Customs revenue cruisers watched for vessels illegally offloading cargo. From 1698, so-called riding officers patrolled the coast to catch smugglers as they beached cargoes and carried them inland, a hazardous job and not one respected by the population at large.

The 1743 estimate that half the tea drunk in Britain was illegally imported shows that smuggling was a highly profitable and universally accepted way of obtaining it. This well organised 'free trade' employed and supplied many people, from paupers to peers. Smugglers have often been romanticised but the reality was brutal. Local people lived in fear of them, with violent reprisals on informers and the murder of conscientious Revenue officers, while corruption enabled captured smugglers to evade harsh penalties. The well-worn saying that there are only two certainties in life, taxes and death, applied in a different way then: excise officers died, certainly, but taxes were happily evaded. Local communities had little sympathy for the murdered public servants, the riding officers, being complicit in and beneficiaries of the illegal smuggling activities. Rudyard Kipling caught the mood in his poem 'A Smuggler's Song':

> *If you wake at midnight, and hear a horse's feet,*
> *Don't go drawing back the blind, or looking in the street,*
> *Them that ask no questions isn't told a lie.*
> *Watch the wall my darling while the Gentlemen go by.*

> *Five and twenty ponies,*
> *Trotting through the dark –*
> *Brandy for the Parson, 'Baccy for the Clerk.*
> *Laces for a lady; letters for a spy,*
> *Watch the wall my darling while the Gentlemen go by!*

> *If you meet King George's men, dressed in blue and red,*
> *You be careful what you say, and mindful what is said.*
> *If they call you 'pretty maid,' and chuck you 'neath the chin,*
> *Don't you tell where no one is, nor yet where no one's been!*

During its early days, the Customs Department was divided into three branches: the Coastguard, the Waterguard and the Landing Service. The Landing Service was responsible for the examination of imported cargoes and collecting any duty payable. Initially Waterguard officers were managed by the Landing Service, but this proved to be a failure.

The Board of Excise is not so ancient. Excise duties are inland charges levied on articles at the time of their manufacture, such as alcoholic drinks and tobacco; duties have also been levied on salt, paper and windows at one time or another. A Board of Excise was established by the Long Parliament, and excise duties first levied, in 1643. The Board of Excise was merged with the existing Board of Taxes and Board of Stamps to create the new Board of Inland Revenue in 1849. HM Excise maintained their own fleet of revenue cutters until January 1822 when they were transferred to the HM Customs fleet. The 1908 Finance Act transferred the management of excise duties and the associated powers and duties of the Commissioners of Inland Revenue to the Commissioners of Customs. The Commissioners of Customs were renamed the Commissioners of Customs and Excise. The Customs and the Excise services were amalgamated by an Order in Council from 1 April 1909 to be administered by the Board of Customs and Excise and became known as His Majesty's Customs and Excise.

As for the famous people, in 1374 Geoffrey Chaucer was appointed Comptroller of Customs and Subsidy of Wools, Woolfells and of Petty Customs of Wine in London ('petty' meaning 'new' in mediaeval language). It was later in his term that he began writing *The Canterbury Tales*. Now my English literature master never mentioned Chaucer's earlier job, but then he had no interest in money, as the state of his gown showed. He also did not mention the role the Scottish poet Robbie Burns played as an exciseman from 1789, just as the French were revolting.

Poetry may be rich in words but not in the bank, and many of these writers chose to join the evolving customs service for money. They did so despite the reputation of the service and the resentful attitude towards it of the general population. At the time revenue officers were viewed generally as nothing less than a scourge upon honest people living in coastal areas, including the likes of local dignitaries, parsons and professional men who were not averse to buying contraband goods. Dr Johnson described excisemen as 'wretches'.

On his appointment as an officer of excise, Robbie Burns wrote to one of his friends:

> I know not how the word exciseman, or still more opprobrious gauger, will sound in your ears. I too have seen the day when my auditory nerves would have felt very delicately on this subject, but a wife and children are things which have a wonderful power in blunting these kinds of sensations. Fifty pounds a year for life and a provision for widows and orphans, you will allow, is no bad settlement for a poet. For the ignomy of the profession, I have the encouragement which I once

heard a recruitment sergeant give to a numerous, if not respectable audience, in the streets of Kilmarnock: Gentlemen, for your further and better encouragement, I can assure you that our regiment is the most blackguarded corps under crown, and consequently with us, an honest fellow has the surest chance of preferment.

Quoted in *Robbie Burns and the Excise* by Gerard Carruthers

Fortunately his tenure was not prejudiced by one of his lesser known (to me anyway) works, called 'The Deil's (Devil) Awa Wi' The Excisman':

> *We'll mak our mau (malt), and we'll brew our drink,*
> *We'll laugh, sing, and rejoice man,*
> *And money braw (many) thanks to the meikle (big) black Deil,*
> *That danc'd awa wi' the Exciseman.*

The motivation was somewhat different for Adam Smith, the moral philosopher and Scottish Enlightenment figure known as the father of modern economics. Smith's seminal work, *An Inquiry into the Nature and Causes of the Wealth of Nations*, laid the foundations of classical free market economics and was reported as being a constant in Margaret Thatcher's handbag. However, during his lifetime the coincidence of the American colonial rebellion (1776–83) and the publication of his *Wealth of Nations* posed serious problems for Smith. He actively sought to influence decision-makers to dismantle the mercantile economy and *Wealth of Nations* spoke out against the American colonial trade under mercantile monopoly laws. By taking the side of the 'rebels' and pressing for free trade, he lost all of his influence in Britain. He therefore decided, rather bizarrely, to apply for the post of Scottish Commissioner of Customs and Salt Duties, in 1777. This was a man who wrote:

A person who, while no doubt highly blameable for violating the laws of his country, if frequently incapable of violating those of natural justice, would have been, in every respect, an excellent citizen had not the laws of his country made that a crime which nature never meant to be. The high duties which have been imposed upon the importation of many different sorts of foreign goods, in order to discourage their consumption in Great Britain, have in many cases served only to encourage smuggling

Perhaps he felt, if you can't beat 'em, join 'em. Or maybe he wanted to influence from within. Whatever, it would take another 216 years to see part of his objective reached with the completion of the Single Market in Europe, although a number of free trade agreements lessened the pain of 'protective' customs duties throughout the 20th century.

Dick Whittington's involvement in customs was more conventional. The real-life inspiration for the English folk tale Dick Whittington and His Cat, he was a merchant and member of parliament, four times Lord Mayor of London and a sheriff of the city too. He had no money problems. Despite being a moneylender he was sufficiently trusted and respected to sit as a judge in usury trials and, significantly for me, he was given the task of collecting revenues and import duties. Thomas Paine, the political activist, philosopher and revolutionary was a contemporary of Adam Smith with very similar views. Famously author of *The Rights of Man*, *The Age of Reason*, *Common Sense* and *The American Crisis*, he was heavily involved in the American and French Revolutions and is regarded as one of the Founding Fathers of the United States, inspiring the rebels in the revolution to declare independence. John Adams, the first vice-president and second president of the newly independent country, wrote: 'Without the pen of the author of Common Sense, the sword of Washington would have been raised in vain.' However his early life started out a little more humbly when he became an excise officer in Grantham at a salary of £50 per annum. In 1765, he was dismissed for 'claiming to have inspected goods he did not inspect'. A year later he requested to be reinstated by the Board of Excise, which surprisingly was granted the next day, a decision they may have later regretted because from 1772 to 1773 he joined other excise officers pressing Parliament for better pay and working conditions. In the spring of 1774, he was again dismissed from the excise service for being absent from his post without permission and he later emigrated to America. The rest, as they say, is history.

I knew little of this at the time of my career choices. I knew enough, however, to tell me that HMCE was more than, in my own inexperienced mind, just another civil service department. It had a rich history at the core of government going back centuries, one that had attracted a wide range of talented and influential people. I visited my brother at work as the excise control officer in Federation Brewery in Newcastle and thought, this is it. I didn't take much persuading to take an extended correspondence course for the university entrance level exams, which I passed two years later after working for Thomas Cook and Son and a brief time in the Ministry of Pensions and National Insurance, one of those 'just another government department'. It was while working for Thomas Cook that I met my future wife, Aurea, who worked in the airline industry.

Despite my sketchy knowledge of the service I was joining, I shall never forget the feeling I had as I climbed the stairs of the historic Custom House on Newcastle Quayside on my first day in the job. It was a mixture of pride and awe. Sitting opposite the Collector and gazing at the long list of his forebears on the wall behind him powerfully reinforced those feelings, feelings I have never lost.

My first years were delightful, working as an unattached officer (UO) standing in for officers on leave or assisting in busy ports, warehouses, tax offices and breweries; and travelling too, albeit only around Northumberland. However there was something missing. There was no villainy. Most of the controls we carried out were just that, controls that prevented brewers from evading duty, pubs from abusing their licences, schools from distilling whisky. In fact I thought many of them were absurd. We were required to visit pharmacies to check the methylated spirit records to ensure there was nothing underhand going on, and to visit schools to inspect the Manesty stills in their science labs. My first such visit involved the Convent of the Sacred Heart in Jesmond. We worked to timed units and we were given five minutes for such controls. When I told the nun who greeted me exactly what I was there for and that I would like to inspect the laboratory still, she disappeared and was gone for over fifteen minutes. She eventually returned to tell me that the Mother Superior had said that the still was all right. Well, that's good then. 'Thank you,' I said, turning on my heel, walking out of the door and never doing another school still survey from that day on.

Things changed for me when the department introduced a new control method to tackle the substantial evasion of fuel duties. Our fuel excise duties were among the highest of all taxes at the time in the UK and indeed the world, and that hasn't changed much. However, allowances were granted to vehicles that did not use, and were not registered to use, the public roads. These included farm machinery such as tractors, harvest trucks, combine harvesters and the like, heavy loaders such as fork-lift trucks and mobile cranes, and so on. These vehicles were able to use duty-free diesel off-road on private premises. This diesel was marked with a red dye to prevent misuse and users were permitted to store this marked diesel on their premises.

It was recognised from the start that the opportunity for farmers, scrap metal merchants and transport, warehouse and shipping companies to use the red diesel from their own storage tanks to fuel their road vehicles would be too tempting to ignore. This was borne out by an analysis, albeit rather crudely carried out in those days, of red diesel consumption figures which suggested that duty evasion was rife. The Board therefore decided to set up a system of random testing, using large vans manufactured specifically for the purpose. This was the birth of the Road Fuel Testing Unit (RFTU), a blue van emblazoned with the departmental portcullis logo and 'HM Customs and Excise' in large letters on each side. Not every Collection throughout the country was issued with one, as the areas allocated to the units were usually much larger, consisting of one or two adjoining Collections, and teams were set up to administer and staff the vehicles. Every van had an office-based control officer, a driver from the Waterguard watcher grade and a junior unattached officer.

The Newcastle unit covered the three northern counties of Northumberland, Durham and Cumberland, as it then was. It was a large area, and for officers seconded to the van for the stipulated period of three months each time it meant several days a month away from home in fairly modest digs, typically boarding houses, as B&Bs were then known. Each van was given a list of places to visit. The list included the companies at each place which had the dual facility of red and full-price diesel, and these were identified, chosen and compiled by the control officer. The RFTU officer was required to visit each place on the itinerary and to test the fully registered vehicles belonging to each of the companies on the list. In addition, tests had to be carried out on parked vehicles in lay-bys and commercial vehicle parks. The tests involved the sampling of the fuel tanks using a suction pump and adding a chemical to the sample to establish whether the red dye was present.

I was the fourth officer since the unit's inception to take over these duties in Newcastle. There had been only three detections of the illegal use of the red diesel over the previous nine months. After a month on the van, without a single detection from checks and the sampling of hundreds of vehicles, I had nothing to show for it, even though I had given up the chemical test after a week since the red dye could clearly be seen with the naked eye. This had the advantage of increasing the number of vehicles I could check at each stop, but it still yielded no detections.

After a lengthy pit stop with my driver, John, at a pub in Middleton-in-Teesdale, I discussed a completely different approach to the work, but without letting the control officer know in case he vetoed it. John agreed to go along. We would approach the nearest police officer or police station in each area we visited and enquire about who they knew or thought were dishonest and who had access to red diesel. I decided to begin there and then and asked the publican where I could find the local village bobby. The next morning we knocked on his door and found the most obliging of men, happy to talk to us all day about his work and the goings-on in the village. Middleton was a small community, he said. Everyone knew everyone, in more ways than one. In his patrols around the village from his grace-and-favour house in the centre, and from his general everyday observations, he saw more people of the opposite sex going in and out of neighbours' houses than went into the pub. 'Put it this way,' he said, 'there are only two things to do in Middleton-in-Teesdale, and there's no fishing in the winter!'

The outcome of this fruity but fruitful meeting was that I got the names of two men he wouldn't trust with his Co-op passbook. One was a farmer on the hill above the village, the other ran a scrap metal yard opposite the village green and a housing estate. This was where we started. We kept observation on the scrapyard from a street on the estate; not easy given the rather bold colours of our conveyance. Nevertheless it paid off. We knew he stored red diesel in the yard. All we had to do was wait until one of his delivery trucks returned to the yard, drive over to the gate to prevent its leaving, and then test it.

We had to wait no more than two hours. A lorry with the company name on the side duly turned up and drove into the yard. John was quietly dozing in the driving seat when the truck arrived. I shook him awake and he drove like a stock car racer the 500 or so metres to the yard. I'll never forget the looks of surprise, nay shock, on the faces of the lorry and forklift truck drivers. Understandably a feeling of optimism came over us as we inserted the plastic tube into the fuel tank of the lorry, squeezed the sample container and saw liquid pouring into it. It was brim-full of red diesel. We had the same good fortune when we later staked out the farm at the top of the hill. We waited until the farmer returned in his Land Rover and found he was up to the same game with his tractor fuel. The memory of these initial successes is as vivid as the village constable's colourful description of the nefarious goings-on in the village, although I must admit I cannot say the same about the name of this indiscreet upholder of the law, which is perhaps just as well.

This new approach of targeting known miscreants, coupled with a decision to use the police to stop vehicles on the main roads, similar to breath-test stops much later on, rather than at rest in lay-bys, netted us a huge increase in the number of detections. I had twelve in my three months and another sixteen six months later on my second stint on the van.

The second major influence that attracted me to enforcement work was a drama series on my twelve-inch black and white television set called *The Revenue Men*. It featured Ewan Solon as the senior investigation officer in charge of the Glasgow office of the Department's Investigation Branch (IB). This was a small band of men based in London and three provincial offices in Birmingham, Glasgow, and Buxton. Their task was to do just what I thought I would be doing: investigating serious fraud and evasion. I was captivated, and resolved there and then to apply to join the IB. I was selected for interview most probably as a direct result of my successes on the RFTU van. I don't remember too much of the interview in London other than the first question Ron Turner, the Deputy Chief Investigation Officer, put to me:

'Do you drink?'

'Yes, beer,' I replied.

I was in! In fact I was placed fourth in a successful intake of eight. However, it would take another two years before I was called up. We eight literally dribbled into the Branch, as it had a fixed complement at the time and so few left. Still, it would be worth waiting for.

3

Omar and the Naked Lady

T HE TELEPHONE RANG. I put out my hand to lift up the receiver but couldn't reach it from my bed. I stretched farther but the instrument remained strangely, infuriatingly beyond my fingertips. Its ringing continued, seeming to get louder and louder, until I screamed at it in desperation. My wife nudged me hard in the back.

'For God's sake, answer that phone.'

I snapped out of my dream, coming awake with the fuzziness and confusion of the first deep sleep of the night, and grabbed the receiver.

'Mike Knox,' I said drowsily.

'Oh, sorry to trouble you this late, sir. This is LAP. Bill Johnson, PO.'

A Customs preventive officer phoning from London Airport.

'What time is it for Chrissake?'

'A quarter to midnight.'

I groaned. 'Not to worry, what's the problem?'

'We've stopped a young woman at inwards, Terminal Two. Last plane from Paris.'

'And?'

'She's wearing an expensive mink.'

'Uh huh.'

'And that's all.'

'All? What do you mean?'

'All, sir, nothing else. No luggage, no clothes, and not even a dress underneath, I think.'

'Nothing at all?' I was wide awake now.

'Well as far as I could tell, sir, because she kept her coat firmly fastened and flatly refused to take it off for me to examine. Oh, and she has a tiny clutch bag with a hankie and some cosmetics.'

'What's her story?'

'She says she is coming over for a party and going back to Paris tomorrow on the afternoon flight. Her ticket shows her booked back on the four-ten.'

'On the game?'

'Could be. She's a looker. Very high class if she is. I'm not so sure though.'

'Then what do you think she's up to?'

'I think she's smuggling the fur. It's worth a lot. I reckon the duty and tax could be in the region of five grand. We've had a few similar movements recently – no luggage, one-nighters – although this is the first seriously expensive fur coat.'

I smiled. It was a familiar story. You can't blame them, I thought. If the Department, in its wisdom, paid rewards to staff for seizures, bench officers were bound to work the system to their advantage. A smuggled mink would attract the maximum reward of £40, not to mention, since this was the last flight of the shift, a couple of hours' overtime to complete the interview, the seizure, lock-up and report. A nice little earner.

But calling in the Investigation Branch didn't fit. If the IB officer took over the investigation, no reward was payable. The preventive officer lost the case and the reward. IB officers already received a fixed annual allowance to cover overtime, rewards, and various out-of-pocket expenses. So why had Johnson rung the IB duty officer?

'Can't you take a deposit to cover the revenue?'

'No, sir, too much. She doesn't have any cash or other security with her.'

'What about holding the fur overnight and returning it to her on the way out?' I hadn't finished the question before I realised how stupid the suggestion was, and the reason for Johnson's call.

'What do you know about this party she's supposed to be going to?'

'She says she was rung up by Omar Sharif and told to get on the first plane to London.'

'What, the Omar Sharif?'

'The same, apparently. He told her he was having a party and he wanted her there. Different world. It takes me all my time to get up from the telly and get down the pub of an evening.'

'How's she supposed to get to the party if she's got no cash?'

'He'll pay for the taxi, she says.'

'Sounds a bit leery to me,' I said. 'What do you think?'

'I know if I was the taxi driver, I'd take her.'

'How old is she?'

'An extremely confident twenty-two.'

'Does she have his address?'

'She has to go straight to the Piccadilly Hotel, where he is in a big bridge tournament.'

I paused for a moment, thinking of a number of possibilities, then decided on the simplest and surest. 'Right, listen, hold her until I get some pants on and I'll be there as soon as I can.'

I put down the phone and stood up. The Egyptian-born Omar Sharif was one of the biggest movie actors in the world, the outrageously handsome star of a string of hits: *Lawrence of Arabia*, *Doctor Zhivago*, *Funny Girl*. This girl's story sounded ridiculously implausible – but there was only one way to find out.

'Don't wake the kids as you go out,' said my wife.

AT THAT TIME I was living in Ewell with Aurea and our three children, in a 1930s semi-detached house backing onto Nonsuch Park, famed as the setting of one of the residences of Henry VIII, Nonsuch Palace. It passed to Elizabeth I, who was said to have used the banqueting hall on a site close to our house. The palace and hall were pulled down in 1682 by Barbara, Countess of Castlemaine, the mistress of Charles II, to pay off her gambling debts. The park remained and was now a delightful place to play with the children and walk our Labrador dog, Rebel.

As I drove away from my more modest if slightly more modern residence, my mind travelled back to my first drive up to Heathrow shortly after joining the branch. London was almost unknown to me in those days. The senior officer had had to explain the route and the layout of the airport, something, he'd said, that I would eventually be able to navigate in my sleep. Prophetic words. But sleep was already a distant memory at the prospect of interviewing this intriguing young woman.

I could smell her almost before I reached the Customs office behind the baggage carousels in Terminal 2. The intoxicating scent of Chanel took the edge off the sour odours emerging from the well-used lavatories next door. As I entered the office, I could see the young lady was not happy; not happy at all. Her agitation somehow enhanced her looks. She reminded me of Catherine Deneuve, or was it Martine Carol? My thoughts flashed back to the first bare breasts I had ever seen on film. I was clearly not going to take the comparison with Caroline Chérie or Belle de Jour any further, as the woman wrapped her fur even more firmly around her slim body.

I nodded to the uniformed preventive officer, obviously Bill Johnson, standing beside her. 'I'm sorry to have kept you waiting, Miss...?'

'Bellard. Look, I don't believe this is happening to me. I've been here over three hours. Why are you keeping me here? It has ruined the weekend for me and my friend, and for what possible reason?

'For an unconventional reason, Miss Bellard.'

'Unconventional? What on earth do you mean? I'm not used to being treated like this.'

'We don't often come across young ladies at baggage control arriving from a foreign country on Saturday evening wearing the most expensive mink coat this officer, Mr Johnson, has ever seen – and he has seen a lot I can tell you – with no luggage, no money, and dressed ready for ... bed?' I saw Johnson wince as I said the last word.

'How dare you!' The voice lost some of its softness as the volume increased. 'How I choose to travel is my affair. It isn't a crime. I demand to be released, with an apology. And my taxi fare.'

'What's your first name?'

'Suzanne.'

'Well, Suzanne, I'll do better than that. I'll drive you to your destination myself.'

I swung past Marble Arch and headed down Park Lane.

'What was the address again?'

'The Piccadilly Hotel. Look, you didn't have to drive me there. I was going to take a taxi.' Her English carried just a faint Gallic accent.

Omar and the Naked Lady

We made an interesting couple waiting in the lobby of the hotel on a cold Sunday morning in Piccadilly: she, tall, radiantly beautiful, wrapped in the luxurious mink over dark brown stockings and black high heels, exuding perfume from every pore; me, a few inches taller, pale-faced under a day's stubble, in leather jacket, jeans and trainers, smelling of stale sweat, garlic and beer from the night before. The foyer was deserted apart from a rather sleepy concierge. The bridge gamers were either tucked up in bed or had gone back to their own hotels.

The lift door on the other side by the stairs opened and, much to my amazement, the film star Omar Sharif stepped out and walked quickly over to us, stubbing out his cigarette on the way.

'Suzanne, darling!'

'Omar!'

'I'm so glad you decided to come. Was your flight delayed?'

'That's a long story.'

He looked at me. 'How much, cabbie?'

'No charge, sir, my pleasure,' I replied without hesitation, then turned on my heel and walked to the car as the two embraced each other. Well you live and learn, I thought, as I headed for the nearest phone box to ring the airport.

'Just make sure she and that priceless fur coat are on the four-ten tomorrow afternoon, Johnson.'

I carried her scent and her close contact with me in an almost dreamlike state on the drive home. I couldn't imagine what was taking place inside that hotel suite. But curiously, a young woman of a similar age, nationality and appearance, although with a different name, was arrested at Frankfurt Airport several months later with an internal concealment of cocaine. Just a strange coincidence? Or the suspicious mind of a budding investigator?

I am glad Mr Sharif took me for a cabbie, though. In 2003, he received a one-month suspended prison sentence for striking a police officer in a suburban Paris casino; he was also fined €1,700 and ordered to pay the officer €340 in damages. He had insulted and then headbutted the French cop when he tried to intervene in an argument between Sharif and a roulette croupier. 'It made me a hero of the whole of France,' he was quoted as saying subsequently. 'To headbutt a cop is the dream of every Frenchman.'

A close shave!

4

Sam

S AM CHARLES WAS NO ordinary man. He was no ordinary investigator. In fact by the time I joined the Investigation Branch, he had
acquired, after twenty years in the job, almost legendary status. It was
a status he thoroughly deserved.

The IB had been formed in 1946, the culmination of a series of
changes that first began when the separate Customs and Excise departments were amalgamated in 1909. That led to the so-called Special Duty
Staff of Customs, who carried out investigations, being merged with
the Detective Branch of Excise to form a new unit, the Special Services
Staff. This was renamed the Special Inquiry Staff in 1921. Gradually the
investigation service of His (later Her) Majesty's Customs and Excise
grew from a small, compact unit of seven officers, assisting their front-
line colleagues with inland inquiries, to eleven in 1927, nineteen in 1936,
and fifty-one in 1949. By the time I joined, the IB had a complement
of seventy investigators and seven support staff – still very few personnel
in a government department that employed over 29,000 in total. There
were only three women: the Chief's secretary and two typists.

The reason for the IB's growth, slow though it now seems, was
the steady increase in smuggling and tax evasion in the UK, which
were only partly interrupted by the outbreak of the Second World
War. As the War progressed it caused chronic shortages of not just
food and drink but also of the good things in life: luxuries like
watches, jewellery, fashionable clothes, silk stockings and the familiar,
to Customs officers, baccy and booze. The introduction of purchase
tax on many items on 21 October 1940 added to the incentives
to smuggle goods into the country and to evade tax. Nor did the
situation improve much after the War, when shortages remained
acute, hence the need for specialist investigators like Sam Charles,
who joined in the post-War expansion.

As the growth slowed, recruitment was reduced to a trickle through the rigorous selection panel, new staff being taken on individually as the need arose. Following this seemingly interminable two-year wait, I attended the long, drawn-out training sessions with a Senior Investigation Officer (SIO) named Paul Butcher, as we awaited a vacancy in an operational team. Butcher was in his forties, of medium height and build with sleek black hair combed back from a high forehead. His large brown eyes peered through thick, black, horn-rimmed spectacles. His appearance, bookishness and role as a teacher attracted several nicknames, 'Prof' being the favourite; perhaps seventy highly competitive egos couldn't stand the thought of, or even allude to, superior intellect in a colleague. Butcher had worked under Sam for four years before his promotion to SIO in charge of training. His tutelage was therefore filled with stories about the 'great' man; about the prodigious hours he worked, the secretive way he ran his operations, about his head-on clash with Scotland Yard. The stories were legion, probably embellished over time and some apocryphal but, depending on your taste, were no less inspiring, annoying or amusing for all that. A favourite was the oft-repeated account by Jack Brisley, Sam's senior hand, of being sent down to Southampton 'to look for a man in a brown hat'. Brisley scoured the city centre without success, then rang Sam and was told perfunctorily to come back as he had 'obviously been spotted'. Such were the mysterious and sometimes infuriating methods of the great man.

There was also the time – Butcher always warmed to this one – when Sam's wife rang the Chief to ask where her husband was. The Chief had no idea and asked why she needed to know. She retorted that Sam had gone off to work two weeks previously and she hadn't heard from him since. She demanded that the Chief find out where he was, and when he did, to tell him that his wife had put his dinner in the oven when he left and wanted to know what she should do with it.

It was his meticulous attention to detail, strengthened by his thoroughness and total commitment to success whatever the cost in man-hours or resources, that set Sam Charles apart from his peers. Sam, it was said, would still be gathering evidence as the culprit was taken down from the dock to begin his sentence. My colleague

Sam

Alan Taylor tells the story of when he was recruited one evening to drive Sam from London into the depths of Surrey and Sussex to interview company salesmen. They had done three or four of them by 11.45pm.

'Just time for another couple,' said Sam.

'Sam, you can't go knocking on doors at midnight, they'll all be in bed,' said Alan, very sensibly.

'Well, we could try,' said Sam.

With great trepidation, the exhausted Alan said, 'I will take you to the next one, but I'm going to drop you off and I'm going home. You will have to make you own way back.'

Alan waited for the explosion, but in the end it was just mutter, mutter, mutter, then, 'We had better get back.'

Sam was the first in the IB to get into really heavy crime, using a series of purchase tax frauds to clobber the east and south London gangs, and was the first to push for telephone intercepts in an effort to compete on more level terms with the police – and to monitor their activities. He was instrumental in steering the branch away from watch smuggling and into more meaningful fields of endeavour. Textile import restrictions, designed to protect this mainly Lancashire-based industry, always featured in his case-load, as well as export prohibitions on weapons and strategic materiel to unfriendly states, sanctions against South Africa and Southern Rhodesia, large-scale purchase tax evasion and, later, drugs – all on his own initiative. But he showed little interest in alcohol or tobacco smuggling, and none in pornography. Butcher again: 'Sam tried a beer once and gave it up, tried a cigarette once and gave it up, and he only has one child!' That one palled after too many airings. But it was typical of IB humour: a grain of truth or totally inaccurate, who cares as long as it's funny? We held an annual dinner in London for the whole branch that was full of it, with entertainment in the form of sketches and songs by the investigators themselves. I took part in many of them, performing and writing scurrilous scripts to send up senior management and colleagues. Some of the jokes were quite blistering – and invariably very funny – but everyone loved it and the event undoubtedly helped to forge the unique spirit of camaraderie of the IB.

He was not perfect. 'There was a big drugs bust, which Sam master-minded,' Alan Taylor once told me. 'This resulted in the detention of a large lorry and the arrest of the driver. The lorry was taken to Custom House Quay. I remember going down there from Knollys House, then the IB headquarters, in Bywater Street, central London, and saw Sam in the lorry using a pickaxe to break open the floor, to reveal long, square sectioned plastic containers full of cannabis. The driver was later convicted and sentenced to a term of imprisonment.

'Time passed and the Custom House staff wanted the lorry removed. By this time the tyres were flat and degraded and the engine was kaput. So it was decided to employ contractors to break it up into manageable pieces and to remove them. The contractors arrived and set to work. After half an hour, one of them called in one of the local Customs officers: "Oy, guv, we think you should come and see this." So he went to the lorry and there was the floor all broken up by Sam, but now the contractors had started on the side panels. Lo and behold they also held the same plastic containers, full of cannabis and still in situ.

'Sam was phoned, and after some hesitation, said, "Leave it to me, I'll take care of it." And that was it. Nothing more was heard about this find and the fact that the master sleuth had apparently missed it first time round.'

So I felt a mixture of fear and excitement when told that at the end of my six-month stint with Paul Butcher I would be working for Sam Charles as the junior member of his four-man team. My strongest feeling, however, was trepidation. I had a wife who was new to London and two of my children were under school age. Excessive and uncertain hours would put a great deal of strain on family life. Nonetheless I could hardly contain my excitement at the prospect of learning from reputedly the best there was at that time, however idiosyncratic. Sam, fifty-two years old, of medium height, with thinning hair and a small moustache, had been in bomb disposal during the war which is, perhaps, why he was so commanding and fearless. His daughter Penny tells me that he was injured in an explosion when he went down underwater in deep-sea diving gear to defuse a bomb which promptly went off, killing two of his companions. He lost some of his hearing and all of his hair, which had always been straight; when it grew back it was curly. Brave indeed.

Sam

It was not easy. The first weeks were spent, I felt, running errands: Companies House checks on suspect firms, vehicle checks on suspect cars, Criminal Records Office checks at Scotland Yard on suspect people, ships' manifest checks on suspect cargo, electoral roll checks on suspect addresses, telephone number checks on suspect lines, unauthorised checks on bank accounts with public-spirited bank managers, similar checks on gas and electricity supplies to areas known to be running illicit stills, access to airline and travel agents' records to obtain advance booking information. This progressed to hours cramped in unmarked, specially adapted observation vans watching premises in south London, counting cardboard boxes of folding umbrellas from Hong Kong into the warehouse and counting cardboard cartons of folding Hong Kong umbrellas out again; in Stoke Newington, watching thousands of Romanian suits wheeled into store and thousands wheeled out again; in Shoreditch, monitoring movements of furs; in Hatton Garden, movements of gem dealers. And at Mount Pleasant postal depot, X-raying postal packets to prove the absence of thousands of watches declared as being exported to Jersey.

I was told very little about the cases any of this hard slog related to. There were no briefings, no updates. I went out on the occasional raid, or 'knock' as they were known, and was given the task of second officer to take the notes and write up the witness statements, the only time when I had the opportunity to discover what was actually going on. With major jobs and those Sam took a personal interest in, not one of his team ever knew the whole picture. Jack Brisley told me that he expended more energy and powers of deduction trying to work out what his boss was up to than on the actual villains. What Jack also said was that, in spite of his boss's infuriating ways, Sam attracted unswerving loyalty from his officers.

During my two years under him he was also heavily and surreptitiously involved in a police corruption case. I only knew it as the 'Kelaher case', a name that became familiar to me from my skirmish with Prichard and Pilcher of the Drugs Squad, but nothing more. Sam never discussed it with me or anyone I spoke to about it, which was probably wise given the nature of the case. He was, in other words, the ideal man for the job.

IF I HAD A pound for every word that has been written about police corruption I would be as rich as Silvio Berlusconi, although hopefully not as tarnished. On the contrary, if I had to live off the words written about Customs corruption, I would be quickly looking for the nearest food bank. That is not to take an arrogant or high moral stance. Customs was far from being a paragon of virtue: we have had, and will always have, a few bad apples. But a corrupt service it certainly wasn't.

In November 1969, the *Times* newspaper published what quickly became a landmark article about corruption in the Metropolitan Police. This was the month I joined the IB from my provincial existence in Newcastle Collection; so provincial that I did not read or know anything about the article, nor about the investigations into the Yard underway by a number of press and TV journalists. That was hardly surprising, as I was adjusting not only to a new and exciting change of direction in my career but also to the overwhelming presence, and the anonymity, of a huge city I hardly knew. Plus, *The Times* was not my preferred reading at the time.

Indeed it was an unusual story for the staid *Times*, which was hardly the *News of the World* or the *Sunday People*, downmarket scandal sheets always looking for newsworthy revelations of corrupt or illicit practices by celebrities. The *Times* was the paper of the Establishment, which made its revelations all the more shocking:

> Disturbing evidence of bribery and corruption among certain London detectives was handed by *The Times* to Scotland Yard last night. We have, we believe, proved that at least three detectives are taking large sums of money in exchange for dropping charges or being lenient with evidence offered in court, and for allowing a criminal to work unhindered…

The *Times* article was only the beginning of the revelations, the tip of the iceberg, which would rock the Metropolitan Police to its foundations and lead to a complete overhaul of the service several years down the line. The so-called 'Fall' of Scotland Yard took place between 1969 and 1972. As a result of what happened in those years, thirteen London detectives went to gaol (yes, that's how we spelt it then) for a total of more than ninety years, hundreds more left the force in disgrace and the old CID hierarchy was severely restructured. The myth of the London bobby I thought I knew, of Jimmy Handley and *The Blue Lamp* and *Dixon of Dock Green*, was badly dented, and a long-standing tradition of detective work was almost completely destroyed. The officers involved were in, or in some cases actually in charge of, the Flying Squad, the Drugs Squad and the Dirty Squad (Obscene Publications).

In 1971, the *Sunday People*, the more usual source of such stories, ran its own story about corruption in the Met. This covered the pornography trade in Soho and exposed the involvement of the police in sanctioning the operation of porn shops for a fee. The article named a number of leading figures in the pornography trade, including Jimmy Humphries, Jeff Phillips, Gerry Citron and John Mason, all four of whom were arrested and convicted several years later and gave evidence in the trials of corrupt detectives in Scotland Yard's Porn and Flying Squads. Humphries and Bernie Silver, the Godfather of the porn trade in London, had struck up relationships with Commander Wally Virgo and DCI Moody of the Yard that involved holidaying abroad together and copious dinner parties. In 1969, a deal had been struck to pay 'licence fees' for bookshops in Soho to their police contacts. To have some idea of the obscene level of corruption, Humphries paid £14,000 for the 'licence' for one shop and £2,000 a month thereafter; this is the modern equivalent of £200,000 and £28,000 respectively. Such bribes to the Scotland Yard teams had been going on for over twenty years, although not at that level.

In 1972, the *People* ran a second series of articles exposing pornographers and again alleging corrupt dealings with detectives. One article which caused the greatest embarrassment to Scotland Yard was a report about Jimmy Humphries and his wife holidaying in Cyprus with Commander Kenneth Drury and his wife. Robert Mark, who was then the Deputy Commissioner, ordered an immediate investigation into the association, but when interviewed Drury said that he had gone to Cyprus – paying his share of the cost of the holiday – in an attempt to obtain information about the whereabouts of the Great Train Robber Ronnie Biggs. This cock-and-bull story was not believed and he was suspended from duty. He resigned shortly afterwards. Drury later wrote an article for the *News of the World* justifying his association with Humphries, who he said was a paid informant – another 'creative' story.

It took a long time and the appointment of Robert Mark as the new Commissioner later that year, with a mandate to clean up what had become an international scandal, for all of the porn barons and corrupt detectives to be tried and sentenced. Jimmy Humphries was gaoled for eight years, Bernie Silver for seven, Commander Drury for seven, Commander Wally Virgo for five, Bill Moody for five and countless others for lesser sentences.

Relations between Customs and Scotland Yard had been strained for many years. The conflict was inevitable once both organisations started investigating in earnest the same criminality, in particular illicit drugs and pornography. Customs had no interest in general crime: murder, robbery, arson, rape and the rest of the long list of bad things that people do to each other were entirely a matter for the police. However, both drugs and porn were usually smuggled in from abroad. This made them a Customs matter. But if there was no evidence of the actual importation – even if it was known that they came from abroad – the offence usually became possession, which was the sole responsibility of the police. Unfortunately, in between those two extremes was a grey area. The police wanted to tackle the big importers too: that's where the glory was. They also felt that if they were working on what appeared to be a possession or distribution with intent to supply, and then discovered evidence of international trafficking too, they should be able to continue investigating the case without handing it over to us. Matters became critical when an ambitious and effective DCI, Vic Kelaher, took over the Drugs Squad in 1968. He persuaded his superiors that the police should take over Customs arrests at Heathrow, since those arrested might belong to international syndicates, the province of Scotland Yard. The Home Office would later criticise the police role at Heathrow, stating that many of their cases involved travellers bringing in minor amounts of drugs where the police follow-up was minimal.

In 1970, the IB became heavily involved with a case that would eventually bring all of this to a head: the investigation of a London-based Bahamian, Basil Sands, who was believed to be trafficking in cannabis. Sam Charles assisted the police, especially Gilbert Kelland, the head of the CID in Scotland Yard, throughout this time. We, his team, knew very little about it. All we ever got was from the press articles and books written by investigative journalists. When I had my brief, although significant, encounter with Prichard and Pilcher of the Drugs Squad, I knew nothing of their backgrounds or activities. I subsequently learned that Norman Pilcher had transferred from the Flying Squad to the Drugs Squad in 1967. 'Nobby', as he was known, became notorious for the vigour with which he pinned possession of drugs charges on pop stars and hippies, and for the dubious methods employed in his undercover operations. He was involved in the arrest of a number of celebrities during the 1960s on drug charges, such as Donovan, Brian Jones and Mick Jagger of the Rolling Stones, and two members of The Beatles, George Harrison and John Lennon. Various celebrities complained that the Drugs Squad framed them or was only carrying out raids and arrests to satisfy the tabloid newspapers.

Det Sgt Pilcher's reputation was further damaged in the early 1970s after Basil Sands claimed, during his drug smuggling trial, that he was innocent and had been working with the police as an informant. After the judge directed the jury to discount any private belief they might have that Pilcher's superior, Victor Kelaher, was at the centre of a drug smuggling ring, since this was something that should be addressed at a subsequent trial, Sands got seven years. Thanks to a nervous complaint requiring hospital treatment, Kelaher avoided subsequent problems with the Home Office. Interestingly, again unbeknown to me, we had previously found Kelaher in the Holland Park flat of a prostitute called Mrs Roberts, who he had helped purchase an expensive watch. She was the former wife of a gaoled drug smuggler, Ghanaian diplomat Kofi Roberts, whom he had previously arrested.

Pilcher and Nick Prichard were belatedly brought to trial in September 1973, convicted of perjury and jailed. Kelaher was cleared at trial but subsequently left the police due to ill health. Sentencing Nobby Pilcher to a four-year stretch, Justice Melford Stevenson famously told the disgraced detective: 'You poisoned the wells of criminal justice and set about it deliberately.' All of this and more was soon after related in an explosive book, *The Fall of Scotland Yard*, by journalists Barry Cox, John Shirley and Martin Short, and in many other print sources. I will go no further. I knew nothing of the Kelaher/prostitute raid attributed to Customs, and still don't. But all of this does provide an important backdrop to some of my cases which involved the police and my attitude and behaviour at the time, as the Clapham case in my opening chapter has already clearly demonstrated.

5

Haute Couture

'BANANAS?'
    'Bananas.'
  'So while you're all stuck into missing traders and illegal arms sales to the Middle East, I've got to look at bananas? You must be joking.'
  'It's no joke Mike. Sam's adamant. He's had some kosher info that the trade is bent. He didn't explain it fully, surprise, surprise. Something about the evasion of import licensing restrictions designed to protect the Jamaican banana trade by misdescribing dollar-area bananas as plantains. But you know what he's like. No matter what we've got on, there's always room for more. And you will continue to be involved with the other jobs.'
  . I shared an office with Jack Brisley. I liked him. He was an East Londoner with only the hint of a cockney accent. He was tall, a little on the heavy side, had just turned forty and was still madly in love with his wife. His sharp features were accentuated somewhat by metal-rimmed glasses. He was always cheerful, encouraging and honest; there wasn't a devious bone in his body. He slavishly followed Sam's instructions and hunches to the letter and had been rewarded with a first-officer role in some of the branch's most prestigious jobs.
  He looked at my crestfallen face with the sympathy of one who had been there before. 'Mike, you're young, inexperienced, a long way to go. The best advice I can give you is to relax. Let it happen. Give it your best shot, of course, but take things as they come. Don't force the pace. It will never work with someone like Sam. But trust his intuition. He's never let us down yet, I can guarantee that.'
  'Bananas!'
  The sound of running feet and the hurried opening of the door

brought our conversation to an abrupt halt. Brian Ellis, the fourth
member of Sam's team, burst into the room, followed by Don Holmans.

'Have either of you got a car here?'

'We both have. What's up?'

'Where are they?' Ellis's high-pitched voice seemed to go half an
octave higher.

'Both in Carey Street.'

'Damn, that's ten minutes away. Never mind, we've no choice. We
have to get up to the airport as fast as we can. We may already be too
late. I'll brief you on the way to the car park.'

WE REACHED THE CAROUSEL in the BEA Terminal just as the luggage
from the 11.15 Paris flight was coming up on the conveyor belt. Three
of us spread out and mingled with the passengers, listening as best we
could to conversations often drowned out by loudspeaker announce-
ments and general clatter. Jack Brisley leant against a wall, taking in the
whole scene.

The information had been vague: haute couture dresses from the
Paris Spring Collection being smuggled in to avoid duty and tax. No
names, no descriptions, just a lot of expensive clothes. Passengers were
grabbing their luggage and making for the Customs benches to make
their individual declarations to one of the two uniformed officers on
duty. After a few words with each passenger, asking whether they had
anything to declare, the officers drew white chalk crosses on the bags
and allowed them to proceed; this was in the days before the Green
('Nothing to Declare') and Red channels were put into effect. Every
so often the officers chose a passenger for a thorough bag examination.
When they were both tied up searching suitcases, the growing queue of
passengers leaving the carousel was waved through unchecked.

As Jack watched the officers work in the unscreened examination
area, his attention was drawn to a large, elderly woman calling in a loud
voice for one of the porters leaning lazily on their barrows near the
carousel. Her twelve-stone frame was covered in a large fur coat and her
round, heavily made-up face was overshadowed by a broad-brimmed
red hat. She issued orders to the skinny little porter as though she were

a duchess returning from her French chateau, pointing out all the heavy suitcases on the conveyor belt she wanted him to lift off for her. Her bluster attracted Jack's attention, distracting him from the wider picture, until he noticed her nod towards a young woman standing beside two large suitcases waiting for the Customs line to move. He turned and watched as the woman picked up the suitcases with some difficulty and walked through the Customs area unchallenged. Both uniformed officers were fully engaged in inspecting luggage.

Jack scanned the remaining passengers and spotted two more young women with the appearance, like the first, of fashion models – slim, pretty, petite – waiting by the carousel for their luggage. The 'Duchess' continued her flow of orders and invective at the browbeaten porter, then again imperceptibly motioned to one of the women, who had retrieved another two heavy suitcases from the conveyor belt and was waiting at the entrance to Customs. Nodding back to the older woman, the young woman picked up the cases and struggled through past the two officers, who were once again immersed in toilet bags, underwear, dirty laundry, and presents. The Customs hall was beginning to look like a jumble sale.

Jack quickly alerted us to the situation. We agreed to split up: Jack and I to go to our cars parked outside the arrivals hall, Brian and Don to follow the 'Duchess' through Customs. It was another twenty minutes before she finally walked through, with the porter at her heels carting three matching suitcases, a hatbox and several smaller bags. Brian followed immediately behind her and Don positioned himself beside the newsagents directly opposite the Customs exit. As soon as she reached the 'safety' of the concourse, she went up to join the young women, who were grouped around their cases. Don counted four and assumed that one had gone through before Jack had realised what they were up to. Two minutes later, three more porters arrived to take the eight cases and accompany the now sizeable and heavily laden party to the taxi stand outside the terminal. It was one of those extraordinarily warm late winter days that takes everyone by surprise, especially the older woman who was now sweating under her heavy musquash coat.

Brian and Don walked as quickly as they could without drawing attention to themselves, and got into our cars parked fifty yards from the taxi stand. We had already established radio contact and had agreed to run the risk of a tail. The 'Duchess' and her entourage were so encumbered that they had to commandeer two taxis, which gave our surveillance team its first headache. Jack radioed that if the two taxis did not stay together on the journey, we should all try to stay with the first. In the event, the tail proved easier than we could have hoped for. The two taxis travelled quite slowly in convoy and managed to keep together through even the densest traffic. The drivers, as innocent carriers, took no interest in our two cars close behind them, changing places from time to time just in case. We had some uneasy moments through Knightsbridge, when three pushy London drivers inserted themselves between us and the taxis, but they all peeled off up Park Lane as the taxis reached Marble Arch. We continued into Oxford Street and, after only thirty-five minutes, turned into Bond Street, where the taxis stopped outside a shop halfway down. Jack drove about 100 yards past and parked, instructing me to hold back a similar distance away on the Oxford Street side.

The disembarkation took a long time. Whether the drivers were charmed by the models, terrified by the 'Duchess' or simply paid enough wasn't obvious but, remarkably for London cabbies, they carried all the luggage into the shop. The shop windows either side of the door displayed a variety of fashion clothes and the sign above simply said 'Yvette'.

Jack let Brian take the lead in the shop. We had given it thirty minutes after the taxis had left to knock on the door. One of the young women opened the door and almost fainted when confronted by four officers brandishing burgundy-coloured wallets with their identification. Most of the suitcases had been opened and what seemed like hundreds of dresses were being hung on rails by the other three women. The 'Duchess', now relieved of her coat and hat, was sitting with her feet up on a stool in the middle of the shop, surrounded by suitcases, clothes rails and unclothed headless mannequins, drinking a cup of tea.

She was remarkably composed. She tried to bluff her way through the first few questions Brian put to her, but when she realised the game was up she admitted that the dresses were second-order garments rejected for the Paris Spring Collection shows. The dresses chosen for the March/April shows always went to the major fashion houses, commanding enormous prices, but second-order 'rejects' also commanded respectably high prices, especially in London. Each suitcase contained over thirty dresses and each dress was worth at least £300. Multiplied by eight – her own luggage was just a cover – and a fraud that she had been perpetrating on her own admission for twenty years without detection, the Charles team had something to celebrate.

The 'Duchess', or Yvette as we now knew her name to be, was cautioned and reported to the Board for her latest importation offence, with the previous evasions taken into account. The dresses, worth over £10 million at today's values and a whole lot more on resale to her regular customers, many of whom could be found in the pages of Debrett's, were seized. She later paid the Department, or rather the Treasury, £30,000 in an out-of-court settlement, and in my book got off remarkably lightly.

I enjoyed the subsequent visits to some of her customers to obtain witness statements providing the necessary evidence of onward sales. The most notable was to a lady in Belgravia, whose wardrobe was as long as a tennis court; in it were hundreds of dresses, coats and more shoes than Imelda Marcos's collection. She showed me the ones she had bought from Yvette, which I then seized. She admitted that the dress she was wearing was also bought from Yvette and I had the unenviable task of asking her to take it off and give it to me. By seized I meant that we sorted them and hung them all together in the wardrobe, with a warning to the lady that they should not be moved. The Commissioners of Customs and Excise, in their wisdom, later lifted the seizure order and she was left to wear the 'second-order Paris fashion garments' for as long as she wished.

6

Nosebleeds

ONLY WHEN SAM CHARLES had no interest or appetite for a particular inquiry did I get any opportunity to carry out a full, hands-on investigation of my own. So-called 'squad' weeks – every fifth week each of the four-man teams, or squads, had to take its turn on seven-day, twenty-four-hour call – gave me those opportunities. While squad weeks were an ideal training ground for inexperienced officers like me, they were an irritant to Sam. He was so heavily involved in ongoing cases that he left his junior officers to deal entirely with what he regarded as dross, without guidance from him. The Streatham and Clapham raids I conducted with the Drugs Squad came through in my squad week. Despite what were forecast to be sizeable amounts of drugs, Sam was sceptical about the information – probably because it hadn't come from an informant of his – and surprisingly gave it to me to cut my teeth on.

When I returned to the office after the Streatham knock, Sam called me into his office and told me to go up to a jeweller's in Hatton Garden to find out what I could about 'off record' sales through their retail outlet. Alan Taylor, a senior officer from another team, would assist. The drugs case I had just been on was not mentioned.

Hatton Garden was just a five-minute walk from our modern office block in New Fetter Lane. We had only recently moved there from a small suite of offices in Knollys House, itself a short walk from HM Customs and Excise headquarters in Kings Beam House, close to the Tower of London. We had outgrown that accommodation and needed more space for equipment, seizures and vehicles. As Hatton Garden was so near to the new offices, Alan Taylor and I decided to walk to the jeweller's.

We crossed High Holborn and entered the narrow street where most of London's jewellery trade had congregated since the 1870s.

The Investigator

In Elizabethan times it had been the orchard of Sir Christopher Hatton's Holdenby Palace, but a place less like a garden now would be hard to imagine. Not a blade of grass, not a single tree to shade the brilliance of the gold, diamonds, platinum, sapphires and myriad precious stones adorning the windows of one shop front after another, over fifty in all, from Holborn Circus to Theobalds Road. Black trilby hats, frock coats, ringlets and beards were much in evidence as we made our way with some difficulty past small groups of mainly Jewish traders talking animatedly on the narrow pavements outside the retail outlets. Inside, behind and above reinforced glass windows, were over 200 manufacturers' premises, with more security systems guarding their entrances and stock, it seemed to the uninitiated, than the Bank of England. We walked up past the passageway to Ely Place, where the Bishops of Ely once resided and which is still technically part of Cambridgeshire, and the Mitre Tavern, where Elizabeth I was said to have danced around the maypole.

I was oblivious to this historic and bustling environment as we reached our destination next to the London Diamond Centre. All I had was Sam's cryptic order. We had extremely limited powers to look at the records and stock of the company. HMCE's famous writ of assistance, which gave the power to enter properties without a warrant, only extended to searches for goods which were liable to seizure because the import duty and tax had been evaded; not very helpful when I had no hard information and only Sam's unexplained suspicions to go on. As we walked through the glass-fronted door, I recalled my tutor Paul Butcher's words: 'Remember, whatever you may be feeling, the clients, even the fierce-looking ones, will always be more frightened of you. You have the power.' Some power, I thought, but at least I considered Butcher's advice wise. I did have the authority of the Government, which was some reassurance.

We were shown into a small, dingy office at the back of the shop by one of the young sales assistants. The jeweller, a short, plump, balding man with gold-rimmed spectacles, stood up and smiled as we came in. He introduced himself as Isaac Jacobs.

'How can I help you, gentlemen?'

'We're from Customs and Excise. My name is Michael Knox and this is Alan Taylor. We should like to have a look at your retail purchase and sales records, if you don't mind.'

'I was not expecting a visit from you for another three weeks, or rather from my regular officer. Is there anything wrong?' said Jacobs, in a mid-European accent.

'We certainly hope not,' I lied. 'We're just carrying out a number of routine checks on jewellers this month and hope you can help us.'

'Of course, gladly,' Jacobs lied in return, with the smile looking a little more forced and an almost imperceptible movement of his Adam's apple giving me a smidgen of encouragement. 'What period would you like to see?'

'Oh, the last quarter will do.'

'You'll have to excuse me.' Jacobs came round from his desk and squeezed between us to reach a safe in the corner of the cramped office. He unlocked it and took out two ledgers. I noticed several other books in the safe and noted the care Jacobs took to re-lock it before returning to his seat.

'Are these all your records?'

'The ones you will need, yes.'

'But I saw a number of other books in your safe. What are those?'

'Oh, they're just my production records and odds and ends. They won't be of any interest to you.'

'They might. Could I see them, please?'

The smile disappeared from the jeweller's face, his Adam's apple increased its movement, and a tiny bead of sweat appeared on his wide forehead.

'Yes, of course.' He squeezed past us again, took out the key and opened the safe. As he did so, Alan, who was clearly on my wavelength, reached past him into the safe and began lifting the books out. Jacobs protested that he was perfectly capable of finding the books we needed himself and tried to push my colleague back towards the desk. Alan held his position and doubled his efforts to secure the books. Both took hold of a large red book and pulled, like two children fighting over a cricket bat in the schoolyard. The brief tug-of-war that followed was pure slapstick, an unequal struggle that ended with Alan snatching the book out of Jacobs' hands, putting his firm behind between the jeweller and the safe, and handing me all of its contents. Jacobs visibly deflated. He seemed to shrink before our eyes as his shoulders dropped and he flopped back into his seat behind the desk like an exhausted marathon runner.

I skimmed quickly through the books as Alan plied Jacobs with questions about his business: who his suppliers were, how much stock he held, his turnover, customer base and so on. He took him methodically through his tax account, reconciling the shop sales with the tax return he was about to submit to the Department. Jacobs replied in a monotone but he was co-operative; there was nothing in his replies or his records to suggest anything irregular. The books balanced and the arithmetic was correct, to the penny. Alan looked at me and gave a slight shrug of the shoulders.

I was not satisfied. I was sure, from the jeweller's demeanour and earlier reticence over the books, that we were missing something. It was probably staring us in the face but we couldn't see it. Each time either of us singled out a transaction from any of the company books, it traced through to the tax account and into the tax return. He had paid, or, for the most recent transactions, was about to pay, all his dues.

An hour into the visit I began leafing through a thin blue book labelled 'second-hand rings'. Jacobs explained that each line in the book represented a second-hand ring bought from a customer. They were of no interest to Customs since second-hand jewellery was exempt from tax. The record showed the date of the purchase, a number, which Jacobs said cross-referenced to the customer's name and address, a description of the ring, the amount paid and the date of sale. Where the sale date was missing, the ring was still in stock. I chose three of the undated items and asked to see the rings. Jacobs called in the young female assistant who had shown us into the office and asked her to find them, not too difficult a task since all of the stock was displayed either in the window or in glass counter cabinets in the shop. 'If it's not on display, it doesn't get sold,' he said. That was something, I must admit, I hadn't realised was the retail jeweller's modus operandi until then.

To my untrained eye, one of the three rings I inspected through the jeweller's magnifying glass appeared new. The other two looked slightly worn. The worn rings had customer reference numbers; the other simply a blue pencil line in the customer column. 'Naturally we clean and polish them thoroughly before we put them on sale. We wouldn't sell them otherwise,' Jacobs assured us.

I then asked to see the customer book containing the names and addresses of the previous owners. Jacobs could not immediately put his hands on it and thought it could be with his accountant. While he was talking I noticed that he moved his briefcase from the side of his desk nearest to us across to the far side.

'What do you keep in your briefcase?'

'Oh, just private papers.'

'Such as?'

'Just personal things.'

I pressed: 'Like what?'

'Insurance documents, letters, stuff like that.'

'Do you mind if we have a look inside?' I had already reached the briefcase as I was asking the question and grabbed the handle at precisely the same time as Jacobs. But before a second tug-of-war took place, a thin trickle of blood ran down from Jacobs's left nostril, over his mouth and onto his chin. Jacobs had a handkerchief out of his pocket to staunch the flow before the first drops could stain his immaculate white shirt, but the briefcase was now in the possession of this young uncivil servant asking politely if there was anything at all he could do to help.

It was only a matter of seconds before I found the customer book in the briefcase and began cross-checking the customer reference numbers against the names and addresses listed there. Jacobs had by now stemmed the bleeding, but each time I asked him to name the customer for each item that had only a blue pencil line in the column, his nose started to bleed again. I switched my line of questioning away from the blue-pencil items for a couple of minutes and then back again, as though I was reeling in a fish. And there was certainly something distinctly fishy about the 'blueys', as we later described them, since I elicited the same bloody response each time I returned to them.

The tiny office had become unbearably stuffy. In addition to the blood spasmodically pouring from his nose, Jacobs was finding it difficult to breathe and his white shirt was no longer immaculate; wet perspiration stains appearing under the arms and across the chest. Alan motioned to me to leave the room with him. I followed him into the outer shop.

'Leave it, Mike, he's had enough.'

I was annoyed at being dragged off my prey. 'But we've got him on the run Alan.'

'Pressuring him more now will be counter-productive. Remember, softly, softly, catchy monkey. I suggest we leave him for the moment and allow him to calm down. Let's go through the second-hand book with one of the sales staff and pull out all the blue-line rings that are still in stock. Then you can put a couple to him and see if we can winkle out the manufacturing details of all this "off" stuff. We'll then have to call it a day.'

It took us about two hours to find all the rings not covered by customer details and work out their value. The sales assistant then helped us to total the value of the remaining sold rings. It came to a staggering £225,000 (over £3 million today) in the five months covered by the books in our possession.

When we finally returned to the back office, Jacobs had recovered his composure and was drinking a cup of tea. There was no sign of the bloody handkerchief. I showed him four diamond rings from stock and asked him for the name of the previous owners, knowing full well they were all blue-pencil-line items. As if by remote control, Jacobs's nose started to bleed again.

I read from my notebook: 'Mr Jacobs, I have reason to believe that you have been selling new jewellery described as second-hand to evade the purchase tax. You do not have to say anything unless you wish to do so, but anything you do say will be taken down and may be used in evidence. The time is twelve-fifteen p.m.'

The hapless jeweller's pupils rolled up into his eyelids, his mouth clenched shut and he slumped forward across his desk in a dead faint.

WHEN JACOBS HAD RECOVERED sufficiently not to require any further medical aid, and the ambulance men had left the premises, we made our way through the outer shop clutching all the documentary evidence we could carry. Outside it was drizzling. We hurried over to Alan's Hillman Imp, which he'd gone to fetch and had driven up from the office while the ambulance crew were about their mission of mercy, and put all the books and papers in the boot. We made one more trip for the rest of the evidence before I turned and said, 'You go on back, Alan, I'd like to walk.'

As my colleague drove off, I took a deep breath of the fresh damp air and walked airily down the street. It could well have been sunny and warm the way I was feeling. The rain had swept most of the traders off the street and for the first time that day I was able to take an interest in my surroundings. I marvelled at the facade of the charitable Bluecoat School with its ornate statues of pupils above the door, sadly all that was left after the Luftwaffe bombing of Wren's 1696 design. The delicious aromas of coffee, latke, and chocolate babka filtering out of Lasky's, the Jewish restaurant on the corner of Cross Street, almost tempted me to delay my return to the office. This was my first real success. I was exhilarated. I felt expansive. I would take Aurea and our children, Suzanne, Julie and Paul, boating on the Serpentine at the weekend. I passed the *Daily Mirror* building into New Fetter Lane and ran up the short flight of steps into the foyer of number 14.

News of the 'nose-bleed job', as it was rapidly becoming known, had spread like an Australian bushfire through the building. The uniformed custodian on the front desk greeted me. 'Mr Charles would like to see you, sir. He said it was urgent.'

Sam's office was Spartan. The grey steel furniture was unadorned. There were no pictures on the walls, not even a calendar. There were no photographs or other personal possessions to provide even a glimpse of a private life. It was like a surgeon's consulting room hired by the hour. Its austerity was the only clue to the nature of the man who occupied it. Sam was standing behind his desk, licking his fingers each time he noisily snapped the pages of the purchase ledger over one by one. Alan was looking uneasily over his shoulder.

'Where are the diamond purchases?' Sam shot at me.

'They're in the purchase day book.'

'I've already been through the journal. It nowhere near covers the number of diamonds he's been using.'

Taken aback, I stuttered, 'Well, we didn't have time to ask him everything before he keeled over.'

'Look,' Sam retorted fiercely, 'we need to know the source and quantity of his "off" diamonds. All the new rings are diamond ones. Get back there and find the diamond records.'

'But he wasn't very well when we left, and…'

'That's his problem. You'll also need to take the branch valuer to prove that all the rings in question are new. Are they secure?'

I looked helplessly at Alan, who jerked into action, 'We had them put separately in one of the safes.'

'And you've got the key?'

'Well, no, not exactly,' Alan replied uncertainly; then more confidently, 'we don't have the power to seize the rings.'

'Look,' Sam Charles was beginning to lose it by now, 'this isn't about seizure. These rings are evidence in a serious case of fraud. What on earth have you been doing? Get back there. Now.'

'Don't say it,' Alan got in first.

'Sod!' I did say it, through gritted teeth as we stood in the corridor outside Sam's room. 'The man flaked out, for God's sake. Blimey, I thought I was being hard on him. You pulled me off, remember? What would he have done? I suppose he would still be interrogating him, putting leading questions to him and then noting down, tellingly, "The suspect made no reply." I give up.'

Alan could not suppress a smile.

From euphoria to frustration in less time that it had taken me to walk back from what I thought was the beginning of an illustrious career on the branch. At thirty-two, I was older than my fellow junior officers, most of whom had joined the IB in their mid-twenties. Whether that made me more impatient to acquire the skills to perform well as quickly as possible, to run before I could walk, or whether it was simply my nature, must have been difficult for my colleagues to discern. They saw a self-confident man with drive and ambition who could be quite irritable when things were not going quickly enough but who soon turned to humour to lighten the mood.

Alan Taylor looked at me sideways as I continued to fume and swear walking back down Hatton Garden, but said nothing. Now where were all those humorous thoughts?

7

Deep Throat

THE OVERHEAD LIGHTS WENT out. The bright white of the blank screen lit up the tiny cinema on the fourteenth floor of New Scotland Yard. I sat back in my seat in nervous anticipation of the likely scenes I was about to watch. A noise behind me broke my concentration. I looked around and, to my astonishment and embarrassment, saw that the twenty or so seats were filled with police officers who had obviously heard that something interesting was being screened and had slipped in without me noticing.

My stomach turned over as the first images appeared on the screen. The film was in black and white, and it took me some time to work out that we were watching an old Laurel and Hardy short running upside down and backwards. This wasn't what they had all turned up to see. I didn't know whether to laugh at the thwarted lascivious appetites behind me or cry at the wasted effort in bringing the films down from the airport.

I wasn't making an auspicious start to my investigation career. A few minor squad jobs that hadn't amounted to much: 3,000 cigarettes picked up in the boot of a car in the centre of Reading by the Old Bill; an empty Omega watch box sent through the post after the watch had been smuggled through controls on the new owner's wrist; the mink coat embarrassment that had done nothing for my reputation; and the glory-stealing antics of Nobby Pilcher. While they were saying that my 'nosebleed' job was the largest on the Branch in revenue terms since the watch-smuggling heydays of the Sixties, Sam was furious at my ineptitude over the diamonds; unfairly in my view, but what did my opinion count?

A ripple of laughter went around the room, but quickly stopped when a new scene began rolling forward, in colour. A beautiful young

57

woman was kneeling down in front of a naked man sitting on the edge of a bed, supporting the largest penis I had ever seen. The girl took the enormous organ in her hand and pulled it towards her mouth, and then, incredibly, proceeded to swallow it, a feat I had never even imagined in my wildest fantasies, never mind seen – or even considered feasible. I sat uncomfortably with a certain stirring in the groin. The man immediately behind me whispered to his colleague: 'It's Linda Lovelace. We've only had one pirated copy of *Deep Throat* in the squad so far. It's only just out.'

Deep Throat was a landmark porn film made in America in 1972. It was apparently one of the first such films to feature a plot and character development, although I'm sure that's not why most people watched it. The basic premise was that an attractive but sexually frustrated young woman, played by Linda Lovelace, is informed by her doctor that her clitoris is located in her throat and thus she can only achieve orgasm by performing a particularly penetrative form of oral sex. You can probably imagine the rest. The film was subject to various obscenity hearings but was openly shown in New York cinemas and became something of a hit, even earning a review in the prestigious *New York Times*. It was, however, banned in the UK by the British Board of Film Classification and would remain so until a DVD version was given an R18 rating in 2000.

The absence of sound from the flickering screen was matched only by the intense quiet of the screening room, apart from the odd throat-clearing, during the sixteen-minute run. The film had a soundtrack but the projectionist had switched off the sound for some unknown reason. The silence made the impact all the more stark and left an impression on me that I would never forget. Twenty or so grown men who had come through the Swinging Sixties now dry-throated by egregious images of heterosexual behaviour. After the film had reached its messy climax and the lights went on, a thickset man in his forties came up to me and introduced himself as DI John Cooper, the head of the Yard's Obscene Publications Squad, colloquially known as the Porn Squad.

'What a stroke of luck,' Cooper ventured. 'Did your blokes realise what they'd stopped?'

I was in a dilemma. The Porn Squad had a reputation, and it wasn't for discretion. Don Holmans had talked, I didn't know how knowledgeably, about them receiving brown envelopes on Fridays from Soho traders

– payoffs to avoid punitive raids – but I had no hard information to rely on. It had come as a profound shock to me to be told, virtually on my arrival from the provinces, that many police officers were, in the then unfamiliar jargon, 'bent'. I'd been brought up in the belief that the police were the incorruptible pillars of society – my *Dixon of Dock Green* analogy. Nothing in my albeit infrequent contact with the police during my early years in the job in the North-East of England had carried even a hint of dishonesty. Now I was in an environment where my colleagues openly talked about collusion between detectives and villains, two Met officers I knew about were under arrest on corruption charges, and Sam Charles was embroiled in a major case alleged to involve the Drugs Squad itself. Stupidly I had not expected company at the film showing, although in the absence of an 8mm projector of our own, I had no choice but to use Scotland Yard's facilities. That was clearly something to sort out for the future, I thought.

'No, it was more than a stroke of luck, John. The examining officer at Heathrow found the film with some American sex magazines addressed to a shop in Soho and asked us to look at it.'

'I see. What do you intend to do now, bust the address?'

'No, not yet. We're going to trawl through our records to see if they've had any previous importations and see what turns up.'

'Good thinking, Mike. Could you keep me informed? We could work on this together. The address of the shop would be useful. We may already have tabs on them.'

'OK. I haven't got the whole consignment here, but I'll let you have it when I get back to the office.'

MY RETURN TO THE office was greeted with a little more enthusiasm than my Hatton Garden foray. I had considered myself fortunate to have escaped Sam Charles's clutches and to have landed three weeks later in Colin Garrett's team. Colin was the antithesis of Sam. No less ambitious, he was however open and encouraging. An ideas man, he liked nothing better than brain-storming sessions with his officers to resolve difficulties and to identify new lines of inquiry. His favourite comment was 'problems are only solutions in disguise'. I never discovered whether the maxim was original or borrowed but I embraced it with a passion and adopted it from then on as my personal credo.

The only similarity between the two SIOs was their medium height. Otherwise they were poles apart. Whereas Sam was slim and muscular, Colin was slightly overweight, with a round, clean-shaven, handsome face and jet black hair, which some said, mischievously, was dyed. Whereas Sam was ascetic, awkward and temperamental, Colin was genial and helpful. He was also ten years younger than Sam and had made SIO two years previously at the age of thirty-five; Sam Charles's eccentricities had delayed his promotion to that rank until he was forty. This still rankled with the older man, who regarded himself as superior in all respects.

'Well done, Mike.'

We were sitting in Colin's homely office overlooking New Fetter Lane and the dozens of black taxis that used it as a shortcut between High Holborn and Fleet Street. There were Hogarth prints on the walls, including a set of eight charting The Rake's Progress from wealth and popularity to destitution and insanity. Whether they were meant as a warning to their owner, I never asked. I knew that Colin was not poor and didn't need all of his Civil Service salary to keep the wolf from the door. He had a reputation for not being as generous with his money as he was with his time and support, another cause of tension between the two SIOs. Sam always referred to him as F22, which Don Holmans explained to me was the tightest aperture on a camera. That was not at all fair or accurate, as I discovered while working for him for three years, but it was hardly the first undeserved reputation in the IB.

I raised my eyebrows and smiled. 'Thanks. I met the head of the Porn Squad at the Yard. He wants to team up with us on this one.'

'I bet he does. What did you tell him?'

'I said I'd speak to you and get back to him.'

'Ordinarily I would have said no. But I don't think they would be so daft as to compromise a live Customs job; although they're capable of anything. No, something else has come up that I want you to look at, so the quicker we get rid of this one the better. And they can take it over if it gets messy or protracted. HQ is dead against us getting too involved with porn anyway.'

'Why?'

'Government policy. Keep it low profile. Don't stir things up. Not a big issue. Bigger fish to fry, so don't spend much time and money on it. Quite frankly I think they're pleased the Met gives it only token attention, even if that gives the dicey officers more scope.'

'Same priority as drugs, then?'

'Their drugs effort is a disgrace,' said Colin, warming to the topic. 'The problem's been growing since the early Sixties and all they've got is a man and a boy in the so-called Drugs Squad, none of them squeaky clean. Hopeless when we need any assistance. They simply aren't taking the problem seriously enough. They'll live to regret it, of that I'm certain.'

'So what do you want me to do?'

'Sort out Laurel and Hardy quickly with the Met and then have a look through these papers. Decca Records has gone into receivership owing us over half a million in tax. We're preferential creditors with the Inland Revenue but we still stand to lose a hefty sum. It has taken the record industry completely by surprise. The market is buoyant with the ending of retail price maintenance and the UK is still leading the world in the pop music field.' It was true, he said, that Decca had been vulnerable to competition, with its reliance on the comfort of guaranteed prices and a catalogue with fading popular appeal. 'But there could be evidence of deliberate, and therefore criminal, bankruptcy in there somewhere.'

I put the papers to one side and got back to *Deep Throat*.

I SUGGESTED A SMALL team for the raid on the Soho premises and DI Cooper agreed: two officers, Cooper and me to make the initial approach when the owner arrived to open up in the morning, followed by the others when required. I would have two of Colin's more senior officers in support. Cooper would also have two of his officers as back-up.

The importer was shown on the Import Entry, the official Customs declaration, as Eros Publications, in Compton Street, Soho. The 5,000 'Laurel and Hardy' films were part of a much larger consignment of soft-porn magazines, with plenty of nipples but not a pubic hair in sight. They were from an exporter in New York under such subtle titles

61

as *Young Wives Fantasies*, *Skirts Up*, and the even more disingenuous *Stockings and Suspenders*.

The law governing the content of imported photographs or films was much more restrictive than national legislation on home-produced material. Customs only had to prove that the imported material was obscene, whereas the police had the more difficult task of proving the material they seized was 'likely to deprave or corrupt', one good reason for Cooper to want to join in a Customs operation. The interpretation of both definitions changed with the times, but it was always much easier to declare an item obscene at any given time and have it accepted in court than prove its deleterious effect on an individual. So pubic hair could be defined as obscene in 1971 but not lead to depravity and corruption. The twin concepts were as confusing to law enforcement agencies as they were to the general public, but legislative changes were sloth-slow (in fact that's an understatement: according to 'Pi' Patel in *Life of Pi*, the three-toed sloth can travel at over five metres an hour, whereas this legislation was inert!).

We were lucky. The importer who had signed the declaration in this case, one Jack Cribb, had telephoned the cargo office a couple of days after I had discussed the operation with Cooper. He wanted the airline to deliver the packages and gave an address in Frith Street, also in Soho. If he had decided to collect the consignment himself, we would have had all the problems associated with inner London surveillance, heavy in manpower and high in risk of losing the tail. As the films were an absolute prohibition, they could not legally enter the country without copper-bottomed safeguards, and so would have had to be secretly substituted by more innocuous material before being released to proceed to their destination. The importer could not then be caught red-handed, as it were, opening the box and taking possession of the actual films. This would make it much more difficult for us to establish the importer's knowledge, the legal requirement of *mens rea* needed for the more serious offence of *knowingly* importing a prohibited good, which carried a maximum penalty of two years in gaol.

Being in control of the delivery made it easier – we could leave the real films in there – but required a slight change of plan. I would accompany the delivery driver dressed in the courier company's livery.

We would sit on the premises until the right time came to knock, not an easy judgement as I knew from one or two parcel post jobs I'd done in the past, where the postman delivered a parcel containing, say, a couple of ounces of cannabis and we all charged in after an 'appropriate' waiting period. The delay was to allow the recipient to open the parcel and handle the drugs, which had been sprinkled with gentian violet, an invisible dye that turned purple when handled. It was always a delicate judgement as to exactly when to steam in.

Cooper was happy to go along with my plan but asked on the phone whether we were going to 'gentian' the films. I smiled as I recalled my first postal job in Hackney as a real rookie. I had been a bit too liberal with the gentian. The door was answered by a black Jamaican, well he had been black: his hair, face, hands, T-shirt, jeans and the towel he was carrying were now all a bright violet. Behind him, his partner's former white dress was violet from hem to hem, while the small child she was carrying in her violet arms looked like a fake blue-period Picasso. I laughed out loud when I remembered the first exchanges:

'Customs. I believe you have just received a parcel from Jamaica?'

'No man, wrong address, try next door.'

'What's funny?' said Cooper, sounding miffed.

'Oh nothing, John, sorry, you just reminded me of my younger days. No, that won't be necessary. Our lads have had a look at the premises. It's a shop in Frith Street that sells girlie mags, next door to a strip joint. There's no back entrance, so it's one door in, one door out. We just have to make sure he has enough time to open the consignment. I would have thought overnight would do it. But if he takes anything out the front door before we're ready, we'll have to nab him.'

THE TWO-DAY DELAY GAVE me time to study the Decca papers Colin had given me. It took me almost three hours to sort through the pile. It was a sorry tale. One of the longest-established companies in the record industry, Decca appeared to have been resting on its laurels, relying overmuch on its traditional classical music base. It had been slow to sign up new artists during the Sixties - infamously turning down a young band called the Beatles - when the pop music explosion offered enormous returns to any company with the foresight to sign up the new bands emerging almost every week and taking the UK, US, Europe and Australasia by storm. The classical music catalogue continued to bring in steady revenue, but without any growth, whereas the middlebrow – standards, show tunes, brass bands, jazz, country and western, folk, comedy – was losing ground; sales had been shrinking fast. Decca had only three recognised pop groups on their books that were good earners, but even with the solid classics sales it was not enough to prop up the rest, which accounted for over 65% of the business.

The directors, most of whom had grown up with the company, had clearly been caught by the ending of guaranteed prices and the increased spending power of the younger generation, who were putting their money into rock and roll, R&B, reggae and pop. They could barely feel the heat of this competition because they were in a different place in the market, a different era. The catalogue was like a hammock: two ends, pop and classics, holding up a sagging middle bumping onto the ground every time the wind blew. The bank had finally cut the ropes and the body had rolled out onto the ground, belly up.

I felt like handing the file back to Colin. It was open and shut, to me: a straightforward case of a staid, unimaginative, short-sighted group of directors being swept out of their cosy existence by an avalanche of change. I saw no evidence of criminality. But I didn't think it would go down too well with my boss if I dismissed it out of hand without giving it my attention for at least a couple of days. A visit to their premises in south London would make my analysis look more respectable, and it would give me a nice day out while I was waiting for Laurel and Hardy to go the right way up.

Decca's finance director, Stephen Hall, was a man in his late fifties who had joined the company as a junior clerk when Hitler was coming to power. When we went through the figures together that afternoon, I was impressed with his arithmetical skills but not with his knowledge of the current music scene. I seemed to know more about the latest developments in the industry – and I had only read the file that morning. An accountant should be more than a just a bean counter, I thought, as we went through the balance sheets and accounts.

We were sitting in his oak-panelled office, looking out onto a sprawling ten-acre industrial complex housing pressing rooms, printing presses, material stores, warehouses, loading bays, recording studios, administration blocks, transport sheds, security offices, boiler rooms and a huge chimney. Despite the liquidation, it was a hive of activity, like an ammunition factory during the war. I had driven past it many times on my trips to and from work but had never realised just how extensive it was. It employed over 10,000 people.

Hall was bitter. His future looked bleak, but at least he had some personal resources to fall back on. His main bleat, on behalf of all the 'loyal workers and staff who have nowhere to go', was against falling standards. The young weren't interested in classical music any more. They had 'no taste', he said. And the newcomers in the business were pandering to the lowest common denominator to cash in on this 'seismic shift in the nation's cultural heritage'. I thought that this was a bit rich, given that a lot of the company's production was mainstream, and much of that pretty banal and sentimental; but I recognised that Hall's only real passion was classical music. My interests were fairly broad but my favourite music at the time was jazz and brass bands. I recorded all the jazz programmes I could from the BBC. But that afternoon I realised I hadn't bought a gramophone record in years.

It was hard going. Hall was not good company, with one complaint following another, and I was relieved when we finally finished the books. After we had shaken hands and I headed for the door, Hall said, 'The people you should be after are the young upstarts. They're unscrupulous. They're tearing the industry apart.'

'Like who? I asked politely but uninterestedly.

'Like Virgin Records.'

THE SOHO OPERATION WAS set up for the first of March. We would make the delivery late in the afternoon, having already stationed an observation van across from the premises in Frith Street during the night, when the streets were empty. From the unmarked Ford Transit our senior officer, George McKenzie, kept everyone amused over the radio with a colourful description of the everyday life of a Soho street. At one stage I had to tell him to restrict his remarks to the whereabouts of the owner and leave the assorted toms, pimps, strippers, punters, traffic wardens and coppers to get on with their life.

His key information was that a man had opened up at 8am. There had been a number of customers during the day most of whom had come out carrying a plastic bag. The strip joint next door had been busier, and the open door on the other side with its three named buzzers – Maxine, Jo and Model – was even more popular.

Our airline courier van approached Frith Street at 4.05pm and I readied to make the delivery. McKenzie radioed that the owner was still in the shop, together with three customers who had been in there for some time. In I went, carrying cartons.

The shop was about fifteen feet square, brightly lit, with racks of magazines from floor to ceiling on all four walls. Most of the titles were familiar – *Playboy, Hustler, Spick, Span, Health and Efficiency* – others less so. But all looked fairly innocuous to my untrained eye. The man at the counter confirmed his name as Jack Cribb and asked us to put the four boxes in a storeroom behind him. The dingy, windowless storeroom was smaller than the shop, with fewer shelves, leaving more space for the large number of cartons stacked one on top of another in no systematic order. We were in and out in five minutes and Cribb gave the driver and me twenty cigarettes each for our trouble. I was quite tickled by that.

McKenzie was surprised to learn that we had seen no customers in the shop. Three were unaccounted for, he confirmed over the air. I was annoyed that we'd let our side down in front of the police and chided my colleague for being sloppy.

'You should have kept your eyes on the punters, not the pros, Mac. Over.'

'I'm not mistaken, Mike,' McKenzie insisted, but didn't press the issue.

'OK, well let us know when the shop closes and whether chummy takes anything out with him. Over.'

'Wilco. Out.'

On the following day, we parked outside the premises from 7am. The door was locked and bolted and the windows boarded up. McKenzie had reported that Cribb had not closed up the previous day until midnight, when he bolted the door and boarded up the windows. Traffic had been especially brisk during the evening and customers had sometimes spent well over an hour in the place. That made me nervous, but Cooper convinced me that Cribb couldn't sell 1,000 films in one night. I was conscious, though, that I had effectively allowed prohibited material to be put onto the home market.

I sat in the front passenger seat of Cooper's car. I was surprised at how busy Frith Street was at that time of the morning; I always thought of Soho as a night-time place. Darkness and sleaze were natural bedfellows; sex wasn't commercial in the morning. But it wasn't the sex industry keeping the narrow streets full of people and traffic: office workers walked from tube stations to their workplaces; chefs and waitresses entered the plethora of Italian, Turkish, French and Greek cafes; film executives strolled to their plush office suites in Wardour Street; booksellers hurried to open up the string of bookshops in Charing Cross Road; bakers arrived at the numerous bakeries, from which mouth-watering aromas and the smell of Cona coffee pervaded the air, enticing the twenty-four-hour car park attendants otherwise bent on getting home and into bed to delay their return. We spotted only the occasional recognisable sex worker, exhausted from a night of taking and giving, and one traffic warden, beginning her shift idly observing the cars rapidly filling up the empty parking meters on her patch. Rubbish trucks, delivery vehicles, black cabs, buses and people aplenty – but no Cribb, yet.

It was a long wait. Then one minute we were discussing Arsenal and their chances in the fifth round of the FA Cup and the next we were watching Cribb opening up the shop. It was 10.35am. We waited some more. Eventually, after four customers had gone into the shop and only one had re-emerged in over an hour, we went in. Cribb was standing behind the counter. One customer was flicking through a magazine. There was no sign of the other two. There was also no sign of the films. Some of the magazines had appeared on the shelves but we could find nothing else, even after an extensive search of the two rooms assisted by the back-up team. Where were Laurel and Hardy, and where, for goodness sake, were the three customers?

8

Devils

'THERE WAS NO PLEASING him. You thought you knew what he wanted. Well, when I say that, he's not the greatest communicator in the world.'

'You can say that again.'

'So you had to guess half of it. You went out, did it, came back, and then he'd moved the bloody goalposts. You'd either done completely the wrong thing or else you'd missed the crucial bit of evidence. It was so demoralising.'

I was unburdening myself on my friend and colleague Brian Hubbard, who had joined the Branch just after me, in our usual watering hole directly opposite the office. The Printers' Devil was in fact a lot of people's usual watering hole in that area: journalists, lawyers, shopkeepers, car-park attendants, IB officers. And yes, the printing fraternity of course: Fleet Street, the home of the British newspaper industry, was just a minute's walk away. This was when drinking in working hours was *de rigueur*, before the real Printer's Devil, in the shape of Rupert Murdoch, put a stop to most of that.

That evening the pub was packed with after-work drinkers and you had to almost shout to be heard over the din, not that that bothered me. I needed to belt out my frustration.

'But I thought the bloody-nose job had gone superbly well?' said Brian. 'Everyone was full of it.'

'It had, until I got back to the wretched office and Sam.'

'What?' Brian cupped his hand around his ear straining to hear over the raucous laughter coming from a group of our colleagues gathered around two of the office typists.

'Back to Sam Charles,' I shouted just as the laughter died away and my words rang out over the temporary lull. I lowered my voice again. 'He said that we'd missed the crucial diamond records and the extent of the fraud wouldn't be known until we had an accurate tally of the "off" diamonds. He also said we had to recover all the customer books from as far back as possible for the same reason. The trouble is, he was right of course, but the client was in no fit state to cooperate when we left the premises the first time.'

'You went back then?'

'Oh yes, he who must be obeyed had decreed, whatever the consequences.'

'Was the client still there?'

'Only just. We were lucky. He had loaded up two briefcases full of papers and had a taxi waiting to take him home.'

'Brilliant, what did you do?'

'Went home with him, of course.'

'What, in the taxi?'

'No, Alan Taylor had his car and we bundled him into that.'

'Didn't he object? You had no powers to enter and search his home did you?'

I smiled. 'Haven't you heard of the Ways and Means Act? Listen I was more concerned about going back to Sam empty-handed than upsetting a little jeweller who was as bent as a corkscrew.'

'So how did it go?'

'Almost one hundred per cent. We spun his drum…'

'You're really into the Old Bill slang already. Didn't he try to stop you searching the house?'

'I think the word is compliant. He was as compliant as a West End tart, less infectious but not as much fun. In fact he was darn right miserable throughout. He'd given up the ghost, actually, and we were able to do as we liked. His wife gave us more of an ear-bashing. She was worked up about his health. The word Gestapo was dropped into the conversation a number of times, but she didn't prevent us finding record books going back over ten years. We calculated that he had been using the second hand fiddle since 1964, more than seven years. Some of it will be out of time for prosecution purposes but we can still collect the back tax. It will amount to a hefty amount.'

'How much?'

'We haven't done the sums yet. Hey but listen, this is history now, since then I've been having some fun up in Soho after my move to Colin's team. Fancy another beer?'

'Why not,' said Brian. 'I've missed the seven-thirty from London Bridge, the next isn't until eight-twenty. My dinner'll be cold now anyway.'

As I fought my way to the bar and waited to be served, feeling a little more at peace with the world, I studied the crush in the centre of the room. The two female typists in the middle of the throng of investigators were clearly in their element. In a male-dominated organisation full of testosterone-filled blokes, they had quite a choice, and had enjoyed a clear field for years. Their first competition had arrived the previous week in the shape of a third typist taken on to cope with the heavier workload being generated by us. She stood a couple of paces away from the boisterous group, being button-holed by Phil Jackson, unaffectionately known by his unimpressed colleagues as 'Jacko', the Branch number one lecher. She looked ill-at-ease and kept glancing my way with a wan smile on her pretty face. She was younger than her sisters-in-type, about twenty-four, with straight sienna-brown hair falling down like a soft silk scarf over her shoulders. Her best features were her finely shaped legs, almost fully exposed under a very short miniskirt.

I couldn't stand Jacko. He was an older officer who'd been on the Branch about ten years and never lost an opportunity to regale the company, any company, with stories of his sexual exploits. He was so self-centred; he always had to dominate the conversation. If anyone managed to get a word in edgeways, Jacko always managed to steer the subject back to himself if, for some strange reason, it had gone off at a tangent away from the Centre of the Universe. The incredible thing to me was that some of the girls fell for it.

When I returned with the drinks, Brian pointed to the couple and commented on Jacko's solipsism and arrogance.

'She's as interesting as he is loathsome,' he said. 'You wonder how anyone can be that self-confident with looks like that. He told me that he believes in the direct approach. Apparently he put his hand on a police inspector's bum last month at a "do" and said, "Do you fuck?" She slapped him hard across the chops and told him he was the

Devil Incarnate. I wouldn't have been so restrained. He was completely unabashed. He said to me that at least he knew where he stood. It saved time: for every five slaps, he struck lucky. Anyway enough of creeps, what about your Soho jaunt? But before we get into that, you said that you had been almost a hundred per cent successful with the jeweller. What about the unsuccessful bit?'

'We didn't find the diamond records. And he wouldn't tell us where he bought them. Still a mystery. But listen, we've enough evidence to sink a battleship. Sam wasn't too happy, but then as I was saying, there's no pleasing him.' I took a swig of my beer. 'So, Soho. I don't know what you've heard?'

'I overheard a conversation in the canteen, so I know about *Deep Throat* and the stakeout. Oh, and the delivery. But apparently you lost some customers as well as the films? Careless. I didn't hear the outcome.'

'It was almost unbelievable,' I said. 'There we were in this seedy little dive, with this creepy purveyor of filth at a complete loss for an explanation. He was no bloody help. When we hit the wall and had nowhere to go but out, he adopted this oily, obsequious manner that got me riled. So riled that I started throwing things around in the storeroom at the back, kicking the boxes, emptying the contents all over the floor. He got quite agitated but I didn't care. It wasn't me at all but I somehow couldn't help it. And then do you know what happened?'

'I'm all ears.' Or rather he was until another great guffaw came from 'our' crowd. Brian looked across.

'Look at that bastard, Mike. He's all over her. He's got hold of her arm now. You can see she doesn't like it. God I could…'

'Brian, she's old enough to take care of herself. Do you fancy her then?'

'No. It's just that…Anyway, tell me what happened next?'

'Oh, yes. Well, one of the boxes that I'd half-emptied – I'd found nothing more than softcore stuff – I threw…'

'Keep the noise down lads! Some of our customers are complaining. Enjoy yourselves by all means but a bit quieter, please?' The manager was a decent enough bloke so a chorus of sorry's greeted his request and the noise level subsided immediately.

'Blimey, am I ever going to hear the end of this story? I don't want to miss the eight-twenty.'

'Sorry, Brian, where was I?'

'I think you were throwing boxes.'

'Right. Well you won't believe it. I threw the box down and it bounced against this block of shelves, and hey presto, it swung open. It was a cleverly concealed door leading into another room. Brightly lit. It was like Aladdin's Cave. It was almost twice the size of the storeroom with shelves from floor to ceiling, and, would you believe?'

'Ali Baba?'

'Ha bloody ha.'

'The three missing customers?'

'Right second time. Give that man an orange. We stood there open-mouthed, I can tell you.'

'I'm not surprised. Was this where the films were?'

'And the rest. Hard porn of every shape and size. Straight hetero – I really don't know why they ban that. A bit of erotica can't do any harm. But the other stuff? Ugh. Fetishists, sado-maso, homo-lesbo, animals. And worst of all, kids. Children as young as five.'

'Bloody hell. Did you nick Ali Baba, then, or leave him to the Old Bill?'

'I would have nicked him but that wasn't quite the end of it. In the corner of the room there were two doors. One was a bathroom. The other led into a bedroom, and off that another bedroom. But they weren't your ordinary bedrooms. The first was lit with a red light and was set up with a tripod cine-camera, thirty-five millimetre SLR, and lighting for filming and photographing the bed. It was unoccupied when we burst in but the bed was covered in assorted lingerie. The further room was almost like a dungeon, with high racks.'

'Racks?'

'You know, like you see in castles. There were pulleys, presumably for hauling people off the ground, handcuffs, whips, scourges, even stocks. And a huge waterbed. This was also fully equipped with photographic gear. And even that wasn't the end of it. It was a veritable rabbit warren. A locked door from the dungeon opened into a corridor which led to three flights of stairs, with a suite of rooms on each used by three ladies of the night – or in this case, of the day, because they were hard at it and it was only twelve o'clock.'

'Wow. But I thought the punters were in the porn room?'

'They were. There was a separate exit from the shop which was also the main access from the street to the girls. They had labels like "Maxine", "Jo" or simply "Model" on the side of the open door. Each notice had its own bell to let them know the punter was about to come up the stairs. I have to say that we left the Met clearing it all up. It was just too messy for us, and Colin wanted me out of it ASAP. He isn't at all interested in non-revenue jobs. You know, Brian, there's enormous potential for huge jobs in the porn field. I'm not talking about the straight stuff but the nasties, especially child porn. It's disgusting.'

'Look, I can't miss that train, she'll kill me. But let me know how it goes next week, will you?'

'Sure. I'll probably be all right for Tuesday, because my squad week ends Sunday evening thank God. See you then.'

I then stood up and turned round. I was surprised to see the pub almost empty. Most of the lads had gone. Jean, the senior typist, had her arm around one of the watch team, and the new girl, June, was backed into a corner of the bar with Jacko still sounding off. I decided to act, and walked over to the pair.

'Sorry, Jacko, time to break up the party. You wanted a lift, June?'

If the girl was taken aback by this surprise statement, she didn't show it. Jacko's thick-lipped mouth fell open.

'Yes, thanks. I've just been saying to him it's time I got on my way. I don't want to hold you up.'

WHEN WE REACHED THE pavement outside, I turned to the girl and said 'I'm sorry to tear you away. I thought Jacko was going to eat you.'

'I thought he was going to kill you! Thanks for rescuing me.'

We both laughed as we walked the hundred yards or so across to my car parked in one the squad bays outside the office. The keen early March wind cut into us and the girl quickly donned the long-waisted black coat she was carrying over her arm. The fashion for long coats that buttoned down almost to the ankles ideally complemented the short skirts the younger girls were all wearing. She had to undo one or two of the lower buttons to get into the car and I heard myself, full of brio and

charged with sexual energy, ask her, uncharacteristically, to undo a few
more if it was a struggle.

She looked at me calmly, then undid all the buttons and opened the
coat to uncover her white lace-fringed top and black skirt. I extended
my hand and said, 'Mike Knox.' She shook it and replied, 'June. June
Farr.'

'I hope you will do.'

'What?'

'Go far.' The three pints had reinforced my bravado more than my
wit. 'Let's get out of here before Jacko tumbles he's been tricked. Where
do you live?'

'Clapham.'

'Great, that's on my way home.'

I backed the car out and drove down New Fetter Lane, through the
lights and onto Fleet Street, heading for Waterloo Bridge. As we passed
the City of London and Westminster boundary, I asked her if she was
married.

She smiled up at me and said that she wasn't and why was I interested.

I smiled back, and then pulled hard on the steering wheel to avoid
a taxi that was overtaking us around the Aldwych. I was beginning to
think naughty thoughts. This wasn't right. I had rescued her from the
lascivious clutches of the Devil Incarnate and here I was entertaining
the same thoughts as him. From one devil to another; that wouldn't do.
When I pulled up outside her block of flats, she leaned across and kissed
me on the cheek, thanked me for rescuing her, and bade me goodnight.

On my slow drive home, my mind was muddled by so many emotions.
Why should I even be considering straying for the first time in over
eight years of a happy, faithful marriage? Whether these thoughts were
the result of an irresistible surge of adrenalin that had been fostered by
the recent experience with Suzanne Bellard, or the exposure to all that
pornography, or simply the attraction of June Farr, who knows? What
I did know was that the Investigation Branch was noted for its share of
infidelities, offering as it did opportunities for indiscretion when one
was so often on call or away from home. Perhaps it was us, and not the
porn merchants we chased, who were the real devils!

9

Virgin Territory

PORTERS WHEELED THE CADAVER through the double doors into the mortuary. A pathologist and a policeman were talking in the corner of the large room waiting for them to lift the corpse onto one of the five examination tables, a flat rectangular marble slab surrounded by a shallow trough to collect the blood and fluids, with a plug-hole at one end to dispose of them.

I watched queasily as the pathologist made his first incision from the centre of the breastbone down to the stomach before I moved away from the glass door of the sample room where we had set up observations. There was little to alleviate my slight nausea as I moved across to the window past rows of jars containing hands, arms, knees, kidneys, brains and a hundred other assorted body parts. More boring as it might be, I much preferred looking out at the commercial premises directly opposite the hospital. Yet Dick Browne and I had been there a week and seen absolutely nothing of interest. We had watched plenty of deliveries into the warehouse and plenty of postal vans taking mail orders out, but had spotted nothing remotely like a bulk export.

After the Decca dead-end, I had decided to follow Hall's pointed finger at Virgin Records, without much enthusiasm it must be said. My mood quickly changed. I found that Virgin had only been going a matter of fifteen months and had already made a significant dent in the marketplace. Large full-page ads of all the latest long-playing albums at a 6.5 per cent discount were appearing in both the musical press and the dailies. While the manufacturers no longer controlled the retail price, profit margins on records were tight, so selling an LP at a 6.5 per cent discount virtually wiped out any worthwhile profit. Looking at it from the tax angle, however, offered a possible explanation. Top catalogue

LPs were being retailed at £2.30. I calculated the purchase tax on the wholesale value as fifteen pence, the exact amount of the discount being advertised. Coincidence or design?

I had arranged to make a visit to Virgin posing as an assistant to the local purchase tax officer. Their premises, in an old warehouse in South Wharf Road directly opposite St Mary's Hospital, consisted of a large storage area on the ground floor piled high with boxes of gramophone records and two rows of benches for the packaging and labelling of mail orders. There were three tiny offices on the first floor, in one of which I had found Richard Branson, Virgin's twenty-year-old owner. Unkempt, struggling to grow a wispy beard on an otherwise hairless face and wearing an old, stained pair of jeans, woolly cardigan and open-necked shirt, he looked like a typical first-year university student – which he was, or rather had been until he dropped out to start up the magazine *Student* in an effort to get into the business world.

He had been polite but had quickly steered me to a rickety wooden desk in the corner, on which the company books had been laid. It took me almost two hours to sort through the chaotic accounting system. The sales were mainly by mail order, but Branson also had acquired a small shop in Oxford Street six months previously. During that period, the sales through the shop had increased to over a quarter of the business. A similar increasing proportion of sales was being exported. One document had aroused my interest: an export certificate stamped by Dover Customs showing 30,000 LPs exported to France. I was interested because exported records were exempt from tax. These ones were declared as being taken out of the country in a Land Rover. It did not take me long, following a look at the boxes of LPs on the ground floor, to work out that it was impossible to fit 30,000 of them into the back of the old company Land Rover parked at the back of the warehouse.

In the three weeks prior to obtaining permission from the hospital administration at St Mary's to set up our observation position in the mortuary, all of us in Colin Garrett's team, including Colin himself, had been engaged in a time-consuming and exhausting exercise. This involved nightly trips on a shared rotation basis up to the premises of EMI, Virgin's main supplier, to mark the records before delivery to South Wharf Road. Colin had thought up the idea of using ultraviolet pencils, invisible to the naked eye, to give each consignment a unique reference number. With the full cooperation of their chief security officer, every night at about 1am, two of our team had entered EMI's main warehouse at Ruislip and been taken to a locked room off the packing hall. The Virgin consignments, as many as 500 LPs at a time – all the Top 20 records from the Beatles to the Kinks, Tom Jones, the Grateful Dead, the Rolling Stones, the Supremes, and so on – were brought to us under the strictest secrecy, for us painstakingly to write the coded number on the record label in the centre of each LP. It was the same idea as tagging wildlife, or prisoners to track their movements, but in some ways not as easy because we couldn't see what we had written.

The undercover operation had borne fruit in less than a week. We had followed up our marking efforts with private mail order purchases to our own homes and had also gone out to the Oxford Street shop and bought the artists and titles we'd seen during our nocturnal visits. Each time a record was brought into the office, Colin proudly pulled out the UV lamp he'd borrowed from the Home Office Technical Branch and placed the label under it. There had been jubilation when the number on the first record, Tom Jones's *She's a Lady*, had shone back at us under the ultraviolet light.

Over the course of the following two weeks, we accumulated forty-five marked records. It was encouraging but hardly clinching. These were only a tiny percentage of Virgin's total throughput during the period and all could legitimately be part of the high proportion of home market sales. Without verifying the actual distribution of the marked records through the books of the company, which was almost impossible given the primitive state of the accounts, there had been no way of proving that tax-exempt exports had been diverted to the home market. Costly as it would be, surveillance on Virgin's premises with continued nightly marking was the only option.

'THEY'RE WEIGHING THE POOR guy's liver!' Dick exclaimed, as he stared through the glass door. 'Are they on piecework?'

'Another postal van,' I said, ignoring him. I noted down the time in our observation log. 'And a taxi.'

'Hang on,' Dick uttered as he came back to the window. 'Branson's getting into it.'

'Big deal,' I remarked sarcastically. 'What I want to know is when is he going to get into the Land Rover and drive down to Dover? He'd been doing it once or twice a week for ages, until we arrived on the scene.'

'Do you think he suspects something? Your visit maybe?'

'No way. I've never seen anyone so laid back and relaxed. Anyway he's used to the Department being around, checking his returns every quarter, verifying exports, etcetera.'

'What about EMI? Could there have been a leak from there?'

'Anything's possible but I would be very surprised. The security guy has a spotless reputation in the business.'

'What, an ex-copper?' Dick laughed.

'Yes, even an ex-copper can go straight,' I replied. We both chuckled, which temporarily relieved some of the gloom that had descended upon us.

'What about the local officer?' Dick did not give up easily. 'You said he was not very helpful. Po-faced, I think you said.'

'Stevens? No, he wasn't very happy when I asked him to make the appointment for me and lie about who I was. He didn't like the subterfuge. He assured me that "his" trader did everything by the book and was completely above suspicion. It was probably a defensive reaction, but I've met this sort of protective mechanism in the past.'

The local officers, or more accurately control officers, were responsible for a number of registered purchase tax traders in their geographic area. They saw their clients every three months to check the records and inevitably became friendly with them, sometimes over-friendly. Not in a corrupt way, but the closer the association, the more difficult it was for them to see an irregularity.

'He couldn't see this kind of fraud just by auditing books anyway,' I continued, 'but he isn't to know that. I represent a threat to his standing. But that doesn't mean he would alert Branson, does it?'

Dick looked out of the window again and did not reply. We both fell silent.

The air of gloom remained for the following two weeks. The pattern was roughly the same. The warehouse was opened up at around nine every morning by one of the office staff. The warehouse and other office people began arriving from about 9.15. Branson himself seldom arrived before ten and, apart from a couple of mornings when he left by taxi, returning late in the afternoon, he stayed indoors until he left for the day at about 6pm. They had an average of three deliveries from the major record companies each day and up to three postal vans taking away the parcels. The Land Rover did not leave the warehouse during the whole time, and neither Dover nor any of the other south-coast ports that we had contacted had seen an exportation of gramophone records in any type of vehicle. Meanwhile we spent our days in the mortuary and our nights in the locked room. The strain was palpable.

COLIN GARRETT SAT LOOKING at the glum faces across the desk from him. We had been tossing the outcome of our six-week effort about for over an hour, but we still hadn't found the solution, which was clearly in heavier disguise than Colin was accustomed to. Nonetheless he had not lost any of his optimism.

'I think we'd better wrap this up now. We've looked at all the options and it is obviously pointless to prolong the agony and add to the cost with more marking and obs. We have no choice but to go back in there and see if the books reflect the activity we've witnessed. We also now have a tax return which covers the period of our purchases of marked records. Mike, fix up through the local officer another "routine" visit as soon as possible.'

I rang Stevens at the Purchase Tax Centre at the Elephant and Castle as soon as I got back to my office. I couldn't believe my ears; he refused to make the appointment. He bleated on about the Department allocating a limited number of visiting hours to each trader, and that a further visit now would prevent him carrying out vital audits later in the year. I was incredulous, in fact speechless for a few seconds, before I gathered my composure and ordered Stevens to make the appointment. Stevens refused and became angry, threatening to complain to his line manager, the Surveyor for the area, and his regional head, the Collector. I shouted, 'Complain to them then; I'm coming over straight away,' and slammed the phone down.

The Investigator

I decided against involving Colin and went over on my own. As extraordinary as the situation was, as unreasonable as Stevens's attitude was, I was confident I could handle it. I had not taken into account the powerful psychology of closing ranks against a common enemy.

The Investigation Branch was not popular with control staff across the Department. They were seen as the Glory Boys: crash, bang, wallop, in and out, leaving the mess to be sorted out after they'd trampled all over some poor officer's home patch, destroying good relationships with traders that had been carefully nurtured over years and which had to continue long after the IB had left to conquer fields anew. I knew the Outfield Service and how they thought. Heavens, I had worked there for nine years before joining the Branch.

I had deliberately avoided joining the uniformed service, but that was where the action was: smuggling in all its guises. The detection, the chase, the arrest, police stations, courts, prisons. Exciting stuff. Intellectually more challenging and better paid the Outfield Service may have been, but it was so strictly regulated that the control systems had become procedural, inflexible, static, sclerotic. Customs meant customs. Traditions. Try changing a control measure that had 'stood the test of time' but had uncovered not a single infraction in thirty years.

The introduction of betting duty in 1968, which was laid to the Outfield, began to change the culture. Real villains began to confront officers unskilled in dealing with them. We had to quickly learn innovative methods, such as undercover test betting, on and off course, where we placed bets that could be checked later against the records; if they didn't show up, it provided irrefutable evidence of evasion. I had cut my fraud teeth on illegal bookmakers, until the bookies got wise and switched their illegal activities to telephone betting. I never forgot the time when I was test betting on a freezing cold and rainy evening at Redcar Dog Track. After placing a bet on each of the first four races, I overheard another punter talking to the bookie:

'Awful night. Not too good for business?' I heard him say.

'Too right, mate. If it hadn't been for you and the Excise officer over there I'd have gone home by now.'

But entrenched attitudes elsewhere did not change overnight. Fraud was still a taboo subject, certainly as far as purchase tax was concerned, where regular auditing and close contact with the directorship of companies was considered virtually fraud-proof.

As Stevens droned on with his spurious arguments for inaction, my attention drifted to the six lanes of traffic I could see from the Surveyor's office window negotiating the complex of roundabouts and one-way systems around the Elephant. It was drizzling, a typically grey day in London, which reflected my mood. I was brought sharply back to the present when the Surveyor, Tony Bradley, endorsed everything his officer had just said.

This put me in a dilemma. How much intelligence should I share with these two recalcitrants, both of whom were clearly on the trader's side and might consider it their civic or even their official duty to share the information with Branson; indeed, might have already done so? We might well have already been compromised, but I didn't know that for certain, and the risk of jeopardising the operation at this stage was therefore still an issue. And how convincing was this intelligence in any case? Discount sales that happened to coincide with the amount of tax but still gave an up-and-coming business plenty of exposure and some profit from higher throughput; exports of more LPs than a 1967 Land Rover could carry that might well have been a misprint for a larger vehicle on the form; marked records sold on the home market that could well be legitimate? No, that wouldn't cut any ice with these two boneheads. Force was the only answer; overwhelming force. The problem was that their Collector, with over 2,000 staff under his command, was a Civil Service Grade 5 and outranked my Chief, who was at that time only a Grade 6; Civil Service ranks descended from Grade 1 (Chairman). At the time of the case, our CIO was a Grade 6, though Douglas Jordan would subsequently become the first Grade 5 CIO. So force it had to be, but force of argument or of personality, or both, to get the derailed train back on the tracks.

I did have another lever which underlay all dealings between the IB and the rest of the Department and which gave us the edge in disputes like this. It was generally only implied and seldom, if ever, deployed. The IB was responsible for carrying out all internal investigations into officers suspected of wrongdoing, from petty theft to full-scale corruption. There was no separate body at that time. Fear was always a useful persuader.

'So let me get this straight,' I addressed myself directly to Bradley, fixing him with what I hoped was a steely stare. 'This has really nothing to do with using up allocated audit hours. What I think you are saying is that you are prepared to jeopardise weeks of intensive investigation work so that you can go back into those premises again in three months' time, heads held high, remaining on friendly terms with "your" man, on the off chance, and I mean off, that you uncover an underpayment of five shillings and sixpence. Listen, Mr Bradley, we're talking thousands here, and criminal evasion to boot. If you impede this inquiry, the Board will be down on you like a ton of bricks.' It was always sensible to pray in aid the top management of the Department when the going got tough. 'Are you saying that this guy's as clean as a whistle?'

'No, we're not saying that.'

'Then what are you saying?'

'We're saying that you have no hard evidence to justify underhand methods that could leave us with egg on our faces and a complete loss of trust. Our credibility would be ruined. Remember, we have to carry on our task long after you have swanned off on other cloak-and-dagger jaunts.'

'Mr Bradley, let me make a deal with you. You make this appointment for me and I promise that I will personally explain to Mr Branson, when we have finished, that all along you were convinced of his innocence and that it was only our nasty suspicious minds that spoilt his day. We'll be the bogeymen. We're to blame. We'll take full responsibility if we have to say sorry. We're used to that. What do you say?'

Bradley paused for a moment and looked at Stevens. I looked at both of them. They were both from the old school. Bradley was in his fifties, small, on the obese side of heavy, with a horseshoe of grey hair encircling his bald pate. His manner was terribly formal. He wasn't going any further up the promotion ladder, I decided. Stevens, aged about forty-five, was much thinner and taller, with a shock of wiry, greying hair over protruding ears. If he carried on like he was that day, he wouldn't even make surveyor. Their first jobs in the Department would have been checking methylated spirits sales in chemists or examining Manesty stills in school labs, as I had done. What they knew about sophisticated tax fraud, I judged, they could get on the back of the cigarette packet Stevens kept fiddling with.

'Could you give me five minutes, Mr Knox?'

'Of course, take as long as you like.'

After a brief absence from the office, Bradley returned and agreed to the visit but said he would make a full report to his Collector that day. Stevens then led us along the corridor to his room, where he was to make the call to make the appointment. He dialled the number and waited.

'Oh hello, can I speak to Mr Branson please. Alexander Stevens from Customs. Yes, of course, I'll hang on.'

Stevens cupped his hand over the receiver. 'He's with a client, won't be long.'

'Richard Branson? Richard, it's Alex Stevens...Fine, thank you, and yourself? Richard, I have that young man who came the other week with me. He would like to make another visit if that's all right? No I don't think so. He's from our Investigation Branch. Something troubling him about your exports, I think. What about this afternoon? Two o'clock? Fine, he'll see you then.'

As the phone went down I blew my top. 'What the blazes do you think you're bloody well playing at?'

'Don't you swear at me. I've got you your appointment.'

'My appointment? My appointment?' I mimicked Stevens's public school voice. 'My surreptitious appointment, my undercover appointment, my "little look to see if we're right without arousing any suspicion" appointment? You've got me my appointment all right, with a guy who's destroying every bit of incriminating evidence he's got in his possession right now. Thanks a bundle. Six bloody weeks work up the spout. You'll pay for this, Stevens. Mark my words, you'll pay for this.'

'STAY IN THE AREA, don't come back to the office.'

Colin's calm reaction over the phone did little to assuage my anger, but it was effective in keeping me focussed. 'Go through with the visit and I'll get someone back into the morgue as soon as I can. I'll also mobilise as many people as I can for an early knock if that's needed.'

'What are we going do about the idiot Stevens, Colin?'

The Investigator

'I'll deal with that. But not right now. Don't you concern yourself about what's done, think about how you're going to play chummy this afternoon.'

That afternoon I climbed the stairs up to Richard Branson's office a second time, on this occasion with my heart in my mouth. How I was going to carry off this visit as nonchalantly as last time, I had no idea.

The young whizz-kid was, understandably, much more attentive and asked me straight away what the problem was. I explained that the last time I had looked at his books I had not seen all of the official evidence of the exports on which he was claiming tax relief. I needed to verify his latest tax return.

'What period do you want to look at?' he asked.

'Oh, just the last three months will do. The period of your last return,' I said.

He sorted through the papers on his desk and handed me a file marked 'Exports'.

My blood pressure rose as I leafed through the documents. The file contained sheaf after sheaf of export certificates, stamped and authenticated by Dover Customs, all of which declared an export of anything from 10,000 to 30,000 LPs – in the good old company Land Rover. I quickly read through the documents covering the period of our surveillance and the declarations were all the same. What was more, the exports took place on the actual days Branson had left the premises in a taxi.

I could only assume that he had gone down to Dover by train, gone into the Customs Office, made the false export declaration, pocketed the certificate and high-tailed it back to Paddington. Our control systems were obviously hopelessly deficient. Most of our resources were being put into intercepting illegal imports, not checking that a Land Rover containing a tax-free load of gramophone records had actually boarded a ferry to go to Calais. Oh dear. Nevertheless, I was now convinced that all those hours through the days and nights were going to pay off. I thanked Branson for providing me with the satisfactory evidence of shipment, told him that I did not need to see any other records as all seemed to be in order, and took my leave.

Back in the office, Colin was already making the necessary arrangements for the knock the following morning. He allocated officers to the examination of the warehouse and the visit to the Oxford Street retail shop, and told me that Dick Browne, who was actually senior to me, would accompany me as my second officer for the interview with Branson. As with all tax fraud cases, we would proceed by what was called information and summons. This involved a report to the Board, the Solicitor's endorsement that there was a case to answer, the issue of an information setting out the offences for the accused and the court, and the issue of a summons to be served on the offender requiring an appearance in a magistrate's court. It was a long process.

I was disappointed. I felt the case was serious enough for an immediate arrest and magistrate's court appearance. Colin was adamant that there was no precedent for that, but I insisted that here was a young man who was just setting out, apparently very successfully, on a possibly long entrepreneurial journey (how did I know?) who needed a sharp shock to bring him back on to the straight and narrow. In any case, I argued, I hadn't arrested anybody since I had joined the Branch and it would be a valuable experience to do it. Amazingly he relented. This meant that we did not need any prior approval from our solicitor and the knock could still go ahead the following day, an advantage given the circumstances and the possibility of a delay convincing our solicitor's office.

On 28 May 1971, Dick Browne and I drove up to South Wharf Road and parked outside the hospital. The rest of the team took up positions to raid the two premises. As we entered the premises and I again ascended the flight of wooden stairs, we were blissfully unaware of the dramatic events of that morning and the previous night. Apparently Branson had been tipped off. In his autobiography written years later, *Losing My Virginity*, Branson would say that a caller, who refused to give his name, phoned him at midnight and warned him that his bogus trips to the Continent had been noticed and that he was about to be raided by Customs and Excise. He was told to buy an ultraviolet lamp from a chemist shop and shine it on the records that he'd bought from EMI, which would reveal the letter 'E' stamped on the vinyl of all the ones that were meant to be exported to Belgium. He also described us as 'rather different from the two dowdy little accountants I had been expecting. They were bulky, tough men, and very threatening.' Bulky and tough was certainly not a description that had ever been applied before to Dick and me; it's interesting how a person's perceptions can change when up against it. He also relates in his book the shock of seeing a man fall out of an upstairs window of the hospital and end up pinioned on the spikes of the steel railings opposite his office as he arrived that morning – some preparation for what was to follow! Certainly he greeted us with a slightly strange look on his face; one of recognition, a little strained perhaps, but not of surprise. I thought momentarily at the time that he might have been warned about our visit, especially after my contretemps with the local staff, but I would have no idea what had actually happened until many years later when I read his book. No matter, I reasoned, we already had the evidence we needed.

In the event, the interview was straightforward. We set out the facts in detail, which he initially challenged. But as soon as Dick told him about his purchase of the marked record he had received at home, and all the other purchases we had made, Branson gave way almost without further encouragement, and broke down. He explained, tearfully, that on a trip down to Dover with a consignment of records he had obtained the necessary export documentation in the Customs office and had boarded the ferry for Calais. On arrival there, he was stopped by French Customs for not having an international travel carnet for his transit through France with tax-free goods to his customer in Belgium. He therefore had no other option but to return to Dover. As he drove home he realised that he still had the export certificate in his possession, already stamped as boarding the ferry and as though he had therefore exported the records. Being an intelligent young man and a natural-born entrepreneur, he thought that this might well be something he could try again, only without boarding the ferry. Branson couldn't believe his luck. Here was a huge hole in the system, and a huge opportunity. He could make as many trips as he wanted and accrue what was a huge profit for an inexperienced young man just starting out in a business and carrying a huge debt, as he had taken on the cost of two premises in central London and a recording studio, The Manor, at Shipton-on-Cherwell, near Oxford. The temptation to clear his debts was just too great.

When I spoke the leaden words informing him of his arrest and rights, he broke down again and asked to make a phone call. I agreed when he told me he wanted to ring his mother. I will never forget the words he spoke when he got through to her, especially given the heights of success he has risen to since. With a slight tremble in his voice, he said, 'Mummy, I've fucked up.' I explained that he was under arrest and being taken down to Dover police station to attend court the following morning. He regained his composure after his mother had clearly reassured him that he would have all the support he needed down there.

We had to drive all the way down to Dover, since that was where the offences had taken place. On the way I realised we needed some light refreshment and agreed with Dick that we call into a pub for a drink. This we duly did and the three of us had a pleasant break from the stressful activity of the previous days. What a contrast my approach to arrest was compared to that of the police. No handcuffs, no police van, no cover over the head: just a quiet drink and a friendly chat before he had to face a night in the police cells in Dover. There was no relaxation for me when I got back to the office though. When Colin Garrett was told of our pub stop, he went berserk. He couldn't believe we could be so naïve. I don't think he realised just how nice a guy Richard Branson was. But as arrests go, I must admit it was a first – and a last.

In court the next day, Branson was released on £30,000 bail put up by his mother. The family, though mainly in the legal professions, was not at all wealthy. His mother was a former air hostess and had little in the way of capital assets, so used her house as collateral. She had faith in him and I am sure she was an inspiration and driving force in the future he then carved out for himself. The Department, following representations from Branson's legal advisers, later dropped the charges against him in favour of an out-of-court settlement of evaded tax and penalty amounting to £60,000, the modern equivalent of over £500,000. Tax fraud in those days was seen mainly as a financial matter, particularly with first offenders, which could be resolved by way of a satisfactory monetary settlement. The major benefit of this for the culprit was the absence of a criminal record. Branson was allowed to pay £15,000 up front and the rest by instalments of £3,000 a month. He went on to develop the businesses so successfully that he was able to relieve his mother of the bail security obligation and pay off all of his debts in under three years.

The Investigator

THE STORY LAY UNDER wraps for some time but eventually became known to the media. I have read various versions of the happenings in that spring of 1971 and find the different accounts fascinating. Tom Bower, the investigative journalist who has exposed many celebrities in biographies over the years, placed the story in the very first chapter of his long biography of Branson under the heading 'The Crime'. His account is colourful but full of inaccuracies about the investigation, which was surprising given that he had spoken to both Dick Browne and myself about the case while he was writing the book. He went on to effectively challenge many of Richard Branson's own recollections.

In *Losing My Virginity*, which was first published in 1998, the future business magnate recalled that when he left Stowe public school at the age of seventeen, his headmaster's parting words were: 'Congratulations, Branson, I predict that you will either go to prison or become a millionaire.' These words came back to him as he languished the night in a police cell, a night that he later decided was 'one of the best things that ever happened to me': He realised that at twenty years of age, he had been able to lead his life in the way he wanted. Prison took that away. He vowed he would never again do anything, in life or in business, to risk his freedom or embarrass himself.

Of course he didn't become just a millionaire but a billionaire. His autobiography does contain a number of inaccuracies about the circumstances of his arrest, and over the years, whenever the subject of his early indiscretion has come up in TV and press interviews he has been gradually watering down the seriousness and size of the offence. I cannot offer any useful comment on the differences in the Bower and Branson accounts, save to say that his subsequent enormous success in business and knighthood shows the mettle of the man and how he has put this youthful, foolhardy episode behind him, which I respect.

10

The Nitty Gritty

TIGHT EXCHANGE CONTROL RESTRICTIONS had been in force in the UK since before the Second World War. Their application became widespread following the financial crises of the early 1930s, with the object of conserving the country's gold and foreign currency reserves to provide maximum benefit to the national economy. The controls were abolished by the Conservative Government of 1959 but a restriction on taking cash abroad remained in force to protect the value of sterling. The subsequent Labour Government reintroduced exchange controls in 1966 but increased the cash allowance of £25 to £50. Those of us of a certain age can well remember these restrictions when taking our hard-earned week's break in the sun in the late 1960s courtesy of Freddie Laker, although in those days most of us actually couldn't afford more than what was regarded as a meagre allowance anyway. It seems strangely quaint, looking back, as money flows are so easy these days, although the downside is the huge increase in money laundering by criminal enterprises and gangs.

In 1972, our commercial smuggling team uncovered an elaborate exchange control fraud involving Italian business people resident in the UK. They were moving large amounts of capital to Italy and had been for years, apparently. Ron Harris, a talented and dedicated officer who later, to my good fortune, came to work for me for a couple of years, was what we called the case officer – quite often the investigator who uncovered the fraud and who was then given the responsibility of gathering all the evidence, reporting the case to the Board and overseeing its completion. He identified Charles Paul Fodrio as the ringleader and driving force behind the fraud. Fodrio was a shipping agent for fine arts, which was at the core of the illegal activity. He deposited money sent to him by a countrywide team of collectors in British branches of Italian banks. He would then pay Italian-based art dealers large sums in cash from these accounts, which they would repay by depositing the equivalent sums in lire in Italian bank accounts to the credit of the UK business network. The Italian art dealers were then able to pay for antiques and works of art in cash in the UK and ship them to Italy, undervaluing them as well to evade Italian customs duties and taxes.

I was part of a forty-man team going out on a co-ordinated knock to interview all those involved. I questioned a husband and wife, owners of an antique business in West London. My interview was essentially with the wife, an attractive, dark-haired woman in her late thirties. She gave me all their records to look at, but when I began to ask her questions about their exports of antiques to Italy, I noticed how her demeanour changed, particularly when I drew attention to certain individual items. It was almost too subtle to spot, but I managed it because she had these beautiful, large, dark brown eyes, which I spent most of my time gazing into as we talked. Every time we got onto Italian exports, I noticed that her right eye watered; just a little, not nearly as dramatically as my nose-bleeding jeweller, but enough to alert me to follow a certain line of questioning. I deliberately moved away from the suspect consignments to innocuous ones, as I had with the nose-bleeder, and then switched back again to the relevant ones that concerned us. It worked every time. The eye watered, dried, and watered again. Quite soon, a confession was forthcoming: when I pointed out her Achilles' heel, she realised the game was up.

In fact, we had success all around: the investigation revealed illegal transfers amounting to £1,750,000 (the modern equivalent of £21 million) and a profit of £70,000 (over £850,000 today) for Fodrio. Thanks to detailed records kept by all and sundry, the subsequent court case resulted in fines, costs and forfeitures of £173,380. Fodrio was made bankrupt.

THE SIGNIFICANCE OF THIS story is that it reveals how important it was to scrutinise the behaviour of suspects during interviews, whether at traders' premises, in police stations, or when caught red-handed. The lessons I gleaned from this I would use to good effect throughout my career, first as an investigator and later as an international negotiator. Interview techniques were never part of the training programme when I joined the Investigation Branch, or indeed at any time throughout my sixteen-year career in the service. You learned them 'on the job'. You came to know what worked and what didn't. It helped if you were encouraging, sympathetic, logical, persuasive or, at the most, coercive, rather than loud, egocentric, aggressive or plain disdainful. Treating your suspect with contempt was the surest way for them to feel the same way about you and clam up. 'Fair' rather than 'fear' was my watchword.

The stereotypical interrogation technique so often featured in the media, crime novels and films – the good cop/bad cop routine – had its merits; but I found that the softer approach was more likely to yield results and obtain admissions, which were so often the vital evidence and the surest way to obtain a conviction in court. However, there was one case I worked on with my senior officer, Tim Back, which shattered this 'hard/soft' theory of mine. We spent almost two days on the road around East London chasing a ship's captain we wanted to interview for cigarette smuggling. He evaded capture by moving from one house to another, sometimes leaving clues; it became a game to him. We eventually tracked him down to a house in Sidcup, arrested him and took him to the local police station. We were exhausted, having hardly slept for thirty-six hours, and began our interview straight away to get it all over as quickly as possible. Our patience was wearing as thin as our stamina and we were no doubt more abrupt than usual. Twenty minutes into the interview, the captain exclaimed, 'Isn't one of you supposed to be the good guy?' It brought me up short and we settled down to a friendly chat, which led to a full admission and a later conviction. He was fined a modest sum, his cooperation, guilty plea and our silence about the chase being taken into account.

Not every investigator had the ability to get 'the cough', to use the police jargon of the day. But some were outstanding. The best of all the ones I worked with was Dick Kellaway, who also had a great number of other attributes which ensured that he later became the Chief Investigation Officer. One of Dick's most successful methods was to take the conversation beyond any admission of guilt. He assumed that was a given – otherwise they wouldn't have been there – so he wanted to know why they had done it, when they had done it, how they had done it, what they got for it, who told them to do it and so on. Not, did you do it?

He might ask: 'So when did you first get the idea of short-dropping the fuel at service stations and selling the surplus for cash to another garage?' Answer: 'It wasn't my idea in the first place.' Gotcha! This was the very opposite of the legal mantra of suspects being regarded as innocent before proven guilty, but it was not improper since this was only evidence to put before a magistrate or a jury, not a presumption of guilt in the legal meaning of the term. And the gullible so often fell for it. Mind you, Dick did have those other assets. He was dashingly handsome, charming, highly intelligent and had an easy sense of humour, which all played a part in persuading wrongdoers to confess.

There were many others with persuasive talent: Terry Byrne, Jim Scahill, Nick Baker, George Atkinson, Dave Hewer, and Dick Lawrence, who also made it to the top job, becoming CIO after I had left the ID in 1985. These were the ones I worked with over the years so to name any more would only upset those I miss out – and those who were pretty hopeless at it. Sam Charles was a prime example of the latter. He made no attempt to obtain admissions. He was very softly spoken, which made it sound as if he mumbled, and although he was a kind, gentle and an extraordinary man in so many ways, he lacked the sort of charisma that would make suspects warm to him, or at least unburden themselves of their guilt. This was, I am convinced, why he relied on gathering all the indisputable evidence beforehand. He knew he could not guarantee getting a confession.

I have to say that admissions were much more common in the early days, especially outside London. Many of the people we dealt with were naïve in the ways of the underworld. As we became involved with more hardened members of the criminal fraternity, and the villains became more streetwise, learning through films and the media, we found them more confident and better informed. Getting a cough became more and more difficult, if not impossible, which is why so much more effort was applied to obtaining the evidence beforehand, particularly through surveillance techniques. But creativity, thoroughness, freedom to pursue individual lines of enquiry unhindered by over-zealous bosses, and, above all, integrity were the hallmarks of the ID, which empowered it and made it the force it was.

11

Pornography

IN 1970, THE *Sunday Times* published an article complaining that there were only thirty-five Customs investigation officers working exclusively on drugs. When I read the article I laughed. At the time there were in fact only five, in a single specialist drugs team with Peter Cutting as the SIO (he later became Chief Investigation Officer). Even that team had not been operating for long. Three months later, thanks to a major reorganisation already in train under the new Chief, Douglas 'Dougie' Jordan, there was a second team bringing the numbers working on drugs up to ten!

From the end of the War and the establishment of the Investigation Branch, there had been five CIOs before Jordan, all having to deal with rapid increases in smuggling and fraud. All were talented and achieved some superb results with limited means. However, some were rather cautious, none more so than Jordan's immediate predecessor, Charles Simison, the Chief when I joined the Branch. A pipe-smoking ex-Waterguard officer, his main concern was maintaining standards, which was a laudable objective. He had, like Sam Charles, an extraordinary attention to detail and the Branch under him turned in some excellent jobs, particularly as he had such people as Sam, John Thwaites, Vernon Cocking, Jeff Smith, Ron Turner, Peter Cutting, Richard Lawrence, Colin Garrett and Alan Taylor, among many others, to come up with the goods. He was firmly against watering down the quality of his bailiwick and therefore was not in favour of expansion, hence the almost fixed complement of officers during his time.

When he retired in 1969, the Board chose not to promote anyone from within but to appoint Dougie, who at that time was an Outfield Deputy Collector. He had, however, been an investigator in the Branch in the 1950s and was the favourite of 'Teddy' Brown, the Chief Inspector, who made the selection. Jordan was tall and, despite suffering from a mild form of scalp psoriasis, was a good-looking man. He was affable and friendly but a person of firm convictions who brooked no nonsense, in every way a commander who gained the respect of the whole branch.

When he took over, he realised that the Board's current policy of involving all branches of the Department in investigation work risked increasing costs without improving efficiency or increasing results, not to mention the danger of serious overlapping, which resulted in lost cases and chaos. So in 1970, after a year in post, he submitted a report to the Board entitled Review of the Organisation and Work of the Investigation Branch. Specialisation became the order of the day. Up until that time, with the exception of specialist watch-smuggling teams, two drugs teams, one hydrocarbon oil team and one purchase tax team, all work was carried out by so-called general teams who took on all types of fraud, moving on to another job as soon as a case was completed. This jack-of-all-trades approach, as investigator Roy Brisley called it in his excellent history of Customs investigation, *Enforcement, Enforcement, Enforcement*, meant that an intelligence-based approach could not be progressed efficiently and productively. Simply dealing quickly with a variety of reported cases lacked depth, follow-up and the acquisition of specialist knowledge. Vital information which could lead to the unearthing of significant fraud or organised criminals was often unused or lost.

Our work often differed from that of other enforcement agencies, such as the police. Major customs frauds seldom arose from what one might call reported crime. We didn't come across dead bodies or plundered banks or smashed jewellers' windows, requiring our immediate attention: the kind of event where you then have to work backwards from the crime to uncover whodunit. Of course customs officers did frequently make seizures at ports and airports but these were mostly dealt with locally and often were not referred to specialist investigators to follow up and look at in depth, or to notate in central records for future use. No, our most important cases came from intelligent research carried out by enterprising officers delving deeply into the trades and people involved. We had to look for the fraud and find the fraudsters.

Pornography

Take drugs, for example. We would often learn of a smuggle before the conspirators got it into the country, either through a tip-off, an informant, suspicious patterns of foreign travel by dubious characters or some other intelligence method. Our job was then to try to track the smugglers and catch them in the act of bringing it in. So instead of working backwards from a crime report, we worked forwards to follow the crime as it unfolded. This was a particularly exciting – but challenging – way of working and was largely unique to the IB.

Jordan's report was endorsed by the Board and led to an enormous expansion of his investigation service. From eighty staff when I joined, the numbers trebled over the next three years. In 1972, the Investigation Branch became the Investigation Division, a much larger body with several branches under its control. This meant the upgrade of the CIO post to Grade 5, equivalent to a Collector, which carried more weight with the rest of the Department. By the 1990s, by which time Dougie had long since left, it had reached well over 1,000 staff. Dougie Jordan could fairly be regarded as the 'founding father' of modern Customs investigation, although that title should be shared with Horace Kimber, a renowned Chief back in the 1930s.

One of the principal reasons for the expansion was the huge increase in drugs smuggling following the free-thinking, freewheeling, licentiously wild 1960s. We then joined the EEC in 1973, and a whole host of new procedures and regulations came into being, most of which had a direct effect on the Department: from the replacement of purchase tax by VAT which was, to the surprise of the Inland Revenue, allocated to Customs and Excise, through to Monetary Compensatory Amounts (MCAs) under the Common Agricultural Policy. But freer trade within the EEC did not mean the end of prohibitions and restrictions.

I benefited directly from this. With the creation of a whole series of specialist teams in a relatively short time, I was lucky enough to be chosen, along with nine others – an unprecedented expansion – to become a Senior Investigation Officer with my own four-man team. I had served only four years in the Branch/Division and at that time I was the most junior, or more accurately, the shortest-serving officer to reach the rank. I must have done something right. I was given the newly created pornography team. Maybe the lovely Linda had something to do with that?

The Investigator

WHEN I TOOK OVER the pornography team, I suddenly came under enormous pressure to get results. It was 1973, a particularly difficult year. The police were investigating allegations of widespread corruption in Scotland Yard, with the porn trade and its links to certain detectives being a major area of concern. Given HMCE's role in dealing with prohibitions, it meant that we had to be seen to be taking the subject much more seriously than before. The Chief gave me three months to break into the big boys of the porn game or I'd be 'back wearing a funny hat again'. He was never one to mince words was Dougie Jordan, although I'd never worn a funny hat in my life.

Jordan stressed that we should only be interested in the major operators, particularly those importing 'the nasty stuff', as he put it. Since he had taken over from the old brigade, who saw the IB as their personal fiefdom to be preserved in aspic and kept as a small, tightly knit elite, the buzzword was expansion. The IB was going to get bigger – much bigger. Yet this went against all our traditions. Typically, investigation officers rose slowly through the ranks. Most, on reaching the age of fifty, returned to the Outfield Service or went into policy jobs in Headquarters; only a tiny minority would eventually take Chief or Deputy Chief positions in the ID. Jordan had been parachuted in from the Outfield. He therefore had only limited investigation experience to bring about seismic change. But change there was.

The world of pornography was becoming much more complicated largely as a result of developments in other countries, notably Scandinavia, the Netherlands and the USA. In 1967, written pornography was legalised in Denmark; films and magazines followed in 1969. The Netherlands also seemed to be open house. The huge number of prostitutes openly offering their services in the windows of the red-light district of Amsterdam when I first visited this so-called Venice of the North in 1970, the unrestricted premises showing hard-core films, as well as the sale of hard-core pornographic magazines and literature in shops there, gave me some idea of their permissive values and attitudes. The situation in the USA was more complicated, given the number of different laws in each state, but the open showing of the movie *Deep Throat* in cinemas in New York in 1971 spoke volumes. It is still a film that would not be shown in mainstream cinemas or on TV in the UK even today, although the mainstream bio-pic *Lovelace* has been on open release.

In England and Wales, the main legislation on pornographic materials were the Obscene Publications Act 1959 and the Obscene Publications Act 1964, to which the Indecent Displays (Control) Act would be added in 1981. Video-oriented depictions of hard-core material, with certain exceptions for works considered primarily artistic rather than pornographic, would remain banned until 1999 when the removal of trade barriers with other European Union member states allowed for the relatively free movement of such goods for personal use. Today 18-rated videos are only available in licensed sex shops, but pornographic magazines are available in some shops selling newspapers and magazines. In 2008, the Crown Prosecution Service unsuccessfully prosecuted a man under the Obscene Publications Act for a textual story on a pornography website involving the pop group Girls Aloud. Also that year, the Home Office introduced legislation to criminalise possession of what it has labelled extreme pornography; these laws are now contained in sections 63 to 68 of the Criminal Justice and Immigration Act 2008. There are restrictions in every country especially when it comes to child pornography and paedophilia, but on the whole, even the nasty stuff, as Dougie Jordan put it – bestiality, sado-masochism – is often available to anyone over the age of eighteen.

THE COLOR CLIMAX CORPORATION in Denmark, established in 1967 when the first legalisation laws came into force, was producing a vast amount of material which was targeted on the UK, the USA and indeed wherever there was a market. Its colour magazines were of the highest print quality and largely depicted straightforward hetero-sexual acts. They could fairly be regarded as extreme, although that changed over time. They were being smuggled in containers along with women's magazines and standard men's mags like *Playboy*, *Mayfair* and *Men Only*, as well as a large number of deliberately mis-described postal consignments. Its mags were in marked contrast to the material available at that time in newsagents, street corner vendors and some of the more salacious shops in Soho: first *Health and Efficiency*, *Tit-Bits* and

Reveille, then *Spick and Span* and, heaven help me, one called *Stocking Tops*. The corporation also began churning out 8mm films and, much later, videos.

My work with the pornography team largely entailed following up seizures made at ports and airports to find out who was behind them. These often resulted in further seizures in warehouses and bookshops and the arrest of a number of minor importers and store managers but no serious people, just a lot of front men for the principal villains, and quite a number of amateurs. We were London-based and saw the inside of some very seedy places and what was a thriving sex industry in the capital. London was at the heart of the Swinging Sixties, a not-entirely-accurate description of the period since things did not really begin to 'swing' until the second half of the decade and then carried on in that vein well into the mid-Seventies, when the Miners' Strike, the three-day-week and a humiliating financial bailout by the IMF brought the party to a morose close. Life then seemed to turn more serious, although interest in sexual freedoms – the permissive society – carried on relent-lessly. The Pill had much to do with that, as well as the pop music scene, daring changes in women's fashion, Carnaby Street, and the growing hippy culture. It was also the time of the emerging feminist movement, which I was not alone in identifying with the remarkable Germaine Greer. I hardly know anyone of a certain age who hasn't read *The Female Eunuch*, first published in 1970.

I admired Greer. She was a highly intelligent woman, so articulate that she literally demolished the arguments of some of the leading male figures of the day in TV, radio and stage debates; and a brilliant writer, with compelling arguments about the role of women in the second half of the 20th century. Many of them are still relevant today. She argued that unacceptable demands were made on women to display the perfect body in order to please others, particularly men, creating expectations as unrealisticc as they were unfair and exploitative. 'Whether the curves imposed are the ebullient arabesques of the tit-queen or the attenuated coils of art nouveau, they are the deformations of the dynamic, individual body, and limitations of the possibilities of being female,' she wrote in *The Female Eunuch*. 'In the popular imagination hairiness is like furriness, an index of bestiality, and as such an indication of aggressive sexuality.

Pornography

Men cultivate it, just as they are encouraged to develop competitive and aggressive instincts; women suppress it, just as they suppress all the aspects of their vigour and libido.'

Imagine, then, my shock when we seized an imported consignment of a pornographic magazine with the non-too-subtle title of *SUCK*. This was published in Amsterdam at the time and the copies we seized had a full-page photograph of a naked Germaine Greer. It would not be appropriate to show the image here, but to give you some idea of its impact, she described it as 'looking at the lens through my thighs'. The close up was of an extremely hirsute…well, all I can say is that it did not quite have the artistic quality of Gustave Courbet's *L'Origine du Monde*, although it did have even more explicit detail. What surprised me most was why she decided to expose herself in this way when she was so opposed to female exploitation. She was obviously making a point but I failed to see it. Perhaps it was her way as a woman of exploiting male weaknesses? An attack on pornography? Attracting publicity for her cause? It certainly did nothing to stop the avalanche of pornography landing on our shores and beginning to be produced in ever increasing volumes around the world. Maybe one day she will explain.

My officers had to sift and pore over erotic material day in and day out, in order to establish cause for seizure, and I became somewhat concerned about the effects on them of being exposed to this tide. We had by now obtained our own projector to screen the 8mm films and so did not have to involve Scotland Yard. I rotated the officers to reduce the exposure and limited their observations to the time it took to establish whether we were dealing with hard or soft porn. I cannot say whether this had a lasting effect, but since the laws on pornography have since been liberalised, even in the UK, society must see it as a lesser problem than alcohol or drugs. I was convinced, however, that such exposure could become addictive. Harmful? Perhaps not, but the spread and easy availability of pornography on the internet and its adverse effect, particularly on children, is a problem which has now got completely out of control. I am only relieved that I was able to grow up through puberty and beyond with the normal influences and desires of the day, without the completely distorted images of sex without love or feelings of respect to guide my early progress to adulthood.

The Investigator

Much of our work centred on Soho, that small, vibrant area of central London that was synonymous with sex. Soho was world famous for it: not just the stationary nudes (moving while completely naked on stage was against the law) in the Windmill Theatre, nor the strippers in Paul Raymond's Revue Bar, but also the even more infamous lines of streetwalkers around Piccadilly Circus and the streets that fanned out from there, before the Street Offences Act in 1959 swept them off the streets into the flats above; the clip joints that fleeced their punters out of large sums to pay for coloured water to watch the gyrations of young titivators; the 3,900 performances of Kenneth Tynan's *Oh! Calcutta!;* the gay bars around Old Compton Street; and the thriving porn trade. Largely unknown to the customers seeking thrills in magazine and bookshops from under-the-counter, hard-core magazines, books, videos, and later DVDs, this trade was in the iron grip of a few porn barons, known to and protected by corrupt police.

Of course it wasn't all sex. The area had numerous restaurants with cuisine from around the world; leading theatres, mainstream cinemas, film company offices, jazz clubs, conventional bookshops, pubs, as well as tree-lined squares, stately residences, Chinatown, and Carnaby Street. Sadly, the first coffee bar to open in England, the 2i's, has long since gone. Where am I going to get those delicious banana milk shakes for one shilling now?

Our work was hampered to a large extent by the police inquiries into their own corrupt relationships with some of the porn barons, and with Sam Charles' secretive involvement in those investigations. Whenever we strayed into their territory, we were warned off. It became so frustrating that I suggested the team be wound up and for us to be given some more fruitful work. So after six months it was agreed that this wasn't a serious enough subject for scarce and costly resources to be used on, and the police were best placed to handle it, if somewhat unreliably – the understatement of the year, given what was emerging from the wave of clean-up investigations under Met Commissioner Sir Robert Mark.

12

Oil

OIL WAS A SUBJECT I knew something about. I had worked in refineries and warehouses as a junior officer, and of course my success in gaining a place in the Investigation Branch arose from my work on the RFTU van in the Sixties. So it was that I was next given hydrocarbon oils as my field of work and the specialist oil team. Their detections up until then had been limited to one oil warehouse at Micheldever in Hampshire and had then dried up. Senior management thought a fresh mind would be the solution, and so they turned to me. When I took over the oil team I adopted the same approach learned in those early incursions into the fraudulent activities of the oil industry.

I was ignorant, however, of the type of frauds that were being perpetrated in the refining, storage and distribution fields. Oil was stored in bonded warehouses and duty was only charged when the oil was delivered to users, mainly garages or service stations. The nature of the product, namely that oil evaporates in storage, meant that every warehouse facility was allowed a 1% loss of product. The measured amounts of loss within that tolerance, when the storage tanks were checked and account taken by the warehouse excise officers at the end of each month, were written off. Duty was charged on quantities over 1% unless a satisfactory reason for the additional loss was given, such as a major verifiable leak in pipes or tanks, which rarely happened. There was therefore no reported crime. If someone was stealing oil, there was no identifiable loss within the 1% limits.

With no reported information upon which to work, I decided to contact Mike Comer, a former IB investigator who, I learned, had left to become the Head of Security at Esso. It turned out to be the breakthrough we needed. Mike not only had film star good looks but also a shrewd brain. Start with the easy ones, he advised. This, you can imagine, immediately resonated with me. Virtually all the delivery pumps in warehouses had been fitted with up-to-date meters which accurately recorded the amount of oil put into tankers for delivery to users' premises. However, there were still one or two that used dipsticks to measure the amount of oil going into each tanker's compartments. Esso had recognised that this antiquated method would allow unscrupulous and unsupervised tanker drivers, or ones in cahoots with their supervisors, to overload their tankers and then sell the extra fuel for cash at garages on their route; hence the major meter upgrade in all their installations, which had still to be completed.

Comer pointed the finger at a small warehouse installation in Lowestoft where there were no meters. Losses from the warehouse were always within the 1% limit but often only just. He and I went to look at the site and I decided to set up a fortnight's surveillance from one of the private terraced houses conveniently situated overlooking the loading bays and pumps. It was a unique opportunity, since most oil installations are large and a long distance away from any local housing or businesses. I was lucky. The elderly lady who answered the first door I knocked on was most obliging. 'Never liked that lot! I bet they're up to no good. Help yourself. Yous'll get the best view from my spare bedroom upstairs. Mine's on t'other side. Can't stand looking at 'em. And the bloody noise!'

We set up surveillance there two weeks later and never went short of cups of tea and treatises on the state of the world, and Lowestoft in particular; a singular experience with a kind lady who turned out to be the soul of discretion. It was certainly a little less gruesome than St Mary's morgue! The observations, however, turned out to be a complete waste of time. All we could see from what was a very good vantage point were tankers filling up and leaving, filling up and leaving, filling up and leaving. We could not see how much was going into each separate tank of the vehicles to enable us to check the company records later. As close as we were, even with the aid of high-powered binoculars, we could not see the dipstick readings.

A council of war was required. Back in the office with Mike Comer and my team, we discussed the various options and possibilities for taking the enquiries further. Should we repeat the observation exercise, only with a mobile surveillance team ready to follow selected tankers on their day's deliveries? Or simply tail without the need for observations? Or tail and then check the records and dip the tanks of the garages en route? Or my suggestion, when we had exhausted the risks and potential for success of each option: crash, bang, wallop! A brief observation from the terraced house and as soon as a tanker had filled up, a radio message to the teams strategically placed on the ground outside the warehouse to move in and stop the vehicle from leaving.

This is exactly what we did a few days later, having seconded a number of investigators from other teams to assist in the quite extensive operation. We decided on the most likely tanker driver, chosen intuitively from our two weeks' observations, to stop and check inside the warehouse. Intuition can be a remarkable tool, and so it proved. The tanker was overloaded in every one of its compartments. We interviewed the driver and his supervisor on the spot and extended the operation to the drivers already on their deliveries, taking each one into the warehouse offices we were using for interviews as they returned during the day, then visiting the garages where they had been.

I was fortunate that I had two of the best interviewers I could have had for the exercise, the previously mentioned Dick Kellaway and Jim Scahill. This was the first time I'd worked with them and I had not singled them out to assist me, since I had no idea of their capabilities, but the successes of the team over the coming months could not have been achieved without them. Their mix of charm, authority, common sense and logic, indeed simply their persuasive power over normally law-abiding citizens, was irresistible. The employees of the companies who were totally unused to law enforcement officers questioning them intensively over lengthy periods had little resistance, and Dick and Jim had no trouble producing the outcomes I was looking for. The Lowestoft operators threw in the towel and admitted the full extent of their fraudulent activities, which went back over several years. They were indeed overloading their tankers and dropping the surplus during their legitimate rounds to their partners-in-crime, co-operating garage owners who paid them between ten and twenty per cent of the standard price in cash. This led to heavy fines on the drivers and garages as well as seizures of vehicles, the restoration of which earned even more money for the Exchequer. It amply covered the £40 we paid the kind lady who allowed us to use her spare room where the forty-watt bulb, she told us, had not been changed in thirty-five years – until we came!

I carried out several operations at oil installations around the country in the following months, from Cardiff in the west to King's Lynn in the east and from Liverpool in the north to Southampton in the south. Since most of them had been upgraded, with meters replacing the antiquated dipstick, the frauds were more sophisticated. The main one was the diversion of oil intended for return to warehouse. The oil was regularly being sent back for a number of reasons: garage closures, over-ordering, incorrect orders. But instead of going back to the warehouse, the fuel was sold and delivered to dishonest clients en route. It often meant a degree of collusion with the supervisors responsible for connecting the pipes from the tanker to the transfer point, fitted with a non-return valve, in the warehouse. A lot of money was involved. At that time the price of petrol was 49.6 pence per gallon, of which over half was duty and tax. And despite this being shortly before the huge mid-70s spike in petrol prices and duty rates, the money being made from the thousands of gallons of stolen fuel had to be counted in the millions of pounds – of which half was owed to the Exchequer. This can only be guesswork since there was never any possibility of calculating exactly how much was involved, given that the losses in warehouse were within the one per cent allowance.

The operations had much in common: there was usually very little to be gained from patient observations and tailing, leaving the crash-bang-wallop method the most likely solution. Even that suffered from the law of diminishing returns as our methods became well known, particularly when it was applied to warehouses, such as in King's Lynn, where there wasn't actually any illegal diversion taking place. During all this time I had the services of my two brilliant interviewers, but the end came in sight when their interrogations at King's Lynn netted a number of drivers who did admit to wrongdoing, only it was for stealing – or 'appropriating' – tins of the hand-cleaner Swarfega, white pumice hand scrubs, solvents, WD40, soap from the toilets, pens from the office, paper, and even cans of Coke. Our aces could charm the birds out of trees to get 'coughs', but this wasn't what we were there for and I realised that I had to call the charmers off. Enough was enough. The approach had run its course and the team folded.

NOT ALL CASES WERE straightforward with satisfactory conclusions. Towards the end of my time in oils, I was pulled off, because of the sensitive nature of the job, to look into the strange affair of Rolls-Royce and aero engine exports to South Africa. This brought me into contact with a minister in Edward Heath's Government – and a dead end.

In 1973 we received information that Rolls-Royce was exporting aero engines to South Africa in breach of the export control regulations. South Africa's apartheid regime had attracted a great deal of opposition across the globe, and although later Margaret Thatcher was not in favour of sanctions, the Government of Edward Heath in 1971 imposed an embargo on any goods that would assist the regime in suppressing the black majority, especially military equipment. These were the days of the iron rule of P.W. Botha and Nelson Mandela was in gaol.

My drive down to Bristol to the headquarters of Rolls-Royce was somewhat daunting. Douglas Jordan had called me in to give me the 'delicate task' of discovering the precise role of Rolls-Royce in exports to the Italian aircraft manufacturer Piaggio, allegedly ultimately bound for South Africa. My remit was to tread very carefully and report back to him personally. I had no idea how I should approach the inquiry. I could hardly go in and turn their offices over to find incriminating documents, as we did in so many tax cases, like the Bloody Nose job. It was difficult enough gaining access to the premises through the heavily guarded electronic gates. However, I did manage to reach the office of the Chief Accountant, who was prepared to give me any documents, including ledgers, day books, orders and correspondence, provided I specified exactly what I wanted to see. That was a tall order but one I achieved after three hours of following the trail from order to sale via licensing approval at the highest level of government. I took copies of the relevant documents back to the Chief's office and discussed the case with him. He asked me what I intended to do next, to which I replied, 'Interview the Minister of Defence.' After a pregnant pause, he just nodded, without adding any further 'guidance'.

My interview at the Ministry of Defence was conducted in the polite and proper way such discussions between ministers and civil servants were held. I was courteous and he was very relaxed, which was hardly surprising since, when I asked the pertinent questions about the authority given by the Government for the exports to Piaggio, he directed me to the Cabinet Papers of the previous Labour Government of Harold Wilson. Cabinet Papers of previous governments are secret: no access was available to anyone, including him and certainly not to a lowly officer of the Crown. I was assured however that Rolls-Royce had acted in accordance with the authority granted by the previous Government, and that authority continued to this day. I had hit a brick wall.

Back in the Chief's office, Jordan suggested that I contact our Italian counterparts and ask them to take over the case. This I did. Case closed. Well, not quite. That November, a question about the matter was raised in the House of Lords by Lord Brockway. Archibald Fenner Brockway, Labour MP for Eton and Slough before his elevation to the peerage, was a veteran socialist, pacifist and champion of African nationalism, hence his interest in and support for the arms embargo on Botha's regime. He was answered for the Government by Baroness Tweedsmuir of Belhelvie, Minister of State at the Foreign and Commonwealth Office:

LORD BROCKWAY: My Lords, I beg leave to ask the Question which stands in my name on the Order Paper. To ask Her Majesty's Government if they have investigated the report of an agreement to sell to the South African Republic fifty military training aircraft manufactured in Italy fitted with Rolls-Royce Viper 632 turbojet engines.

BARONESS TWEEDSMUIR: No, my Lords. The supply to South Africa of military equipment made in Italy is a matter for the Italian Government, who have denied reports that they intend to sell these aircraft to South Africa.

Oil

LORD BROCKWAY: My Lords, is not this proposal a breach of the understanding that while there should be supplies in defence of the Cape route they should not be made available for internal suppression? Is it not also a repudiation of the United Nations decision to which Italy was a signatory, forbidding such sales? Is the noble Baroness really saying that Italy has now decided that these sales will not be allowed?

BARONESS TWEEDSMUIR: My Lords, we are following the practice of the previous Government in not trying to impose conditions over the export of locally manufactured Rolls-Royce engines from Italy to South Africa or to third countries.

LORD FRASER OF LONSDALE: My Lords, is my noble friend aware that many of these pilots have to fly extremely sophisticated jet aeroplanes from Cape Town to Durban and round into the Indian Ocean, that they survey 1,000 miles of coastline which is absolutely essential to the life of Europe and especially of Britain, and is it not a very good thing that these pilots should be trained on Rolls-Royce engines, which are the best in the world?

BARONESS TWEEDSMUIR: My Lords, I would agree with my noble friend that Rolls-Royce engines are the best in the world. I understand that the Italian firm Piaggio have manufactured these aero engines under licence from Rolls-Royce since 1960.

LORD BROCKWAY: My Lords, while it is a little difficult to understand the significance of the noble Baroness's reply, which I think I welcome, is it not the case that during the period of the Labour Government the Piaggio company undertook not to sell planes equipped with Rolls-Royce engines to South Africa?

BARONESS TWEEDSMUIR: No, my Lords; as I think I said in an earlier reply, these particular aero engines have in fact been manufactured under licence from Rolls-Royce since 1960. It would be an entirely separate matter were this country to be considering The Export Of An Engine Direct To South Africa.

LORD ALPORT: My Lords, would my noble friend agree that if we refused to sell anything to any country of which the Labour Party disapproved we should not in fact be conducting any trade at all in the world?

BARONESS TWEEDSMUIR: Yes, my Lords.

LORD BLYTON: My Lords, can the noble Baroness assure us that South Africa will be given spare parts; that the Government will not do what they did to Israel?

BARONESS TWEEDSMUIR: I think, my Lords, that is another question.

THE MARQUESS OF WINCHESTER: My Lords, would Her Majesty's Government further agree that it would be in the interests of the United Kingdom for South Africa to be able to defend itself, and therefore that she should be equipped, whether from the United Kingdom or elsewhere?

BARONESS TWEEDSMUIR: My Lords, we are in terms of the Question asked about equipment made in Italy, and this is a matter for the Italian Government.

LORD BROCKWAY: My Lords, I want to get this quite clear. Do I understand from the noble Baroness's original answer that these planes are not to be sent to South Africa?

BARONESS TWEEDSMUIR: Yes, my Lords.

There you have it. The information we had received that Rolls-Royce was exporting engines to South Africa was not true. The engines were being made under licence by the Italian company, who could well have been exporting them in breach of the embargo but I had not found any evidence at Rolls-Royce to confirm or deny this nor that they knew or suspected that their 'licensed' engines were being used in a way which, if true, would presumably have been in breach of that licence. What I did find out was that the Government of the day had been brought into it at the most senior level. Why, I could only speculate. The lucrative nature of the business? The importance and reputation of Rolls-Royce? The actual authorisation of the licence, which was questionable? Information such as that we had received about its possible illegality? Had this been leaked to us by the new Government to encourage us to make enquiries that would inevitably lead to this impasse, or cause mischief? The record of the discussion in Cabinet was a state secret which could not be accessed by ensuing governments nor by a member of the permanent Civil Service.

No matter. I had no evidence to establish what the Government or the company knew at the time, and the incoming administration had declared that this was a matter for the Italian Government. As an investigator I would have chosen to visit the Italian company in an attempt to establish the facts of the case and to discuss the question with the authorities there, but I was instructed simply to advise them and leave it at that. I heard nothing more. The case was now definitively closed.

13

The Watch Smuggler

WHILE STILL UP TO my eyes, metaphorically, in hydrocarbon oil, I was summoned into the presence of my mentor, tormentor and idol in equal measure, Sam Charles, now one of the two deputy chiefs. I was to see an informant called Sammy Lampert with a fellow SIO, John Cooney. I had been called in because the case officer, Dick Kellaway, had been taken ill that day. It had apparently been Dick's suggestion that I stand in for him.

When I first joined the Branch, the big subject was watch smuggling. Our two 'target' teams were employed full time on the surveillance of watch gangs, well before drugs became the priority. Sam Charles had been one of the SIOs then and had been in charge when Sammy Lampert was arrested for attempting to smuggle watches into the country through Folkestone, for which he had received a suspended prison sentence of twelve months. I was told that Lampert, a watch wholesaler and importer who lived in Switzerland, had now come to the office to see Sam and, to everyone's surprise, wanted to inform on himself.

During our subsequent interviews, Lampert explained that he had been directly involved in undervaluing watches imported into the UK to evade purchase tax. He had been importing watches since 1968 and in July 1971 was involved in setting up a company, MFS (Importers) Ltd, with three other men, including Jones Flood, to take over the importations. Lampert did not make himself a director of the company, his key role being to supply false invoices on genuine Swiss exporters' stationery to MFS. Lampert would telephone Flood every evening to ascertain the company's requirements. He would then place an order with the manufacturers, who would provide the genuine invoices through a shipping agent. Lampert would finally prepare false invoices for Customs inspection at half the true value.

Why, then, walk into our office and blow the whistle when there was no ongoing investigation into his fraud, with everything seemingly going smoothly and, more importantly, when he knew he would be charged with tax evasion himself and could even land up in gaol? Money, of course. Flood had refused to pay Lampert the true cost of the watches, asserting that the false invoices were the actual value despite knowing full well what the arrangements were. At the time Lampert came to see us he was owed £49,000, the equivalent of over £500,000 today, by MFS and could not pay the manufacturers what was owed. When thieves fall out! Lampert convinced us that he could obtain the cooperation of the Swiss manufacturers to provide us with the evidence needed for court proceedings. He was prepared to meet us in Switzerland and to introduce us to them, which was no small thing given the renowned secrecy imposed by the Swiss authorities in financial and trading matters.

In May 1974, Dick Kellaway and I flew to Zurich and then went on by train to Bern. It was my first visit to Switzerland. Sammy had booked us into the Hotel Schweizerhof, one of a Swiss chain of five-star hotels, so we weren't going to suffer (this from a man who wrote to Dick setting up the visit: 'Things are so expensive here, you best bring some sandwiches and a flask of tea'). What struck me was the beauty of the city, both in its location, with the snow-topped Alps as a perfect panoramic backdrop, and with its historic buildings: the magnificent mediaeval Clock Tower, the Cathedral, the Historisches Museum, and fountains everywhere; over a hundred, we were told. Not that we were going to have much time for sightseeing although we did get to the bear pit, an astonishing circular concrete bowl twenty feet or so below street level in which a couple of brown bears, the city's symbol, strolled around, occasionally standing on two legs to look up at the dozens of tourists staring down at them in wonder and incredulity. I believe they were moved later to a more bear-friendly habitat, the Bear Park, on the banks of the River Aare. I loved the red trams and I was particularly struck by the overall cleanliness of the place, as well as by the appearance of efficiency (we would see about that). We rang Sam from the hotel after he had left a message at Heathrow for us to ring him. All he said in his typical economical way was: 'Just be careful!'

We had arranged the visit through the Foreign Office and were to meet the Counsellor, Gillian Brown, at the British Embassy to finalise the details. Miss Brown, as we always called her, was a delight. A good-looking lady, she was every inch the diplomat. Highly educated in intellect, culture and manners, an Oxford graduate, she was later to become the ambassador to Norway and was made a Dame. For now, she was just Miss Brown who greeted us warmly and confirmed the details of our visit, pointing out the voluntary nature of all our enquiries which had been approved by the authorities. In the nicest possible way, she told us that we did not have overall permission to carry out enquiries in Switzerland and could only obtain evidence and information with the express agreement of the individuals and companies involved. The person whom we had to see first was one Pierre Schmid of the International Judicial Aid Department of Justice and Police, who had organised our visit.

At 4pm the same day, we went to Schmid's office, where he confirmed the names of all the companies involved that had agreed to our visit and were fully cooperative. He also outlined the wishes of the local Cantonal police, some of whom wished to accompany us to company premises; others who were not interested. Our programme had already been arranged: we were to see three companies on successive days and a fourth whenever we chose. It meant travelling to Biel, where Lampert lived and where we would book into a more modest hotel, as well as Basle, Grenchen and Liestal. The local police had refused access to only one company, Nisus SA in Neuchatel. We were to meet Lampert in Basle for our first visit the following day.

All went well the first two days and we obtained copies of relevant documents and took voluntary statements from directors. Only one director was not available, as he had gone to Lugarno for a week's stay, but he was prepared to see us there. Unforgettable was our first report back to Miss Brown in Bern when we said we would have to go additionally to Lugarno. She replied in her beautiful cut-glass accent: 'Oh how lovely. Let's all go to Lugarno.'

On the third day, during our visit to Rendex SA in Liestal, we heard a kerfuffle at the door of the outer office and in walked two officers from the local Cantonal police force. Not mincing words, the senior officer said, in his impeccable English: 'You do not have permission to be here.'

'Of course we do,' I replied.

'Who gave you this authority?'

'Herr Schmid.'

'Who is Herr Schmid?'

My heart sank. Herr Schmid. Mr Smith. It was like using a common alias. And our forthright police officer looked decidedly unimpressed.

'Herr Schmid of the International Judicial Aid Department.'

'We have not been informed of this by your Herr, who?'

'Herr Schmid in Bern. Please telephone him and he will explain.'

The police officer, one Herr Kummer, duly rang Pierre Schmid after I gave him his contact details. He came off the phone and apologised for the intrusion, explaining that there had been a misunderstanding between two divisions in Bern. He asked me to visit the police station in Liestal on the completion of our business at the company so that he could explain how this had happened.

When Kummer had left I phoned Schmid, who apologised profusely for the inconvenience and told me that this had happened because he had telephoned the Court in Basle about our visit but the Court had not informed the Cantonal police. He assured me that the matter had now been cleared up and we could proceed to Lugarno as arranged.

While Dick was taking director Otto Meyer's statement, I told him I was just popping into the police station to receive their apologies. I then left him to complete the statement. Things went decidedly downhill after that. The attitude of the police officer in the station, another Herr Meyer, became quite formal. Far from apologising for the misunderstanding, he began, through an interpreter, Herr Sutter, by asking me for proof of my identity and official documents proving that I was a Customs official. Sutter explained that they simply wanted to ask a couple of questions about our visit to Switzerland. I told him that they could obtain all this information from Herr Schmid. This led to an animated conversation in German between the two men, during which Meyer showed Sutter a long telex message. Sutter then explained that the Attorney General's office in Bern had not been informed of our visit and in the opinion of that office we should not have been given permission in the first place. I asked why permission would have been refused, to be told that only criminal matters could be investigated in Switzerland. I said that this was a criminal matter, to which he replied that tax evasion was not a criminal offence there. Meyer then began tapping at his typewriter. I was refused access to Herr Schmid and only reluctantly, after lengthy discussions between my two inquisitors, given the phone to speak to Dick Kellaway so I could ask him to come to the station as soon as he could.

I asked what they had in mind and what was going to happen. Sutter said that we had to cease our enquiries in Switzerland forthwith. He said that it was an offence under Swiss law for a visiting official of a foreign government to make enquiries in Switzerland without permission, although they recognised that we were in no way to blame and had not committed an offence up to that time.

When Dick arrived, he saw straight away the predicament we were in and refused to make a statement when asked to do so. He was told that I was making a statement and that they also needed to take a statement from him and Sammy Lampert, who was in a café nearby. I told them that I was not making a statement and that I wanted to speak to Herr Schmid and the British Embassy. I asked Sutter if we had been arrested. He replied, 'We received instructions to arrest you. Herr Meyer did not do so because you are brother officers.'

I was livid. How could Schmid have got it so wrong? Dick was also fuming and dug his heels in further. He was the perfect support. After a great deal of discussion, most of it beyond our comprehension in German, it was eventually agreed that I could speak to Herr Schmid. He was again full of apologies and explained that he had not contacted the Public Prosecutor's office before our visit and therefore they had issued the order for us to cease our enquiries. The Liestal police had also not known of our visit because the Tribunal at Basle had not contacted them.

I then spoke to Miss Brown, who was most disturbed and said that she would take the matter up with Herr Schmid and inform the ambassador. We agreed a form of words on the phone for a statement saying that we would cease our enquiries immediately. Miss Brown had only a couple of changes to suggest: 'Can you say "errors" instead of "mistakes", and the Swiss "authorities" rather than the departments concerned?' I handed the polished, typed and signed statement to Herr Meyer as our get-out-of-gaol card. We were then free to leave the police station and told that we could stay in Switzerland as tourists but not as investigators. Now we would have all the time in the world to see all those beautiful sights, although with somewhat less enthusiasm than on our first day. I was not to enjoy the attractions of Lugano for another thirty-five years.

There followed a series of meetings between the embassy, including the ambassador, Mr (later Sir) John Wraight, and the various police and judicial authorities, some of whom tried to shift the blame for the 'misunderstandings' and breakdowns in communications. The embassy took pains to avoid apportioning blame and a number of apologies were received. It was significant, however, that throughout all these contacts and discussions, the Public Prosecutor's Office distanced itself, placing the responsibility for the 'misunderstandings' on the Police Division and saying that the Federal Police Department should therefore be approached, not them. During long and detailed discussions with the Federal Police Department a number of concerns were raised, including their fear that the watch manufacturers would be 'blacklisted' by the UK Government. While they were reassured that this was certainly not the case, they insisted that all the signed witness statements and other relevant documents and photocopies taken up by us should be handed in to their office and that no copies should be taken. Fortunately, the Swiss agreed to allow the manufacturers to come voluntarily to the UK to give evidence in any court proceedings and that the documents taken up would, after careful study, be returned eventually to the manufacturers.

When we rang Sam to tell him about our 'arrest', all he said in his gruff voice over the phone was: 'I told you to be careful.' He later rang Dick's wife, Ann, and told her that her husband would not be coming home that night. Ann asked who she was speaking to and he said, 'Never mind.' However, she insisted on knowing who he was.

'Charles.'

'Charles who?'

The phone then went dead; end of conversation.

We returned home and I resumed my specialist duties. Meanwhile Dick reported the case to the Board and in due course the Solicitor approved the issue of warrants for the arrest of Lampert and Flood. Given my substantial part in the investigation, I took part in the arrest of Sammy Lampert, who had returned to Heathrow voluntarily from Switzerland on 13 October 1975. We took him up to West Drayton Police Station where we were obliged to wait in the charging sergeant's office while another prisoner was to be given precedence and charged first. After a short wait, the door to the office was flung open with a crash and a young man was literally hurled into the room by a uniformed police officer. When the policeman saw us, he quickly picked the prisoner up, straightened his clothing and patted him reassuringly on the back. He was then told to stand before the sergeant for the charge to be read out.

'Mr Robinson, you are charged on diverse dates with being in possession of a British Rail uniform valued at five pounds without the permission of the said British Rail…'

We sat aghast alongside our calm and cooperating prisoner, one of the biggest watch fraudsters in the country. When it was finally our turn to parade Sammy in front of the desk, I handed the charge sheet to the sergeant. I don't think either of us will ever forget the look on the police officer's face when he read out: 'Mr Samuel Lampert, on warrant granted by the magistrates of the Uxbridge Court on the ninth of October 1975, that you did, on diverse dates between the first day of October 1971 and the thirty-first day of December 1972, at London Airport and elsewhere, conspire with MFS (Watch Importers) Ltd and Jones Flood to cheat and defraud Her Majesty of some fifty-one thousand pounds of purchase tax on watches imported into the United Kingdom. Contrary to common law.'

It was worth the wait, we thought.

On 17 March 1976 at Middlesex Crown Court, Lampert, who had pleaded guilty, was sentenced to five years' imprisonment, his earlier one-year suspended sentence to be put into effect concurrently. Flood, who had pleaded not guilty, was sentenced to four years. These sentences were reduced on appeal, for Lampert from five years to three and Flood's from four years to two.

The Investigator

Some time later, Dick decided to visit Sammy in Wandsworth Prison to see how this very nice man, despite his criminality, was faring; a kindness on Dick's part but also to repay Sammy for owning up, helping to bring his fellow conspirator to book and being so decent about it all. This led to a series of letters from Sammy to Dick to keep him informed. Here are a few of the best extracts:

> Dear Dick,
>
> I must take this opportunity of thanking you for your unexpected and welcomed visit of last week. I should ask if you have had a good Easter as I know you have been working.
>
> Give Mr Knox, Mr Charles and Mr Cutting my regards and it would be nice to hear from them from time to time, it helps the time to pass more easily.
>
> We had a very quiet Easter, up early and to bed early. At least that hasn't killed anybody yet,
>
> All the best
> Sammy
> Wandsworth Prison

> Dear Dick,
>
> Having been in the army helps in situations like this. Whether you believe me or not I have given up drinking, and have very nearly given up smoking.
>
> I have sent off the Appeal from my Solicitor and I'm sincerely hoping that some reduction will be made.
>
> I am seeing the senior doctor as my Hiatus Hernia is doing me no good. At night I do a lot of belching from the acid etc in my stomach and the noise is very loud. Then the other prisoners in my block start to shout, SHUT UP, FUCK YOU and all that sort of thing. Even here there's never a dull moment even if it's not pleasant.
>
> Should you find it possible Dick perhaps you and Mike can come here for a visit and perhaps enlighten me. I keep thinking to myself, every time I went to see you I always used to offer cigarettes to two blokes in the office as you walk in.
>
> Now I feel like telling them to give them back to me.

Thanking you
All the best
Sammy
Wandsworth Prison

None of the monies owed were ever recovered. MFS was made bankrupt and neither HM Treasury nor Sammy were paid. Sadly, not long after his release on parole after only two years in gaol, the last period in Ford Open Prison, Sammy Lampert died. With the introduction of VAT in 1973, this was the last purchase tax prosecution in the Investigation Division.

14

Morocco

B Y THE EARLY 1970S, the authorities were just beginning to take drug
abuse seriously. Cannabis was the main drug of misuse; frightening
cases of the effects of heroin addiction and the immense problems
associated with hard drugs were still virtually unknown to us. Not
surprisingly the re-organisation of our branch into the Investigation
Division placed most emphasis on cannabis smuggling, with a total of
six teams dedicated to it, backed up by the use of existing telephone
intercepts, informants and intelligence. Only one team was set up to
focus on hard drugs and it took a long time to get into its stride and
achieve results.

In 1975 I was moved into the drugs branch to take over Drugs
H, the Hotels. They were the Moroccan cannabis team dealing with
reported cases of smuggled pot intercepted at ports and airports and
then referred to the Investigation Division. At that time, Morocco
was by far the leading source of smuggled cannabis imports into the
UK, and one of the most interesting cases during my spell at the
Hotels concerned the discovery by the Waterguard of fifty kilos of
resin – a large seizure in those days – hidden in the fridge of a camper
van intercepted at the port of Southampton. The suspect proved to
be particularly unhelpful and denied any knowledge of the drugs,
which he said must have been planted. He pleaded not guilty at the
magistrate's hearing. In his luggage I found a photograph of a farm
in what he said were the Rif Mountains in Morocco, where he had
been on holiday. I obtained permission to visit Morocco to obtain as
much information as I could to prove his deliberate involvement in
the case and to verify his ferry and hotel bookings. For this I needed
a *commission rogatoire*, a legal document allowing us to make specified

enquiries abroad, which I obtained through the Foreign Office, and the invaluable assistance, as it proved to be, of my second officer Ken Stott.

The guidebook I read and re-read on the plane from London described Morocco as 'the tantalising lower lip on the mouth of the Mediterranean Sea, a Muslim land so rich in mystique it seems to hover like a magic carpet somewhere between myth and reality. Tangier, Casablanca, Marrakesh… just the names of these places should stir a hint of spice in the nostrils of the most geographically travelled, and spur them to extol the country's unique living history, its shimmering light, its art.' Even this atmospheric description does not prepare you for the scene that confronts you: living history, yes, but more of the fictional kind, invoking images of Humphrey Bogart walking across the tarmac from the cluster of low wooden buildings surrounded by coconut palms. Nothing seemed to have changed from those scenes in *Casablanca*. It was timeless, dishevelled, almost primitive; and at the same time, unreal. The police officers with machine guns watching the passengers disembark were real enough though.

We decided to take a bus into the capital, Rabat. There was a long queue at the bus stop outside the terminal, but a helpful young man, seeing that we were foreigners and anticipating the possibility of a tip, led us up to the door of the bus to board without waiting. I was dismayed when our cases were loaded onto the roof when it was obvious the bus was full, only to see two poorly clad men unceremoniously turfed off to provide us with seats, despite vigorous protestations on my part. We had to board because our cases could well have gone without us. There was no tip!

While on Moroccan soil we had sufficient cover with our *commission rogatoire* once it was signed by a local judge. It would allow us to obtain evidence from hotels and ferry companies as well as the police in Tangier, so long as it was for a genuine case that was coming to trial. However, in conversations with the First Secretary at the British Embassy in Rabat, I was warned to take extra care as there was substantial corruption involving the police and the cannabis growers in the mountains. At that time there were police posts on the road leading up into the hills to check vehicles into the area, but more significantly on their way back. The information, given by arrested British nationals languishing in Moroccan gaols, was that the police in the 'border' posts stopped and searched all foreign vehicles at the checkpoint and seized any cannabis they found. After the smuggler was convicted and gaoled, the drugs were sold back to the growers at less than they had sold it for originally, making it a win-win situation for the police and growers alike. Our man's concealment in the fridge of the camper van was clearly a little too sophisticated for them – but not for our boys at Southampton!

I got on very well with the local police commander in Tangier, Inspector Meskali, who was assisting us with our hotel checks and took no exception to my suggestion of a bit of 'sightseeing' on our own while we were in his beautiful country. I neglected to inform him that my real intention was to try to locate the farm where our suspect had been 'on holiday'. Although this latter was most definitely not covered by the *commission rogatoire*, Ken and I took off for the hills. The Rif Mountains stretch across the north of Morocco. Except in the highest elevations (7,000–8,000 feet), they are generally hot and dry. The terrain is rugged. The slopes are steep and rocky, often dropping several thousand feet to narrow canyons below. Small, scanty fir trees survive on the upper slopes while shrubs and grasses grow in the valleys lower down. In the central region of the mountains is a small flat plateau. The town of Ketama is located at its western edge.

Approximately 150 km south-east of Tangier, the growing area of the cannabis, or kif as it is known, was and I believe still is contained in a triangle formed by an imaginary line drawn east to west from a point approximately 10 km west of Tarquist to about 10 km east of Bab Taza. The legs of the triangle converge in the area of Taberrant to the south. The area included in this triangle is approximately 1,000 square kilometres. Only a very few sealed roads led into and out of this triangle, allowing the police to set up a limited number of checkpoints at strategic locations. Ketama, right in the centre of this triangle, was reputed to produce the most kif in either Africa or Asia.

We had been told by our diplomatic colleague that various Berber tribes populated the area. Despite their historically nomadic nature, the Berbers had a strong sense of property ownership and knew exactly who owned what. The various families through the generations had

127

built and maintained the stone-terraced fields that sat precariously on the steep rocky slopes, cultivating a number of crops such as wheat, corn, tomatoes and melons, as well as kif, by far the largest crop, on earth that was more rock than soil. Efforts by the Government to solve what they called the 'Berber problem' by encouraging alternative cultivation (how seriously one can only wonder) had been unsuccessful over the years; the barren, marginal soil on which little else would grow, on rugged terrain with poor roads and communication coupled with the tradition of tribes resisting any outside influence made the task virtually impossible. When these factors were combined with the large vested interests of traffickers in transport and distribution, as well as chronic unemployment, it was plain that the Berbers of the Rif would continue to rank high among the world's suppliers of cannabis long after I had any responsibility for the subject. Many of the people could not speak any language except their native dialects; they often could not even speak Arabic. In most towns Arabic was spoken but more importantly for us, occasionally French and Spanish as second languages. To say that this idea of mine was a gamble would be something of an understatement.

It was a long journey. However, as we climbed the steep road leading up to Ketama we were entranced by the wild beauty all around us. Or at least I was; I did not realise until much later that Ken's thoughts were of a different order. Chillingly steep canyon valleys fell away from our road on all sides. Many of the valleys were inaccessible by motorised vehicle. Apparently the cannabis was brought to secondary dirt track roads by donkey for transport to the farms and storage areas.

When we finally reached Ketama, we drove into what looked to us like a ghost town. Hardly a soul around, a dry dusty street running through a motley collection of whitewashed buildings passing, on our right, what looked like a hotel or bar. Our Arabic was not quite up to knowing what the various signs outside meant, although the graphics and a bit of French seemed to suggest that drinks and coffee were being served and beds were available for the night. We went in to lubricate our parched throats and to see if we could enlist the help of someone who might recognise the farm we were looking for from the photo. We did not have long to wait: two foreigners arriving in the kif capital of Morocco were a magnet for any locals involved in the hash trade.

But we were particularly 'lucky'. A young man in the bar came over to us, dressed casually in shorts and T-shirt rather than the traditional garb of the region, and asked in good French if he could help. I showed him my photo and asked him if he recognised the area. Almost without a pause, which should have alerted us straight away, he said that this just happened to be his uncle's farm. Of course I was sceptical but he offered to take us there, or rather direct us outside of town to a winding dirt track leading down to the farm in question. So I went along with it and he got into our car.

He left us at the top of the track and pointed to the clutch of buildings in the valley below. From the shape of the long undulating mountain backdrop, the vegetation, the dryness and the distinctive colours of the landscape at this, the highest point in the range, it certainly resembled the photograph. We drove down this dusty track for about half a mile to a group of farm buildings, passing on the way an overturned car near the bottom being examined by a group of young men. We were greeted by a middle-aged man who, like the young man in the bar, was not dressed traditionally and who spoke French. His burnt-almond complexion, moustache and manner clearly identified him as Moroccan though. In a welcoming, friendly manner, he showed us into the house without asking us why we were there, who we were or what we wanted, offering us some tea and what he described as a local delicacy, cinnamon biscuits.

It was as we were waiting, sitting opposite each other in this darkened old wooden farmhouse, that I noticed Ken's demeanour for the first time. He looked ashen and was breathing heavily. I asked him if he was all right but he struggled to speak. When our host returned with a full tray, Ken began to shake and started wheezing, clearly finding it very hard to breathe. I was so alarmed that I stood up and told the man that we had to leave, as quickly as possible, to get medical help. Where I would find a doctor in the middle of the Rif I had no idea, but I virtually carried Ken to the car and got him into the front seat, while he gulped for air. Over the protests of the farmer, who shouted after me, 'Kif? You want kif?' I started the car and drove up the slope, skidding in my haste on the dusty track. I got as far as the car we had passed on the way down. It was now upright but parked lengthwise across the track, blocking our exit. Five young men stood in front and at the side of it, two of them dressed in the traditional djellaba, one with a red fez on his head, the others in rough Western garments, although to be frank I was less interested in their dress than the ancient rifles slung across the backs of two of them. One of the gun-carrying characters approached the car with a menacing look on his sallow, moustachioed face. He spat a few unpleasant-sounding words in Arabic, or a local dialect, who knows, the only one of which I understood was 'kif'.

I shouted at him in the best French I could muster in the situation: 'Bougez votre voiture. Mon ami est malade, gravement malade. Je dois l'emmener a l'hopital aussi tot que possible. Si je n'arrive pas, il va mourir!' '*Move your car. My friend is ill, seriously ill. I have to get him to hospital as soon as possible. If I don't he will die!*'

Whether because he understood my execrable French or simply saw the state Ken was in – by this time almost unable to breathe and with the start of convulsions that suggested he was heading for a paroxysm – I don't know, but miracle of miracles the leader turned around and ordered his band of brigands to move the car. Instead of assaulting and robbing us, that fierce little band downed their weapons, gathered around the car, lifted it by hand and turned it around so that we might pass. It was a sight I shall never forget, nor shall I forget the profound emotion I felt at the time. I have been asked later whether I was scared. Thinking about it, I don't think I was. Why I cannot say, other than to surmise that I was more worried about Ken's state of health than anything these blighters might do to us. They were in a very lucrative business after all, relying heavily on foreigners for their livelihood. Very little of that went through my head at the time though. I just wanted out of there.

We reached the main road in minutes and I turned right, down the steep mountain road. The farther away we drove from Ketama, the better Ken seemed to be. The town is almost 5,000 feet above sea level and as we descended his breathing started to come back. By the time we reached the police checkpoint it was normal. I doubt that it was just the lack of oxygen that had induced this hyperventilation: the stress of our situation must have played its part. The police took no notice of us (had they been warned by their partners in crime, I wondered) and our drive back to Tangier was uneventful. Neither of us spoke throughout the journey, Ken presumably recovering and wondering what brought all that on, me questioning my judgement in doing such an unnecessary, foolhardy thing – and for what? The misplaced bravura of a thirty-seven-year-old savouring new adventures?

We expected to find safety and calm back at Tangier police station; instead we were greeted by bedlam. We drove into the police yard to see a crowd of men, women and children standing outside the main door talking animatedly, some shouting at the incumbents inside and making it extremely difficult for us to get through the entrance. We came in for quite a lot of abuse ourselves as we forced our way through but, not understanding a word of their dialect, we were unable to take offence. Mercifully Ken's breathing difficulties did not return. Once inside, I had some idea of why the locals were looking so distressed. As we made our way up the concrete stairs to Inspector Meskali's office on the first floor, I could hear muffled screams coming from underneath the building. Somebody was being put through the wringer.

But my most pressing need at that moment was the toilet. Meskali greeted us like long-lost brothers, with embraces and triple kisses, and then escorted me down the wide corridor from his office to the lavatories. As we approached the lavatory door, two uniformed policemen came towards us with a woman prisoner between them being led by the arms and in handcuffs. They stopped immediately and motioned for me to go ahead into the men's lavatory. I was directed to one of the closets, a typical French one with a hole, no seat and two foot places on which to stand or crouch. Meanwhile the poor woman in her loose haika dress and handcuffs was marched in behind me and told to turn her back to the men's latrine up against the far wall. She had her dress pulled up to her waist and then had to relieve herself with her bottom pressed against the steel trough. How thankful I was of (a) not being a woman and (b) not being under arrest in a Moroccan police station!

We obtained all the information we required from the ferry records, which showed the dates of our suspect's visit and the vehicle registration number. When we returned to the UK, I re-interviewed Mr Campervan, showing him the ferry records and recounting our visit to the cannabis farm in the mountains. He conceded defeat, making a full confession, and spent the next two years in prison. I saw him some time later in prison to obtain some useful intelligence information on distributors, and during our long conversation I happened to mention his good fortune at not serving his sentence in a Moroccan gaol. He replied that at least it would have been only for three months, at the most. He was clearly a knowledgeable young man. But for me there was some comfort in being able to make use of our 'interesting' day's outing to the Rif.

15

The Cornish Lady

'I T'S DARTMOUTH. ON THE River Dart.'
   'I know where it is, for Christ's sake. When?'
   'We don't know. Can't be long though; Ray's got a wedding at the end of the month and he says he needs to be back for that.'
   'Do you know any more?'
   'No, only that Jamaica is involved. I'd be surprised if things didn't start moving soon.'

My colleague Dave Raynes walked out of my office and left us in a quandary. His information was too vague. However we were convinced another job was on its way. This was awkward. It meant we had two jobs running at the same time and both were seemingly now active. There was the crowd from Streatham, south London, about whom we had few firm details; that meant we would have to launch long-term obs on them, which would tie up our team indefinitely. Then there were the people from Hornsey, in north London; if they started moving around now, we wouldn't have the resources to cover both. It was four months since we had become interested in the two smuggling gangs and now both jobs seemed to be coming to fruition at the same time. Why were we always surprised?

I swivelled round to face the window and looked down from my third floor office onto the steady stream of black cabs taking advantage of the shortcut between High Holborn and Fleet Street, outnumbering the other London vehicles by a ratio of about four to one. The ID had moved into the former press building in New Fetter Lane some eighteen months before, when we outgrew our two floors next door to the Customs HQ near Tower Hill. My office was reputed to have been used by David Bailey, the fashion photographer, but the photos on my desk were rather more prosaic. I turned back to examine the large black and white photo on the top of the pile, and frowned. The photo showed a tall, thin man with a drooping moustache leaving an Edwardian terraced house, followed by the shadowy, indistinct figure of a much smaller woman. As I picked up the phone, George Atkinson, my number two, walked into my office through the open door with that relaxed ease of familiarity.

'George, the Streatham crowd are on the move. I need to speak to Terry.'

THE RADIO CRACKLED INTO life, shaking us all out of our torpor.

'Tango One and Tango Four are out of the premises. They're moving towards a VW Caravanette, registration number Romeo Charlie Oscar Four Seven Three. Tango Three is into the driving seat…Lift off, we have lift off.'

'Who the hell's Tango Four?' Phil Matthews asked his navigator.

Mike Stephenson looked down at his crib sheet. 'Bob Stafford, Johnny's brother. Where's Brenda, then? I thought she was on this jaunt.'

The radio crackled again as if it had heard them and a female voice came over the airwaves.

'The Tango vehicle is doing a U-ey. A U-turn. It's stopped. All mobiles remain static. Tango Two is coming out of the premises and joining them.'

'Brenda! At least that's right.'

'We have lift off again. Tango is headed north along Ruxley… he's doing a left, left, left, a left, left, left into Shortlands Avenue, and then a right, right, right into Streatham High Street.'

'What's all this "left, left, left" crap, "We have lift off" and "All mobiles remain static"?' asked Stephenson, mimicking my commentary in the lead car.

'Weren't you at the briefing?' asked Matthews.

'No, I was in court. I wouldn't be here now if he hadn't changed his plea at the last moment.'

'It's slow moving…we have one for cover….All Saints Church on the left, the Lamb and Flagstaff on the right. No deviation.'

'No deviation?' Stephenson echoed. 'That's the understatement of the week.'

'Baker's just back from a surveillance course in Canada,' explained Matthews. 'Didn't you hear about it? We've been training with the new procedures for a couple of weeks already. They sound odd, very American, but they're bloody effective.'

'We're stopped in heavy traffic. Still one for cover. Traffic lights in a hundred yards. We'll peel off there. Position mobiles?'

'India Bravo Two…right behind you, ready to take eyeball.'

'India Bravo Four…four vehicles back.'

'India Bravo Five…opposite Lamb and Flagstaff.'

'India Bravo Six,' Stephenson spluttered into the microphone. *'We're stuck in Shortlands. The traffic is appalling.'*

'Get off the air Bravo Six and get off your asses. Tango through the lights… we're doing a left, left, left…over to you Bravo Two.'

'Thanks Bravo One, we are through the lights and we have eyeball. We have four for cover. Traffic easing, moving up to twenty-five mph…keep up mobiles… Bravo One, are you back in line?'

'Affirmative. We should be Tail-end Charlie but we haven't a clue where Bravo Six has got to.'

'Bravo Six from Bravo Two, position please?'

'I'm not sure, Bravo Two, we're…' Stephenson stuttered.

'Here, give me the mike.' Matthews grabbed the microphone and spoke in clear, crisp tones: *'India Bravo One has rejoined the convoy just ahead of us. We're all through the lights and we'll stay Tail-end Charlie.'*

'Received, Tango Six.'

'Sorry, Phil,' said a rueful Stephenson. 'I wasn't prepared for that. Mike's going to kill me.'

'Don't worry. You can only die once. Look, at the next lights take over the wheel and I'll handle the commentary. You'll soon pick it up. Just remember the aim is to avoid the target seeing the same vehicle behind him for any length of time. It allows the eyeball to be right up his jacksie if need be, so long as he peels off at the next intersection. That way we don't lose him at traffic lights the way we used to. Or roundabouts.'

'What if there isn't a natural break? A long straight road, for instance?'

'Use your imagination. If it goes on too long, overtake and take a left at the first opportunity as soon as you are out of sight. Motorways are less of a problem. You don't notice if a following car is travelling at the same speed, especially if you're both right on the speed limit. But don't overtake otherwise you could be forced to go on to Leeds when he took the Bradford exit.'

'*Reciprocal! Reciprocal!*' Atkinson shouted across the air. '*He's gone right round the roundabout and is coming back at us. We're having to pass him. We can't follow. Bravo Four, can you make up ground?*'

'*Negative, Bravo Two, we're stuck behind a lorry.*'

'*Bravos Five and Six, stop, stop, stop.*'

Our target was canny. He had obviously been tailed before and he kept making 180-degree turns around roundabouts to see if he was being followed or to shake off any possible tailing team by making them think they had been spotted even if they hadn't; thus defeating the main purpose of the exercise and causing the tail to be abandoned.

The new method we had been trained to adopt largely took care of this, provided there was no panic. The main reason for calm was the number of vehicles used in the convoy: at least five if available and a motorbike if at all possible. These were the days before mobile phones, GPS tracking and the new technology which eventually made such close tailing with large two-way radios obsolete.

Our target resumed his journey after the test U-turn, which seemed to reassure him, and we stuck to his tail successfully, changing positions in the convoy as necessary all the way down to Dartmouth in the West Country, where a mix of mobile and foot surveillance became necessary. Foot surveillance ideally required a team of at least four people: two spaced apart behind the suspect, one ahead and one on the other side of the street or away to the side in a park or similar. This was again to allow for positions to change so that the target did not keep seeing the same person nearby. The suspect led us to a boat harbour on the River Dart. It did not take us long to ascertain that he was there to charter a sea-going yacht, and this enabled us to set up longer-term static observations. At this point I left them to it. There were two of us in charge of the two target teams, Drugs B and C, or India Bravo and India Charlie. After my first stint on the Moroccan cannabis team, I was now in charge of target team B. The two cannabis target teams worked to information and intelligence. It was a significant step up for me and even more so to work alongside the incumbents, notably Terry Byrne, the SIO in charge of the sister Charlie team.

The Cornish Lady

At the weekend I made a trip down to see how things were going. I have never been allowed to forget the occasion, particularly by Charlie 1 and Charlie 2, Terry Byrne and his senior officer Nick Baker. I had decided to take advantage of a troop visit to take my wife away for the weekend to a hotel in Plymouth, and made the unforgivable mistake of turning up on the Saturday at the observation point dressed in a blue blazer, complete with cravat, grey flannels and blue sailing loafers. Now who was the Charlie? However I did take the opportunity to liaise with a local RAF Commander about the possible use of their unique surveillance capabilities, in case we needed to track the yacht up the Channel on its return. Aurea thoroughly enjoyed all the cloak and dagger stuff as she sunned herself by the pool at the hotel. Terry's car passenger, Phil Matthews, was less than impressed when I radioed to find out exactly where they were so that I could join them.

'We're currently in the middle of the river,' he retorted brusquely.

Annoyed, thinking that they were messing me about, I asked for a more helpful – and respectful – answer. The reply came back the same only even more curtly, as they were actually in the middle of the River Dart on a little chain ferry that transported cars across from one side to the other. I was present, however, on observation with the teams when our suspects took charge of their rented yacht, the *Cornish Lady*. It then sailed, we learned later, for Morocco.

WE HAD BEEN ON edge from the moment the plane touched down at Casablanca airport. Nick Baker and I had good reason to be. While on Moroccan soil we had sufficient cover with the *commission rogatoire* to obtain evidence from hotels and ferry companies. We had difficulty, though, in putting out of our minds the international ramifications that would arise if the Moroccans discovered our main purpose for being there, for which we had absolutely no legal or political authorisation. I had done it before with my trip up to Ketama and got away with it. This promised to be a much more prolonged and difficult operation.

After the yacht's departure from Dartmouth, the smuggling team, led by Kenneth Kitchen, a fine arts lecturer in normal life, had gone to ground. He and Mike Marsland, his partner in crime, had moved from their centre of operations, an Edwardian terrace house in Streatham. Our only chance of staying in the game seemed to be to sit on the house in the hope that it had not been abandoned. But I had come up with another idea, a long shot I knew but one that was worth a try: to fly to Morocco and carry out a search for the yacht, along the whole coastline if necessary, from Agadir in the south, around Cap Spartel to Tangier on the Strait of Gibraltar; then on, if the yacht still remained at large, right into the Spanish enclave of Ceuta in the far north-east. It was a bold proposal and too radical for my bosses, who turned it down flat. Undeterred, I latched onto an already planned trip by another drugs team which I had heard about upstairs in the canteen. I got the green light, or rather more of an amber hue, since neither my Assistant Chief nor the Chief Investigation Officer himself, to whom the application had been referred owing to its unprecedented nature, was prepared to support me if things turned nasty.

My main concern was the certainty that the Moroccan police would insist on accompanying us throughout our stay. It was not going to be easy to get away on our own. At least we were not being met at the airport, so were free to travel to Rabat under our own auspices. I waved aside the blandishments of the taxi drivers in their large Mercs outside the so-called terminal building and headed for the tiny railway station. I wanted to savour the country again close up and save the Government some money into the bargain.

Last time we had taken the bus. Somewhat wiser now, I bought two first-class tickets for the hour's ride into the capital, but recoiled when we walked up to the first-class carriage, hooked up to a hissing 1930s French steam locomotive at the front of the train. The carriage was full to overflowing. Men in white tunics, women in chadors, children in all kinds of garb occupied every seat and filled the corridor. There were no Westerners and what seemed like no room for any. As Nick was tentatively suggesting that we might as well opt for a more civilised form of transport, I threw our suitcases through the first door by the toilet and boarded.

We did not have to make any special effort to soak in the smells and atmosphere of Morocco; they were all around us. I drank it all in and remained in good humour throughout the almost unbearable heat of the journey, even when the train stopped in the middle of nowhere and two Moroccans climbed in with a live sheep and a chicken, held firmly upside down by its legs and squawking to be released. I conversed animatedly in French with the people crowded around me and blithely ignored the contents of the chicken's stomach as it vomited over my shoes.

After arriving in Rabat, it took us two days and both bottles of our duty-free whisky to convince Chief Inspector Abdullah, the international police liaison officer, to leave us to travel to Tangier on our own to meet our police counterparts. The *commission rogatoire* could not be signed for two days in any case and we could 'use the opportunity to do a bit of sightseeing'. We hired a car from Avis. Nick walked around it in the dusty street in the centre of Rabat, pointing out all the dents and scratches on the Renault 5, to the puzzlement of the agent, who clearly thought he had a touch of the sun, and to my amusement too, as I had adjusted more readily to the casual ways of North Africa. This was not London or New York.

Once mobile, we lost no time in scouring all the harbours, beaches and inlets on the coast. The task was easier than we thought. Morocco is not the South of France. The beaches were long and deserted and you could count the number of yachting marinas along the western coast on the fingers of one hand. In many places the littoral was sandy and flat as a billiard table, enabling us to see the harbours with a good pair of binoculars from the road, saving precious time. It was also a great help to have seen the yacht, chartered by three of the smuggling team as it left Dartmouth two weeks earlier, before the information dried up. Not only did we have a clear image of it in our minds and photos of its departure in our pockets, but the 45-foot ketch had a distinctive double gyroscope on its masthead. We were both convinced we would recognise it anywhere.

We had set off from Rabat in high spirits. However, as each successive marina drew a blank our optimism waned; and it had deserted us entirely when the yacht was nowhere to be found in what we had considered would be our best prospect, the Royal Tangier Yacht Club. I vividly recall us lying naked on our single beds in the heat of our hotel room that afternoon, staring gloomily up at the ceiling for inspiration, when

Nick, spotting a mosquito, jumped up with a towel in his hand and leapt up and down across beds, tables and chairs in a vain attempt to swat it before it landed on him, his unrestrained genitals wobbling up and down and from side to side with every lurch until I cried out to him to stop, choking with laughter. A plunge in the pool after that and a superb dinner of couscous and Moroccan wine revived our flagging hopes and we decided to press on the following morning to Melilla and Ceuta.

On the last morning of the last day available to us, we drove down a winding road lined with olive and orange trees, through the Spanish customs post into the whitewashed town of Ceuta. We made for the busy harbour, where a huge variety of craft lay straining at their moorings and glinting in the midday sun. Anxiously we scoured the berths. There were barks, motor yachts, fishing vessels of all shapes, colours and sizes, but no white 40-foot ketch. We had almost given up hope when, amazingly, the distinctive gyroscope came into view. The yacht was partly hidden by an old dredger moored alongside the central jetty. We both let out whoops of joy. I told Nick to park the car beside a restaurant opposite the jetty and suggested taking up observation inside the restaurant so that we could keep an eye on the boat and enjoy a leisurely and well-deserved lunch at the same time.

We went into the restaurant and ordered a three-course meal with a bottle of wine. We had plenty of time now. We could ring the RAF in Gibraltar after lunch to get the air reconnaissance organised and still be back in Tangier on schedule to meet up with the chief of police the following morning. Ordering was a comic affair. We were now on Spanish soil and my French was making no headway with the monolingual Spanish waiter. After a lot of gesticulation and pointing, the first course, a gazpacho, finally arrived. I was lifting the first spoonful of the cold summer soup to my lips when I glanced out of the window and to my horror saw the yacht move. It was preparing to sail and we had as yet taken no photos or identified any of the crew.

The Spanish waiter looked startled as we rushed towards the exit. We couldn't explain and we didn't have any pesetas to give him. We dodged the man like rugby wing-halves and ran out onto the quayside, where we knew we then had to assume the nonchalant, sightseeing role of tourists – not easy with an irate Spanish waiter on our heels, but the yacht was gathering speed and would be out of sight around the headland in a few minutes. Without this evidence, our trip could be a complete waste of time. We were therefore compelled alternately to run and walk as the cover of boats, cars and people allowed. Fortunately the corpulent waiter gave up the chase after a hundred yards and we eventually reached a suitable vantage point on the path approaching the headland, as the yacht headed out to sea.

Desperately trying to look for all the world like tourists mildly interested in the coastal scenery, Nick lifted his camera, pointed it at the yacht and pressed the shutter release. Nothing. He tried again. Again, nothing. The battery was dead. I was speechless.

We did then return to the restaurant to resume our ordered meal, to the relief of the exhausted waiter, and offered our profound apologies to him in English and French, hoping that our body language and tone were enough to appease him, which I am sure they were – as was our generous tip. However, neither of us spoke on the drive back along what passed as the main highway to Tangier. We were both lost in our own thoughts. Nick was worried. Uncomfortable with anything that could even vaguely be described as technology, he was a man who still found the telephone a mystery. 'A miracle of modern science' was his favourite expression. He applied it liberally to every item of equipment from cameras to two-way radios.

Nonetheless I had to admit that he had chalked up a number of significant successes in the two years he had been in the Charlies, picking up lost tails and charming vital admissions out of villains against the odds. His intuition and superb interviewing technique made him an indispensable member of the team. Sensibly I took great care to ensure that he never became directly involved with the technical side of our highly sensitive, intelligence-based operation. But I had felt safe in choosing him to accompany me on the Moroccan trip above other worthy candidates. Why had I entrusted the camera to him then? Why had I brought him at all? I knew why: I liked him. (Years later, Nick would become the ID's principal expert on hi-tech surveillance.

A loud bang shook us both out of our reflective mood. The car swerved violently towards a tree on the left-hand side of the road, before Nick yanked the steering wheel hard down on the right and sent it in the opposite direction, careering towards a large rock on the other side of the road. He jammed on the breaks and the car slithered to a stop in a cloud of dust, just short of a granite boulder.

'What the hell was that?' I screamed at him.

'Puncture,' he replied more calmly.

'Jesus! That's all we need. How the blazes are we going to get a message out to Gib now?'

'I'll fix it,' he said with more confidence than I'm sure he felt.

I grimaced, but before I could utter the stream of invective collecting in my mind, he was out of the car onto the deserted road and fishing in the boot for the tyre kit. He couldn't fathom out the enigma of the wheel jack or how to remove the spare wheel but after I had unravelled the mystery he knelt down and began the arduous task, under the baking hot sun. I took an unkindly satisfaction in the sweat running down my errant colleague's cheek and the dirt from the dusty road accumulating on his white suit, bought especially for the trip as part of the government's lightweight suit allowance.

When we got going again, across the parched landscape, I realised that whatever happened to the yacht after it left the harbour, wherever it was going either with the cannabis on board or to pick it up along the coast somewhere (which is apparently what it did), it was beyond our reach and would not make the UK coast for at least a week. I got over my annoyance and we still managed to ring the office through the embassy and arrange for an RAF flight from Gibraltar to see if we could have the yacht checked as it rounded The Rock on its way north. Unfortunately it eluded the RAF too.

We were cheered up by Inspector Meskali's remarkable hospitality. He took us to his home, which we felt was a real honour, to meet his wife and family and we enjoyed a traditional Moroccan dinner: the other face of Morocco.

THERE WAS NO MOON. Clear skies on the previous three nights had flooded the harbour and coastal waters with its pale, monochromatic light, but tonight the strong westerly had brought in a blanket of cloud so dense that it was difficult to see the outline of the harbour wall, let alone the charcoal-grey river flowing slowly past the Custom House out to sea. I was in two minds about the moonlight. It solved one problem: if the yacht arrived, it would be easier to follow it up the River Exe and observe the landing. Then again, if our quarry were more visible we would be equally exposed. Darkness had its advantages. But the river curved away from the road half a mile from the mouth, which would mean abandoning the cars and following on foot across dark and dank farm fields. And the team had only one night-viewer.

I was not at all sure that this newfangled piece of kit would work on such a dark night. The Home Office lab had explained that the instrument enhanced all available light. A lighted cigarette would turn night into day. It would even be effective in 'dull starlight', which they said meant a cloudy, moonless night. I couldn't think of anything darker than that. What light source was there to enhance? The whole thing had sounded rather implausible to me.

I did not dwell too long on what were, after all, only potential problems. Tonight was no more likely to be the night than any of the other long nights already passed in mind-numbing inactivity. Boredom was becoming a greater cause for concern: how to keep twelve officers on their toes and alert for the final operation. We had been on this case for over six months and had been holed up in the small Custom House and on standby nearby every night for over four weeks since tailing the opposition team down from Streatham.

It had been a difficult tail even with five cars. The last Saturday in July was always the busiest of the year on the holiday routes to the West Country, and the summer of 1976 was heading for the longest period of hot weather England had seen for over 100 years. We had been nose-to-tail in suffocating heat for most of the way. There had been little opportunity to change vehicle positions to minimise the risk of showing out. Even with the now standard practice of ensuring that one vehicle did not stay too long in the target's rear view mirror, we'd had two dramas on the way down. We had almost abandoned the tail when the target had once again circled that roundabout in Streatham, twice. Fortunately the couple we were tailing in a blue VW campervan had simply missed the exit for the A30 and were blissfully unaware of the drawn-out convoy of vehicles behind them. Then Ray Smith's Ford

Cortina had overheated. I had been forced to pull him out of the convoy and hand over the eyeball to Nick, who was four cars further back. We lost contact for several heart-stopping moments. Nonetheless we had finally managed to follow the couple to a car park on Exmouth beach and then, a couple of days later, to a blue and white cabin cruiser, the *Maiati*, moored beside a jetty in the River Exe, about a mile from the mouth.

Nick and I were taking the night watch while the rest of the team remained on standby. There was no indication from our information or the movements of the opposition team waiting on the cabin cruiser that the yacht we had seen leaving Morocco, presumably laden with cannabis, was any nearer to its final destination. To add to Terry's and my concerns, we only had the services of HMCC *Vigilant*, the customs cutter lying off shore, for another three days: it was then scheduled to be in Plymouth for a four-week stint patrolling the Straits of Ushant at the westerly entrance to the English Channel – or entertaining the local management with trips round the bay, more like! We were not enamoured of a policy which allocated cutters to regions for specific periods rather than have them attached to Investigation Division teams, where they would be infinitely more effective.

The exceptional weather and the beginning of the school holidays meant that every hotel we had tried was full, but Nick's silvery tongue and the prospect of a lucrative booking courtesy of Her Majesty's Treasury had eventually persuaded the owner of the Hotel Nelson to postpone his planned refurbishment and reopen his establishment for as long as we needed it. It was the only accommodation we had managed to secure. It was conveniently situated about a mile from the Custom House, however, in a terrace of other large, eighteenth century houses on Beacon Hill, overlooking the palm-lined Esplanade and Straight Point, which strews the shore with yellowish sand that threatens to block the estuary at times. As the hotel was only three doors down from the house where Lady Nelson spent thirty lonely years, it brought to my mind the number of days she must have waited for her husband to return from sea – or from Lady Hamilton. I felt a kindred spirit, but it was small comfort in our own prolonged vigil; and she hadn't had to worry about whether the night-viewing equipment would work.

The Cornish Lady

The brass marine clock on the wall was showing 8.46pm. The heat of the day had left the Long Room, where the Customs import declarations and cash were received during the day, stiflingly close. Perversely the pleasant smells from the old ledgers, oak panelling and leather chairs, together with the old prints of sailing ships, bygone cutters, gauging instruments and officers in long-outmoded uniforms lining the walls, eerily illuminated by the flickering blue light of the CCTV screen, made me uneasy. The Department's overweening attachment to tradition had troubled me from my very first day. In one sense this heavy emphasis on historical roots was comforting and a source of pride; in another it stood in the way of progress, of a more professional approach to our work. In so many ways, the cutter policy being just one example, the Department was complacent, resting on its laurels, sticking to what it knew from its long experience. But the world was changing. Harking back to the days of Chaucer, Coleridge, Adam Smith and Robbie Burns while holding on to a myriad of antiquated practices, stood in the way of the root-and-branch reorganisation of culture and methods which, I was convinced, was essential if we were to get on top of the drugs problem before it grew uncontrollably. In this mood of disquiet and defiance I sank back in the Cashier's comfortable armchair. I closed my eyes and allowed my thoughts to wander back over the extraordinary events of the previous two months, leaving Nick to keep his gaze firmly on the screen.

I was jolted from slumber by Nick suddenly exclaiming that the yacht, our yacht for certain, had just passed the point at the entrance to the river and was sailing upstream. The marine clock was now showing just after midnight and I must have awakened other dozers when I radioed for everyone to scramble and prepare to go up river to follow the yacht. Assembling all the vehicles and beginning the surveillance in the darkness was no easy task and was made harder, as we knew, by the river veering away from the road at least a mile from where the *Maiati* was moored. As anticipated we had to park up all the cars at the bend in the road and set off on foot across muddy fields to reach the river again. To cap it all, Mike Stephenson relieved himself before we set off and, taking aim in the darkness, soaked my trousers.

We were in for a shock. As soon as we reached the river we spread out along the bank between a sea wall and the main railway line from

Torquay, but the yacht was nowhere to be seen. No lights, no hulk visible, other than a boat lying on its side on a sandbank near where we watched. Terry Byrne had the night-viewing equipment and used it to scour the river, again to no avail. A yacht could not just disappear: it must be still making its way up river. Yet that did not seem feasible given the speed with which it passed the Custom House. Something might have happened to impede its progress. We must wait. And wait. And wait. Although it was early August, it was damn cold.

Fortunately Terry was familiar with this part of the river, having reconnoitred the area some weeks before. He told me how he had got the shock of his life while peering over the sea wall near the main railway track between Exeter and Plymouth, when first he heard, then he saw, a train hurtling headlong towards him, forcing him to drop and lie face down between the track and the wall. This may have still been on his mind but it did not prevent him from noticing, at about 3am, something stirring in the river. It was the tide coming in. Then to the amazement of us all, the boat that had been lying on its side on the sandbank began to re-float; and after about an hour it was fully upright. It was ours! They had clearly lost the draught needed to stay afloat, as the tide had receded on their sail up from the mouth and they had just keeled over. They had sensibly switched off all their lights and settled down to await the tide's return, not even lighting a cigarette to help us. They now emerged and set sail again under our watchful, if strained eyes. Terry, armed with the night viewer, kept us informed with his commentary.

About a hundred yards from the *Maiati*, the two-man team on the yacht dropped a rubber dinghy over the side and began to transfer heavy sacks from the yacht into it. They then rowed over to the motor cruiser to load them into the keeping of their accomplice, Marsland. When our boys boarded the cruiser half an hour later, they found Marsland relaxing naked relaxing on seven sacks of cannabis, each weighing a half-hundredweight. He looked up at George Atkinson and all he could say was, 'No!' To which George replied, 'Yes! You're nicked.'

The yacht itself set sail again down river after the delivery. Terry, Jim Jarvie and I ended the night standing on the side of the road at around 6am, looking out past the wide mouth of the Exe to the open sea with the sun just rising above the horizon. We watched as the yacht reached the mouth of the river. The crew were blissfully unaware of our interception upriver and were no doubt enjoying thoughts of freedom after successfully completing this daring and imaginative smuggling venture. They sailed straight into the clutches of the cutter we had called in. As the Customs vessel hove into view, its grey outline seeming to fill the mouth of the Exe, we toasted our success – with pints of milk purchased from a passing milkman on his morning deliveries.

Four members of the gang were later each sentenced to seven years' imprisonment for importing cannabis worth £300,000. Much of the post-knock action Terry and I left to the team as we headed for a well-earned rest and to switch our attention to the other pressing case. We had more fish to fry; or rather, a switch from the sea to the air.

16

Geronimo: Terry the Brave

'**M**R KNOX?'
'Speaking?'
'Oh hello, I'm so glad I've reached you.'
'Can I help?'
'I'm sure you can. My name is Peter Davenport. *Daily Mail.*'
'Uh-uh.'
'Yes, I was most impressed with your recent success down in the West Country. The yacht capture. Great work. Congratulations.'
'How can I help you? We gave a full account of it all at the time and it received a lot of press coverage. What more can we say?'
'I would just like to meet up with you to discuss your work for a piece I'm thinking of writing. Your office is quite near to mine. I wonder if you would like to meet for a coffee or something a little stronger in my drinking hole, Scribes? It's just off Fleet Street.'
A couple of days later I walked up to Scribes, unknown territory to me. Davenport had described it as a relatively new wine bar owned by one Geoffrey Van-Hay, known for his controversial stewardship of the famous El Vino's wine bar farther down Fleet Street, which I did know. His exclusion of women journalists had led to violent protests which naturally received full press coverage, not to mention several well-known male journalists being physically thrown out for drunken behaviour. Who didn't know El Vino's? Now he had set up his own wine bar in a well-appointed cellar in nearby Carmelite Street, funded by loans from journalists, hence the name Scribes. It was packed when I arrived, no doubt full of reporters and press moguls, all properly dressed as was his rule. I was pleased to be wearing my office suit. The concierge pointed out my reporter sitting at a table in a quiet corner of the bar.

Peter Davenport was a handsome, charming young man who very quickly struck me during our conversation as highly intelligent and worldly wise. And today he professed to be interested in me; or rather, what I was up to. What he was really after was a scoop. Well, fair enough. He was a reporter for a major tabloid, after all: that was his job. He asked me what we were currently working on. Here I was in some difficulty. There was no way I could tell him about our current work, particularly the smuggling team we had under surveillance which was in the process of organising a cannabis run from Jamaica. It was far too sensitive and anyway our rules on press contact were strict; they were unwritten but nevertheless clear and came direct from the new Chief, Peter Cutting, who had succeeded Doug Jordan when the latter left to take up a Commissioner post with Hong Kong Customs. Press releases had to be unbiased, meaning no single media outlet could be given an advantage over any other. They therefore had to be channelled through the Department's press office and Reuters, the international press agency. However, I had been concerned throughout my time in investigation work about how unfair media coverage so often turned out to be. Two beat bobbies in attendance with us on a raid and it was 'Police Swoop!' with not even a mention of Customs, when we were invariably the main players in the case. Clearly the police had better contacts than we had and were not constrained by requirements of neutrality.

Davenport was no fool. When he realised that I was not in a position to provide him with the edge he needed to beat the opposition, he came at it from a different angle.

'All right, I recognise that you are constrained and that ongoing investigations must remain confidential until everyone is under lock and key, but all I would need to know is where the investigations are taking place and the likely location of the bust.'

'That's just not possible,' I said. 'We never issue press releases until all the suspects have been arrested. Quite often, after we have arrested the people directly involved in the case, we may still need to apprehend others elsewhere, at large as it were. And if there is a prospect of closing the case after you guys have gone to print late in the evening then we might release overnight. However we are particularly concerned about radio bulletins which go out every half hour. So the likelihood is that a late finish will not get released until the following morning.'

'I understand that. But there always comes the time when you have rounded up everyone you usefully can and you then come out to the media. This is the moment I am talking about. All I need to know is where the main arrests will take place. Roughly. Which part of the country. Not the police station. Not the border crossing. Just the town or even the county. This would enable me to get to the area ahead of time and be ready almost on the spot when the news breaks.'

I had another sip of my wine and was thinking about his request when he added, 'I can give you my phone number and all you have to do is ring me when it is safe to do so and say "Liverpool". Or "Dover". No more than that. I would only report what comes out in the press release but I would be able to get myself into a hotel in the area and be close to the scene of the action for some interesting background stuff. What do you say?'

What could I say? It was a golden opportunity for us to get one up on the police and ensure full press coverage in one of the most widely read newspapers of the day – and without breaching Cutting's 'fair play' policy.

'OK. Agreed.'

Little did I know what a story this was going to turn out to be. Nor could Peter Davenport have imagined in his wildest dreams what would happen.

WE LOST THE TAIL. Not surprising really. London is probably the most difficult place to carry out covert surveillance, other than the Sahara Desert. A little more crowded, certainly. The car wasn't difficult to follow – it was a large American Chrysler. But the complexity of the congested roads made it impossible for any of our convoy to stay right behind it for long. It just took one traffic light to go against us at the wrong moment – and that was what happened. All we knew was that he was going north.

That did not add much to the sum of our knowledge. We knew that the gang were planning to bring cannabis hidden in boxes marked 'Engine Spares' into Luxembuorg by air, and to transfer them into a light aircraft for an officially authorised flight to Middlesbrough. The clever ruse was that the plane would stop over on its journey north on a private airstrip somewhere between Luxembuorg and Teesside, where the boxes would be off-loaded into a waiting car and exchanged for identical boxes containing genuine engine parts. These would then be flown on to the declared destination. Simple. There was no risk of a search at Luxembuorg airport for goods in transit; no risk at Teesside airport, where genuine parts were being imported; and little risk at one of 1,000 private airstrips in the heart of the country, although dodging the official radar controls for the unauthorised landing would be tricky. The problem for us was: which airstrip? Hence the tail, now failed. We were stuck.

Over several weeks we had made a number of sorties into possible landing areas but without any positive indications that we were on the right trail. We carried out a series of extensive surveillance operations around the general area where we thought the plane would land, entailing many tedious hours of driving around the East Midlands countryside, mainly Lincolnshire and Nottinghamshire, to check a number of possible sites. We narrowed it down to about eleven possibles – if that could be called narrow. A combination of hard yards, information, intelligence and intuition narrowed it down even further to two: Langar, in Nottinghamshire, and the more likely Blyborough, beside Blyborough Hall in Lincolnshire, a stately home that was seldom used by its wealthy owner, Patrick Dickenson.

When we lost the tail we all headed straight for Blyborough except for Terry Byrne, who made for Langar to check it out for any sign of our targets. It took two hours to drive to Blyborough, and when I arrived in the area and drove along a road that turned out to be about a mile away from the airfield, I could hardly believe my eyes. There was the Chrysler, parked up and overlooking the flat landscape. Owing to Lincolnshire's almost complete lack of anything one could call a hill, this had been an ideal location for RAF planes to operate from during the Second World War. After I had driven past the Chrysler, I met another car coming in the opposite direction and saw one of our intelligence officers, Dave Raynes, in the driving seat. I gave him the thumbs-up and the grin on his face told the whole story. What an inspired piece of detective work by everyone!

When every one of our surveillance teams finally arrived in the area, I discussed tactics with Terry, who had now joined us. We needed a covert observation point from where we could see the airfield and watch the landing and could direct the interception vehicles. But where, in such level terrain? Dave Raynes had noticed a 13th century church close by in Grayingham, and had told one of our officers, George Atkinson, before Terry and I arrived. It seemed ideal: the church tower would give us the height we needed. Deploying the cars was more of a problem. Our target was arriving by air and would therefore have a clear sight of the whole area around the landing strip. Six cars positioned around the field would be something of a giveaway. We decided to park all the cars in places that would not attract attention from the air, stationing them inconspicuously around a nearby small housing estate where we were confident that there would be no chance of the aircraft pilot spotting anything unusual. However it was some distance from the airstrip, where speedy actions might be needed. Dave Thomas was the case officer and one of our most trained mobile surveillance officers and was thus chosen to be the lead car when it was time for us to move in for the knock.

The next step was to get into the church tower. We needed the permission of the church. This we managed to get by knocking on the right door. The Reverend Eric Thornley, vicar of the parish of Kirton Lindsey, in which St Radogan Church was situated, was only too happy to oblige when we told him quite openly what we were trying to do; although he did look a little sceptical. That was the easy bit. Getting into the belfry was the next challenge for Nick Baker and me. I don't think anyone had been up there since the 13th century – except the pigeons. Ancient wooden steps led up into the top space and the pungent smell of accumulated bird droppings. While the church had been renovated a number of times between the 17th and 19th centuries, the tower was still original. Almost knee-deep in what the pigeons hadn't needed over the years, we surveyed our resting place for the unknown number of hours ahead.

It may have been uncomfortable but it turned out to be the ideal observation point. We had 360-degree vision for as far as the eye could see through ancient window openings on all four sides. It took us only a few minutes to identify the airstrip, which we could see clearly through one window, and to make radio contact with everyone on the ground. The weather was clear. We waited.

At about 5.15 that afternoon we heard the faint sound of a plane some distance away. I had given Nick the job of observing events through the window while I kept radio contact with Terry and the troops on the ground. We had been a successful observation pair in the Custom House in Exmouth so we felt pretty confident. And Terry and I had made a good leadership team, though we were as different as chalk and cheese. Terry was not noted for his patience; his short fuse was notorious. He was more likely to rasp out a stark command or a devastating putdown than a word of encouragement. Yet most of the team would follow him anywhere and act on his orders without question. His qualities – forceful leadership, outstanding analytical skills, quick thinking and decisiveness – had made the overwhelming contribution to the success of our two teams, Drugs B and C, then regarded as the Division's elite, and filled us all with confidence. Moreover his emotional attachment to 'his lads', whom he protected at all times from unwelcome external criticism even at the risk of his own popularity, earned him unswerving loyalty. He also had a great sense of humour. To the lads, I was something of an object of fun. I was also, I like to think, a calming influence, a counterbalance to more assertive attitudes and a wise counsel to let off steam to. However my main contribution was in my regular dialogue with Terry and the joint decisions we made. We seldom got it wrong. Though there was always a first time!

With his binoculars, Nick was able to identify a small aircraft arriving from the south and beginning to circle the area. He began to give me a running commentary which I immediately radioed to the ground troops.

Baker: *'Light plane arriving from the south. Circling…Another circle.'*

Knox: *'Bravo One to all mobiles. We've got contact. Plane arriving. Plane arriving and circling. Stay off the air.'*

Baker: *'It's coming in to land on our strip…Landing'*

Knox: *'Approaching and landing.'*

Baker: *'Taxiing. Ford Granada driving onto the field.'*

Knox: *'Suspect Ford Granada approaching the plane on the airstrip.'*

Baker: *'Crates being unloaded from the plane and put into the car…two crates being lifted out of the car and carried to the plane.'*

Knox: *'Two crates being swopped. Two crates taken to the car, duplicates being carried to the plane.'*

Terry later described my commentary as verging on the poetic: pigeons fluttering around the church tower; grey clouds; a red and white light aircraft circling the field; the plane turning, descending, touching down and taxiing to a stop; a large brown Ford Granada estate coming down the lane and onto the field; the pilot out of the aircraft, two men out of the car, greeting each other; moving to the plane, opening a hatch, lifting out a large wooden crate, and carrying it towards the estate. And all the while my finger was holding down the radio transmit button, cutting out anyone else from interjecting. It reminded him, he said, of a wonderful John Arlott cricket commentary. As I announced over the radio that the car boot was closed, the pilot was going back to the plane (with the smuggling delivery complete), I momentarily took my finger off the transmit button – and an exasperated Terry seized his chance to speak, loudly, and remind me that I had forgotten one rather important thing:

'Bravo One, shouldn't we be knocking?'

The nearest car was a quarter of a mile away from the airstrip. He realised well before me that they needed to get moving, and fast. Shaken out of my commentary which was simply following Nick's observations automatically since I wasn't actually witnessing the movements below, I had inadvertently got the timing wrong; I had actually been lulled into a sense of timelessness. I was on autopilot, which the pilot of the plane clearly wasn't.

'Uh, yes. Hit! Hit! Hit!' I rasped out.

The action on the ground was swift and chaotic. Dave Thomas was in the lead car and got there first but had only managed to reach the lane beside the airstrip as the Granada was leaving. The plane was about to take off. The Granada evaded Thomas as he entered the airfield and Dave, in the heat of the moment, turned around to follow it rather than stop the aircraft taking off. The Granada accelerated down the lane towards Terry's Triumph 2000, the next car to reach the scene. Terry turned his car across the narrow lane to block its exit. Fortunately the

Granada stopped. Apparently it was the passenger who got the car to stop; it emerged in a later interview that the driver had been intent on ramming Terry's car and trying to escape.

Terry got out of his car and ran about 100 yards down the lane towards the airfield, hurling abuse at Dave Thomas as he passed him.

'Get onto the field. Get that f—ing aircraft!' he shouted.

Thomas turned around as quickly as he could in the narrow lane and drove back onto the field. Meanwhile Terry had reached the plane. Without hesitation, he jumped up onto the wing and had begun to berate the pilot, Hugh Hutton, through the cockpit canopy even as he started up the Piper Aztec. Terry's action so startled Hutton that he hesitated momentarily, and by the time he went to rev up the engines to taxi for the take-off, Thomas had managed to drive round in front of the aircraft and block it.

The two suspects in the Granada were arrested. Although we had two police officers on stand-by in the vicinity in case of serious trouble, our own, unarmed guys who had arrived just as Terry blocked the Granada's exit simply grabbed and pulled them out of the car without involving the police at all.

DURING THE LONG WAIT in the belfry, I had decided to call Peter Davenport. I simply said, 'Scunthorpe'. No more. The airfield was only about eight miles from there, the nearest large town. He would be able to hole up in a hotel until the press release was authorised, whenever that would be. Scunthorpe was in fact where we took the three suspects for interview after their arrest. Only one remained at large, the Chrysler driver who had high-tailed it out of the area when all the action began. We managed to arrest him later.

We assembled after the knock back at an army base in the area, where we had set up our control room. The phone rang and I answered it. I then hastily handed it to Terry saying, 'It's for you.' In his innocence he took the phone and said, 'Hello.' To his astonishment, he told me afterwards, it was a journalist, displaying surprising knowledge of our knock that had only gone down shortly before. He asked Terry for further details. Terry asked him how he even knew of the job. 'Oh, we've had an anonymous phone call from someone nearby,' he replied. At that moment, Terry thought it would look foolish and obstructive not to confirm the knowledge we had and then to give some further details. The call ended and, still a little taken aback by the journalist's knowledge, Terry handed the phone back to me.

'It was a journalist!' he said. 'He had an anonymous call, he said, tipping him off about the job.'

'Yes,' I whispered, 'that was me. I gave you the phone because I didn't want him to recognise my voice.'

The look on Terry's face was matchless.

When the interviews were successfully completed or well on their way, we sought the authority of the Chief to issue the press release to Reuters. It went out at about eight o'clock that evening, which would mean no press coverage until the following day, enough time to sweep up the remaining loose ends. Brief radio news broadcasts, if there were any, would not jeopardise the operation.

At breakfast in our hotel the following morning I was absolutely shocked by the copy of the *Daily Mail* that Nick Baker thrust into my hand: it had a full front-page story of the case, complete with a photo of the Piper Aztec on the field. And the reporter? None other than Peter Davenport. No other papers carried the story but his immediate action and coverage after the Reuters press release led to an avalanche of press interest, so much so that a full press conference was convened for later that day in Scunthorpe police station. I don't think there was a newspaper, TV or radio reporter missing. Later Jon Snow, covering the story for ITV, flew over the airfield in a hired light aircraft to film the location. There had not been so much press attention in Scunthorpe since the blast furnace explosion at the steel works in 1975.

Not to be outdone, though a little slow off the mark, the *Daily Express*, the *Mail*'s arch-rival, took a two-page spread the following day under the now famous headline which attracted news agencies around the world: 'GERONIMO! IT'S TERRY THE BRAVE.' What was interesting about the *Express* story was the name of the job. We were asked at the press conference if the case had an operational name. Customs did not give cases names in those days, so the press invented one: Operation Red Indian. This provided the extraordinary headline. I was amused by the description of me in the *Express* as 'a 40-year-old Londoner chewing on a seldom lit cigar'. Me, a Newcastle lad, called a Londoner? Heaven forfend! But the cigar was accurate. I had found a box of Cuban cigars in the effects taken from the plane and helped myself to one. I did not light it until after the press conference.

The pilot, Hugh Hutton, aged forty-one and described by the *Daily Mail* as 'the bankrupt playboy son of an admiral', was later gaoled for three-and-a-half years. Fellow conspirator Peter Goodsell, thirty-eight, who lived in Bayswater and was manager of the pop group Black Gold, got thirty months. Other main men were Michael James, forty-one, gaoled for four-and-a-half years and Kamal 'John' Mitha, aged thirty-seven, the Chrysler owner, who got three years. With the publicity the case generated, we could be forgiven for thinking that we had knocked that particular method of smuggling on the head, and could direct our attentions elsewhere. So it was with a sense of *déjà vu* that I read an article in *The Times* thirty-six years after Blyborough:

> Small private airfields, helipads and even farmers' fields are being used by smugglers and people traffickers as a weak link in Britain's border security.
>
> Microlights, helicopters and private business jets are being used to fly drugs, guns and explosives to remote or unstaffed airstrips where security is weaker or impracticable. Illegal immigrants are also being transported in this way, police say.
>
> There are more than 3,000 small landing sites in Britain, from private aerodromes and small flying clubs to old bomber bases and grass strips surrounded by farmland. There are 20,000 light aircraft and almost 47,000 licensed pilots.
>
> Growing concern about the use of the landing sites by organised crime gangs has prompted an appeal for help from people living near private airfields by the National Crime Agency, UK Border Force and the Association of Chief Police Officers. They want people to report the appearance of windsocks or lights at odd times, unusual activity around an aircraft once it lands, aircraft that are covered in mud, or packages being dropped from low-flying aircraft.
>
> People who fly from or work at private airfields or flying clubs have

been urged to report aircraft that have been modified to adapt their range or load or carry extra fuel, unexplained damage to aircraft, or pilots joining a club and flying to unusual destinations, especially long-distance foreign flights with only a brief stay. Suspicion may also be aroused by pilots who are determined to fly in poor weather or low light, who land short of their notified destination, who disguise flight plans, or who are evasive about passengers or routes.

Plus ça change. Incidentally, young Peter Davenport went on from the *Daily Mail* to join *The Times*, becoming their Defence Correspondent and covering terrorist campaigns from Northern Ireland to the Middle East. He met and interviewed luminaries as diverse as popes, prime ministers, presidents, trade union leaders, military commanders, pop stars and terrorist leaders during his distinguished career – and managed not to be taken hostage, in the days when the jihadists were a little less active and barbaric.

17

The Mounties

T HEY SAY THAT NO battle plan ever survives contact with the enemy, and so it was on drugs jobs. You could guarantee that somebody would lob a spanner into the works at just the wrong time. A classic example came when we were focusing on a gang who were developing plans to deploy deep sea divers to attach magnetised metal waterproof containers filled with cannabis under a ship in Canada. Their extraordinary plan was to have the containers cross the Atlantic without the carrier's knowledge – a sort of clandestine hitch-hike – to be taken off the vessel as it berthed in Liverpool by another team of divers. It was either a highly imaginative idea or pure fantasy – who knew? But they were serious operators with a track record.

To keep us on our toes we then had a little distraction. We learnt that one of the team was organising a cocaine run from the UK to Vancouver. His eighteen-year-old girlfriend was prepared to carry the stuff in a body belt. Our problem was how to deal with this while still keeping our main objective in place. It required two immediate actions: we had to contact our Canadian counterparts to alert them to the run; and to seek authorisation for me to follow the girl to Vancouver, where I could hand over the surveillance to the locals for her arrest. Our opposite numbers in this case were not Canadian Customs but the Royal Canadian Mounted Police, with whom we had been working. My reason for going, however, was not only to point out the courier to their team, but to prevent them taking down our ultimate targets at the same time. They were more than ready and wanted to do just that, but we weren't. The most unusual development came when we learned of the appearance of the female suspect, who we followed to Heathrow: she was a black girl with a head full of tight red curls. We didn't think they would have had much difficulty picking her up at the other end. However, our second objective meant I still had to go with her, obviously a big sacrifice on my part. Flying over the northern Great Lakes, the Great Plains and the Rockies, into warm and luxurious Vancouver to meet up and work with the Mounties, my childhood heroes. Some sacrifice!

The tension didn't end there, for either of us. The pilot announced soon after take-off that owing to 'technical difficulties' the flight was being diverted to Calgary where, after a short stay on the ground, another plane would take us the rest of the way to Vancouver. There was nothing I could do. We knew that the girl was going to be met by a guy with the other half of the $20 note that she had been given to carry, which would prove their identities to each other. The RCMP surveillance team were ready and waiting at Vancouver Airport – and I couldn't contact then.

The boarding was hairy. After check-in, we had to file through a small, narrow room in a line. Each passenger was subject to a cursory customs and security check by a male and female officer; not quite the x-ray, shoes and belts off, separation of computers and liquids of today and therefore not a real problem. I was a few paces and two passengers behind the girl, let's call her Sonia, when the female customs officer stopped her and started to rub her down. She very quickly felt the body belt around her waist under her dress. I felt my mouth go dry. All I could do was try to attract the attention of the male officer to let her go through. Fortunately he saw me, read my lips and pulled his colleague away. What the passengers behind me thought of all these shenanigans I can't say but, after I explained my action to the officers and thanked them, the rest of the boarding went smoothly, even to my finding a seat four rows behind her. She had obviously been shocked by the rubdown, which showed when she ordered and downed a double brandy as soon as she could after take-off. She then went to the toilet. I was concerned that she might dispose of the drugs in there but all I could do was wait and then go into the cubicle after her to see if there were any signs. There was nothing I could see, and she hadn't been in there for long.

When we touched down at Calgary, I had difficulty in following her as closely as I would have liked. We had to disembark, cross the tarmac and join a very long queue in the terminal building up to immigration control, among a milling crowd of passengers. I found myself about twenty passengers behind her. Now my heart was pounding. I turned to a man dressed in a smart suit and carrying a briefcase alongside me and asked him if it was always like this at Canadian immigration controls. He turned to me and said, 'It's OK, Mike, we just want to get a look in her bags.' My heartbeat slowed back to normal. What a relief. We did not speak again until we were through immigration, after which he steered me to a door twenty yards away and I entered what I could only describe as a film set. Inside this large room were countless numbers of plain-clothes officers gazing at television monitors directed by a senior team of RCMP officers, who were now introduced to me. The leader, Jack, quickly explained that they had our girl under surveillance and a female officer was standing by to accompany her into the ladies' toilet should she need that. The object was to befriend her if the officer could and then keep her company all the way to Vancouver. My surveillance task was over. I was off the hook – for now.

This meant that I could enjoy the delightful views out of the window as we crossed the seemingly endless Rockies on the hour-long flight to Vancouver in the safe hands of what I discovered over the coming days was a highly professional service. I was met by a cheerful Inspector Bill Campbell at Vancouver Airport, who explained that everything was under control. The courier apparently had been booked into a hotel in the city centre by her Canadian contacts and the RCMP had set up observations in the room next to hers. He would take me there after we held the urgent discussions I had asked for. We went immediately to the RCMP HQ, where I met the Chief Superintendent. Two hours and a bottle of my malt whisky later and we had a deal: no extended raids on the rest of the gang when the delivery took place and the two $20 holders were arrested. They had enough evidence of drugs smuggling and dealing to use this as their climax to a long operation but they graciously accepted my plea for them to hold their fire.

Their observation arrangements in the hotel were nothing short of incredible. A fisheye lens had been planted in the room next door. Simple, Bill said, they had just drilled a hole through the wall and positioned the barely visible lens in the wall above the bedhead, providing them with

180-degree vision around her room. They could see everything except the bathroom. He regaled me with similar operations involving fisheye lenses, where they broke into suspects' apartments or drilled through walls. On one occasion they had to drill while the occupant was still in residence. 'We just got the army to drive past with two of their tanks to block out the noise of our drilling,' said Bill. And I had thought we were ahead of the game.

We did not have too long to wait. The following morning, after a restless night for Sonia, a man turned up at her hotel reception, and the desk rang through to tell her she had a visitor. She gathered up her things, including her handbag and purse containing her half of the vital $20 note, and took the lift downstairs. She met a lean young man, in T-shirt and jeans, in the lobby and, after a brief conversation during which he seemed to be explaining he didn't have the other half of the note but that it didn't matter, they made their way to the lift. I was a little surprised when the surveillance team took the decision to pounce and arrest them before they entered the lift and she had handed over the drugs. They took both of them upstairs to recover the drugs, which they found in the bathroom. Six plastic bags of white powder were poised precariously around the seat of the lavatory, ready to be pushed into the bowl and flushed away if it all went horribly wrong. When I questioned the timing to Bill, he said that they had entered the room surreptitiously the previous day and that morning, had seen what she had done and had photographed it. Of course. Oh me of little faith!

Back at HQ it was their turn to push out the boat with some excellent British Columbian Mission Ridge reds and whites. One further surprise awaited me during our celebration. On each of the desks in the main office was a tape recorder. When I asked curiously if they recorded interviews with suspects in the main, open-plan office, they looked surprised. No, these were to record telephone intercepts, which each officer monitored from his own desk. These recordings were subsequently used in court proceedings as evidence against the accused. You could have knocked me down with a feather. Yet they could not use surveillance evidence gathered by mobile units on the ground, from tailing and so on. For me, as complete a reversal of our national laws and practices as it was possible to imagine. Strange customs.

Before we had imbibed too much, Bill asked me if I would like to phone England. Vancouver was eight hours behind the UK so I declined his invitation to phone the office which I would do first thing the following day, but I did give him my home number and asked him to ring my wife.

'Hello, Mrs Knox? Oh hi, this is Bill Campbell of the RCMP ringing you from Vancouver…R–C–M–P , the Royal Canadian Mounted Police …Vancouver…Canada.'

Bill cupped his hand over the speaker and whispered to me: 'She doesn't know where you are Mike!'

I took the handset.

'Oh, hello, darling. I can explain…'

WE REPAIRED FOR LUNCH to one of the main wharves in the harbour, to the fishermen's café – more like a canteen – that Bill said was renowned for its food. 'Have you ever had their multi-fish dish Mike?' He pronounced it the delightful North American way: mult-eye. So I tucked into a huge plate of lobster, crab, prawns, salmon and white fish washed down with a glass of Red Truck Lager, which cost the RCMP a princely $10. During lunch Bill promised to take me fishing off Vancouver Island the next morning. Fishing wasn't really my thing and he was going to pick me up at 4am, but how could I refuse?

As it turned out the weather was too stormy to take to the water. I therefore enjoyed a long lie-in before final discussions that morning, followed by an 'official' lunch in a posh uptown restaurant with the whole friendly team who had worked so brilliantly. At the lunch Bill presented me with a whole salmon which had been caught the previous day, as compensation, a second best, for my cancelled fishing trip. I thanked him profusely and thought how the devil was I going to get that home. He read my mind and added that all I had to do that evening when I boarded the plane home was to ask the cabin crew to put it in their fridge, then to wrap it in ice for the rest of the journey from the airport – which is exactly what I did. Aurea was taken aback when I gave it to her on my arrival home to her warm greeting: Bill's final smooth words when I had finished talking to her on the phone had clearly had the desired effect.

Two days later I received a fax message at the office:

'Hi Mike, Sorry to have to report that the lab test has shown the substance we seized to be Novocain, a harmless dental anaesthetic. Sonia released and free to travel back to England. Great to meet you. Good luck with the big boys. Bill.'

After Sonia's red hair and my wife's confusion about where I was, it was the third surprise of the trip: a Novocain scam. We were all duped.

The main gang who we had thought were so professional were actually inept and I think they eventually just faded from our sights: we did not have the resources to maintain surveillance on seemingly inactive 'firms' or time-wasters. My time in B and C was also coming to an end.

18

The Problem

A s HE LAY ON the dishevelled bed in the corner of the darkened room, he saw the indistinct shape of someone walking slowly over to him. The figure came to a point where he could make out the outline of a woman's head, her long black hair contrasting starkly with large white opalescent breasts and thumbnail-sized nipples jutting out between strands of hair. One hand was caressing her thigh, the other gesturing, inviting him to touch her. He began to sweat profusely. He yawned and began shivering. Sweat ran down the side of his face from his forehead, trickled from his stomach into his pubic hairs and between his buttocks onto the filthy grey sheet. A watery discharge began to pour from his eyes and thin mucus oozed from his nose, running down into his mouth like boiling water. The woman was no longer visible through his widely dilated pupils, only a watery haze, and the hair on the skin on his arms stood up as if attracted by a magnet. His skin was cold and covered in goose pimples. To add to his misery, his bowels erupted. Thunderous gas bubbles exploded in his intestines, escaping with a roar and a smell so putrid it reeked of cadavers. His bowels began to act with extreme violence and he was unable to control the flow of watery faeces running out of his body onto the already foul sheet on which he was lying, writhing. His whole body was now shaking and twitching as his muscles went into spasm and he spewed out a stream of bloody vomit adding more colours to the nauseous canvas beneath him.

He was exhausted. But it was impossible to sleep, the painful muscular cramps keeping him ceaselessly tossing on the bed. He cried out repeatedly. No one came. His only company were lascivious images of whores and men with knives and poison, intent on harming him. The frequent sexual hallucinations caused him to orgasm. He became weaker. The enormous quantity of water secreted from his body over the past twenty-four hours since his last fix had emaciated him; so much so that he couldn't have raised his head even if he had wanted to.

It was this filthy, unshaven, befouled sub-human that confronted the paramedics when they reached the block of flats. The stench was dispersing gradually through opened windows, but the three police officers in the room were not yet prepared to dispense with the protective handkerchiefs held tightly over their mouths and noses.

'Hi guys. We found this pathetic specimen an hour ago. I doubt you can do anything for him, he looks beyond it to me. Pity, we needed to ask chummy a few questions.'

'You'd be surprised. It's amazing what a shot of morphine can do to a heroin addict. Give us a couple of hours. We'll be in A&E.'

Was this the real world of drug abuse? Before my period in the drugs branches, I'd had absolutely no personal experience of drugs and very little contact with them in my working life. The drugs of choice in my day were tobacco and alcohol which were bad enough. The cases I investigated were confined to the world of so-called soft drugs: marijuana, cannabis, Indian hemp, hashish, pot, weed, grass, you name it. This graphic description of a heroin addict, recounted to me in 1977 by those impressionable paramedics who questioned him at length afterwards, was an eye-opener for me. I didn't question the vividness of their account, and its accuracy was confirmed for me when I later read the work of the eminent biochemist Sir Robert de Ropp, who knew all about the subject and whose 1957 book *Drugs and the Mind* described the experience of cold turkey in a similar way.

It left quite an impression on me. So whenever I was asked for my views on drug enforcement, I was somewhat equivocal. To me, there seemed to be too much emphasis on cannabis smuggling in the early days of our drug investigations and not enough on heroin, cocaine, and the new experimental drugs like Ecstasy being taken up by the youth of the day. I felt that our seizure record, while impressive, had little impact on the availability of drugs on the home market and called into question the amount of effort we expended on it. However I felt that all the then-extant categories of illegal drugs were dangerous, and that must be the most important message to convey to the general public.

If that meant seizures, arrests, fines, and incarceration, especially of the 'bad guys', so be it. Only if the medical and social evidence showed that some of the substances were not as harmful as others and could be decriminalised could we, as a leading enforcement body, relax our controls, as we had done with pornography. Enforcement does not stop murder, rape, burglary and a host of other crimes but that does not mean that perpetrators should not be pursued and brought to justice.

Of course it was not for HMCE to make unilateral decisions on the priority it should give drugs, and different classes of drugs, without the direction of the Department with responsibility for overall drugs policy, the Home Office; and more importantly Home Office ministers. Terry Byrne, who took over HMCE drugs policy as the Assistant Secretary in 1992, recognised immediately that his role was to determine, within the resources allocated to the Department, how and where best to deploy those resources to deliver operational drugs policy. Nevertheless he was often forcefully pressing his Home Office counterpart to get him to address the issue of the priorities the Department should pursue between hard and soft drugs; how successfully, I cannot say.

The question of legalisation was forever being raised. On this, Terry's view was unequivocal. The fundamental issue was not between prohibition and legalisation. Legalisation would send entirely the wrong message and would create an environment in which drug use would increase. But prohibition should not mean unthinking absolutism. He believed that it was perfectly feasible to have a framework set by prohibition – thus making all supply and use criminal – within an overall policy that dealt with appropriate activities, such as individual use, through understanding and the provision of treatment facilities. This essentially meant a programme of all the various agencies – law enforcement, health, education, care – acting in a coordinated, mutually supportive way.

Much earlier than this, in 1988, *The Economist* ran a series of articles entitled 'Getting Gangsters out of Drugs'. This so resonated with me that in 2000, four years after my retirement, a statement by Prime Minister Tony Blair about the continuing need to keep the misuse of drugs illegal, including cannabis, inspired me to write to The Times. It was published along with five other letters under the headline:

FACING THE HARSH REALITIES OF CONTROLLING ILLICIT DRUGS

Sir,

Illicit drugs rank in value, alongside oil and armaments, as among the world's most traded commodities. But unlike oil and armaments, the trade is exclusively in the hands of criminals. Legalising cannabis would go some way to getting gangsters out of drugs. It would also discourage users from committing crime to feed the habit.

The current debate seems to be concentrating on whether cannabis is harmful or not. This misses the main point that, whatever the harmful effects of any particular drug, and few suggest that cannabis is without harmful effects, prohibition has failed. Legalisation is the better of two difficult options.

Yours faithfully,

Michael Knox

Five days later that former colleague of mine, David Raynes, had the following letter published in response:

SLIPPERY SLOPE OF LEGALISED CANNABIS

Sir,

I am not sure why Michael Knox concludes (letter, October 14) that 'legalising cannabis would go some way to getting gangsters out of drugs'.

I spent many years in the Customs and Excise Investigation Service catching and disrupting those very gangsters, and by gangsters I assume he is not talking about the small local dealers.

The gangsters I know about have, in recent years, shown scant regard for commodity. Their motivation is all about profit. They seem now to care not one jot whether the commodity they traffic in is cannabis, cocaine, heroin or worse. Thirty years ago things were certainly different; then some, even most, 'gangsters' were quite happy to 'shop' anyone who dealt in drugs of any kind and even the cannabis traffickers of the time tended to keep to their commodity. Not so now. I have concluded, after 37 years in the anti-smuggling business, that if society were to remove or soften the legislation against cannabis we would find an increased emphasis by traffickers on other more objectionable and more socially damaging drugs.

Cannabis does have harmful effects. Legalisation (even if it were unilaterally possible in the UK, which I doubt) would surely lead to an increase in consumption and, more dangerously, would send a signal to users and non-users alike that drug abuse had become acceptable. Has it? Would legalisation of cannabis not lead to an increase in the consumption of other drugs as well? It is a slippery slope. Once we start down it there will be no retreat.

David Raynes

(Assistant Chief Investigation Officer, HM

Customs and Excise, National Investigation

Service, 1995-2000)

I later learned that this letter led to Dave Raynes being approached to contribute to a whole series of debates on TV and radio, parliamentary committees, lectures and speaking engagements all over the world including Brazil, USA, Ecuador, Turkey and Bulgaria. He has also been sought out to this day by all the UK political parties as a result. It was certainly an impressive counterpunch to *The Economist* arguments that illegal drug trafficking was one of the biggest commodity industries in the world and that 'recreational' drugs should be decriminalised and treated the same way as other addictive substances like tobacco and alcohol. His arguments have held sway with successive governments even to the point of ensuring that cannabis remains a Class B drug and is not reclassified as Class C, as many proponents of relaxation have proposed. These proponents have recently launched further campaigns to change government policy as several examples of soft drug legalisation in different parts of the world have appeared in the media. Holland led the way, of course, followed by Denmark.

In July 2014 this letter appeared in *The Times*:

Sir,

The so-called war on drugs has been a failure at every level. After more than 40 years and an estimated $1 trillion spent, it has done nothing to reduce drug supply or demand around the world, not to mention crime. At the same time, as the WHO, UNAids and the Global Commission on Drug Policy have repeatedly shown, the ongoing criminalisation of drug users contributes significantly to the spread of HIV/Aids, hepatitis and other diseases.

No one denies the correlation between illicit drug use and crime, particularly in the case of heroin or crack. However, not even the Home Office study Mr Clark [the Home Secretary] cites links the decline in UK crime rates since 1995 to the ongoing criminalisation of drug use or tougher sentences.

The idea that anyone is advocating a full-scale legalisation of heroin or crack cocaine is a typical straw-man argument. Mr Clark may know that heroin is already available on prescription in the UK. Access needs to be expanded to more users whose health and recovery could benefit from it, but no one is calling for heroin to be legally sold in shops.

Perhaps most importantly, we know from prescription initiatives around the world, including in the UK, that those with access to them commit far fewer crimes. The obvious reason: they don't have to fundraise to pay the inflated cost of street heroin any more. No one is breaking into homes or robbing people to buy alcohol.

It's time to get our priorities right. The best way of reducing drug-related crime is to treat drug use as a public health issue. Decriminalisation of drug use, as well as access to treatment, clean needles and harm reduction services are our best options to ensure that acquisitive crime is reduced and people struggling with drug addiction can get back on their feet.

Sir Richard Branson

Commissioner, Global Commission on Drug Policy

Understandably I was particularly attracted to this, given the name of the author and our earlier association. Yet only recently a six-year study has revealed that smoking extra-strong varieties of cannabis could be the cause of a quarter of all new cases of psychotic mental conditions such as schizophrenia. Researchers found that about 60,000 people in Britain suffered hallucinations and paranoid episodes brought on by the use of high-potency skunk. Daily users of skunk were five times as likely to suffer psychosis as those who never used it. The findings prompted claims that smoking cannabis was like playing 'Russian roulette with your mental health'. Psychiatrists said that there was now an 'urgent need' to educate the public about the risks.

The Problem

The pros and cons of legalisation are complex and have been the subject of endless debate, filling books, newspapers, magazines, academic papers, reports of Commissions of Enquiry and so on, amounting to millions of words on the subject. I am still somewhat ambivalent about the question. There are respectable arguments on both sides. If I had to vote on the subject at this point in time I would probably be in favour of maintaining the status quo, more from a fear of the unknown – the unintended consequences – than a sound intellectual case. However I leave the subject with an interesting extract from a letter written to the Canadian Commission of Enquiry into the Non-Medical Use of Drugs:

> In his bid to solve the 'generation gap' our middle son brought a packet of marijuana to us for a Christmas present a year ago. I was slightly horrified because I hoped, like most other parents, that my children were not using it. I was not prepared to try it then. However, with the same sort of persuasion that had previously won him the permission to keep a live garter snake, paint his room in odd colours, and study art instead of mathematics, I tried it as did his father, brother and sister.
>
> Not too much happened the first time, except that a kind of mellowness settled over the family. We smiled a lot and listened to music that somehow seemed less forbidding than when the kids played the records previously. The next night we smoked the rest of it, and the place started swinging. It was really marvellous. Everyone managed to talk together, about trivialities mainly, there was no tendency to put down anyone. Opportunities to complain or dig at the lack of academic diligence that was always part of the previous conversations with this boy were ignored, and father in particular listened to some of his ideas with a semblance of civility. That alone made the experience worthwhile. The family that night was closer together than anytime I can recall. I was greatly surprised to see that what had seemed to be many hours was only an hour and a half. We were all very happy together, and went off to our rooms feeling as if we loved each other for the human beings we were, not for mere points on a scale of achievement.
>
> For the first time in years my husband and I talked for an hour or more about work, plans, memories, problems, and possible solutions – all

things never discussed with each other because of the old scientist/ humanist conflict and the rivalries that develop between people in conflicting fields of interest. The miracle is that he seemed also to be a human being, and not only a work machine that ignored people, and particularly his family. I must have seemed somewhat more reasonable to him too, as he did not try to deprecate my interests.

The real miracle followed when we had intercourse. Instead of the dull, perfunctory act it had become, usually indulged in on my part because it made it possible to get out of it the next night, sex was something splendid. All the old routine thrust and counter thrust to get it over with as soon as possible disappeared. The sensation was extraordinary, each second was a kind of new adventure, each movement an experience, and the climaxes were beautiful beyond description. It was far more beautiful than the first weeks of marriage, and the glow of fulfilment lasted throughout the day. It was both a physical and intellectual rediscovery between two people who knew each other too well for too long.

Gosh, after reading that I began to wonder what I'd been missing all those years. Instead I have just led a life full of all the usual human experiences with highs and lows, ups and downs, vicissitudes, happiness, sorrow, love, anger, prejudice, argument, dialogue, good and bad relationships, sporting and leisure pursuits, world triumphs and disasters surrounded by an extended and extending family; in other words, all the daily experiences of a complete and satisfying life seen through clear open eyes with the normal human perceptions and emotions we are given. Why on earth would I need a false distortion of reality provided temporarily by a drug? And how could I conceivably choose to be 'under the influence' with the extraordinary work I was doing. No thank you!

19

Warrenpoint

A T THE END OF 1978, I was asked to take over a newly created specialist team to look into EEC fraud. It meant that I missed the next great B and C cannabis job, involving a prolific trafficker called Howard Marks. A number of books have been written about that one, including his own, *Mr Nice: An Autobiography*. Instead I faced a new challenge. Knowledge of deliberate fraud against the European Community was very thin on the ground. Whereas the excesses of the European project, such as grain, butter and dried milk mountains, and wine lakes caused by over-generous agricultural subsidies, were well known, fraud was at the time not a subject of any interest to the press or, it seemed, the authorities. However, pressure must have come from somewhere for me to have been given this brief; this empty file.

After a period of settling in and contact with our local Collection Investigation Units (CIUs), I very quickly confirmed that information was indeed extremely sparse but not, to my surprise at the time, entirely absent. Northern Ireland, it seemed, was an ideal breeding ground for cross-border smuggling. It was mired in sectarian 'troubles' and shared the only land boundary in the UK with our nearest EEC neighbours, the Republic of Ireland. Anything from arms, explosives, drugs, people and, as far as I was concerned at the time, grain, was illegally crossing that border.

Why grain? Well, you have to look no further than the EEC's Common Agricultural Policy (CAP). Food, being the essential requirement for life, was regarded as an industry that had to be maintained at all costs. An elaborate system of subsidies was designed to ensure all productive farmers were supported in good times and bad. Anyone who has to rely on weather for a living would readily appreciate that, although not so the current body of supermarkets in the UK, which is putting dairy farmers out of existence by driving down the wholesale price of milk to below the cost of production, allegedly so they can stay competitive with the cheaper new boys on the block – but that is a different story. In those heady days of generous subsidies, the farmers, especially the smaller ones in, for example, France, were seen by much of the UK population as being featherbedded. This was the case over farming subsidies in the UK even before we joined the EU. But now mountains of grain and butter grew, lakes of wine deepened and the cost of the CAP escalated. Reform was a long way off.

Within this system, adjustments were needed between each member state. I'll try to keep this as simple as possible – they certainly had to make it simple for me when I first encountered it! The EU had agreed to set a floor on the market price for certain key foodstuffs – sugar, cereal grains, beef, butter and skimmed milk powder – and would buy any amount of the commodity offered at that price regardless of the state of the market; this was known as the 'intervention price'. However, in the days before the euro, intervention prices were set at a fixed exchange rate called the 'green rate', which differed from the normal floating exchange rates between the various currencies of the EU member states. In order to account for any difference in the rates, a system of border taxes and subsidies was introduced, called monetary compensatory amounts (MCAs). Basically the system subsidised exports from strong-currency countries and taxed exports from weak-currency countries. Or, put even more simply, MCAs were a safety net for farmers who could rely on selling their produce whatever the market conditions, complicated by the different exchange rates between member states well before the euro was created. Such a system was an open door for villainy. Cereal grain moved from Northern Ireland to the Republic, for example, attracted a levy of £15 a ton. I bet you are beginning to realise where the opportunity for monetary gain was. And who might be involved.

When I arrived at Belfast Airport, on a cold rainy day in April 1979, I was struck by how unsophisticated the terminal was compared to Heathrow, where I had just left. Everything seemed too small, too crowded. There was little room to collect bags from the carousel, which was more of an industrial conveyor belt and where a bit of pushing and shoving was needed to retrieve one's things. I found it quite depressing really, although it reminded me a bit of Casablanca. My spirits were lifted by the approach of a handsome young man with a broad smile on his face and his hand out in greeting: 'Hello. Ray MacAfee. You must be Mike Knox?' Ray was the senior executive officer (SEO) in charge of the Northern Ireland Investigation Unit. These units were not part of the ID and were concerned with smaller, local cases that came to their attention. They had been set up after I joined the IB as part of the expansion programme in the early 70s and there was one in every Collection throughout the country.

On our way down to town, Ray began to fill me in with the information they had about grain smuggling across the border, and continued in his office on the second floor of a bank building in Lisburn Road. It had been known for a long time that the IRA were using the largely lawless border region of South Armagh, particularly around the town of Crossmaglen, as a conduit for the supply of arms and drugs from the south. There was little Customs could do. The area was a hotbed of IRA activity with a substantial proportion of the population sympathetic to 'the cause'.

Nevertheless Customs had tried over the years to bring cases to court, often without success. Ray regaled me with an extraordinary story of pigs being smuggled across the border, or rather under the border through purpose-built tunnels, to evade duty and tax. They had kept surveillance in fields adjacent to the tunnel, at no little risk, and witnessed the pigs being shepherded into the tunnel on one side of the border and a little later being taken out and loaded into trucks 100 yards away on the other side, albeit in the same field. The border was after all just a line drawn on a map at the time of the partition of Ireland, with no respect for geographical features or indeed houses. Some properties straddled the border with their kitchen in the north and their living room in the south. They put the seemingly open-and-shut case to the departmental solicitor, based on the observation evidence on both sides of the invisible border line. Unbelievably, he advised against taking it to court. He said that there was no evidence to prove that the pigs that had been put into the tunnel in the north were the same pigs that were collected and loaded onto trucks in the south! A conviction would therefore be highly unlikely.

On hearing that, and before I heard the latest suspicions about grain smuggling, I realised we might have a challenge on our hands. This was made abundantly clear when Ray described the security conditions in this border area. The army and the police often had armed personnel hidden undercover in fields and barns, keeping surveillance on suspected IRA movements and operatives. Despite that, I was to be taken around the whole area by his senior officer the next day to see for myself the site or sites of the suspected smuggling operation. That is if I didn't mind the risk? Of course…

Information had identified two crossings where farms straddled the border. Maize was being imported in ships from France through the large northern port of Warrenpoint. Articulated lorries, or semi-trailers, loaded the grain directly from the ships for delivery, ostensibly to mills in the north. However the trucks allegedly made for the bandit country of South Armagh during the night to the relevant farms, avoiding the main routes south to the border. Under cover of darkness the trailers were unhitched from the tractor units, and Irish units from the south, already positioned and waiting, would take up the trailers and drive to mills in the south. By so doing, export MCAs of £15 a ton were evaded.

The main suspect was a stocky, granite-faced farmer called Thomas 'Slab' Murphy. He lived with his three brothers on their land which lay on the border between County Louth and County Armagh. Murphy lived in the Louth part of the farm, in the Irish Republic. He was suspected of being a leading member of the IRA in South Armagh, an allegation he always denied. The question was, how could we acquire the evidence to put a stop to the traffic and bring the suspects to court? 64,000 dollars came to mind.

The Unit officer drove me down the main N1 road to Newry after breakfast the next day. It was most relaxing to drive through such beautiful, peaceful countryside. After Newry we headed off towards Crossmaglen and the border. He spoke on the radio as he drove; I had no idea to whom but what he said was alarming, to put it mildly: 'I have Mr Knox of the London Investigation Division with me. He just wants to look around the southern border so I am taking him on a tour of the area.' When he came off the radio I asked him what the devil he thought he was doing. I was supposed to be undercover and the last thing I wanted anyone to know was who I was or why I was there. He said that it was important for all those who might be listening to know that we were Customs and not the military or police. It was for our safety. Customs was a non-sectarian organization, employing both Catholics and Protestants. This was recognised by the IRA and absolved us of any responsibility for the oppression of the Catholic population for whom they were fighting. We were therefore not targets. And for the military and RUC, we were not the Provisionals. Well, that was the view then.

Nevertheless I was shocked by his action, taken without consulting or, at the very least, warning me. It was to be not the first time I would be taken by surprise, or indeed amazed, in this totally unfamiliar territory. However the trip was most useful in setting the scene for me and identifying the routes the trucks were taking from Warrenpoint through to Dundalk, a key focal point in the south, via the 'staging' points.

Back in the Unit office, Ray MacAfee explained that his officer was right to announce our presence on the radio. The area was effectively a war zone, crawling with combatants. Both sides in the dispute were very active, using all the sophisticated methods they had at their disposal. This was further confirmed when the discussion turned to our possible approach to the investigation. Based on the trailer-switching information, my immediate suggestion was to mount a surveillance exercise on the routes out of Warrenpoint all the way to the farms and through to Dundalk. Ray's reply had resonances with Sir Humphrey's reply in the TV series *Yes Minister* to a ministerial suggestion: 'That would be very courageous, minister!' Ray took a deep breath and said that conventional surveillance was out of the question. There was no way we could follow the trucks nor keep observations around the farms. Not only would that be extremely dangerous, exposing officers to the risk of being mistaken for 'the other side', but also it could draw Customs into a conflict from which we were currently detached.

Our discussions lasted well into the evening but a few beers at a local bar finally helped us to come up with a Plan B which we thought could work. First of all, the only observations we could keep at Warrenpoint were from the Customs office on site. Ray would speak to Ivan Toombs, the senior officer, to make the arrangements and seek his agreement. There was a good view of the departing trucks from that office and the presence of a couple more officers there would arouse no suspicions. Second, there were two lay-bys that could be used, one on the main N1 road from Newry before one of the Crossmaglen turn-offs and the other back onto the N1 into Dundalk in the south. The observation vehicles would have to be changed regularly, again for security reasons.

Our operation (unnamed as was our practice) began on 1 July 1979. Our team was booked into the Slieve Donard Hotel just outside Newcastle, at the foot of the appropriately named, as it turned out, Mountains of Mourne. Now we didn't choose it because it was 'a grand four-star hotel with breathtaking views of the County Down coastline and mountains'; nor because it had 'superb spa facilities, including a 20-metre pool, in 6 acres of grounds leading down to the Royal County Down Golf Club'; nor because the 'comfortable en-suite bedrooms combined classical elegance and modern luxury'; nor because the 'oak-panelled restaurant offered superb cuisine made using only the finest local produce'. No, it was chosen for us as a place to be safely away from the scene of our work activities. Until, that is, I was warned by Ray that it was decidedly unsafe. We happened to be the only residents in this huge ageing Victorian pile, which had a rather faded, run-down appearance (the quotes above are taken from its latest tourist literature, following an expensive refurbishment in recent years). That wasn't the problem, however. A member of staff was suspected of being associated with the IRA, and could well be feeding back information to the local brigade. So a week later we moved to more modest accommodation in Newry.

OUR FIRST SURVEILLANCE PROBLEM arose from the nature of the smuggling operation. With the trailers being switched at the border, there was no way of identifying the truck that we observed leaving Warrenpoint with the one that was travelling on the other side of the border in the south. The trailer would be the same but the tractor units would be different. Number plates were therefore redundant. My senior officer,

John Chapman, and I sought the advice of the Home Office boffins at their lab in Sandridge. They came up with a spray that was visible in the dark and could be used to mark the trailers with identifiable codes. However I devised an alternative system. Although unmarked, none of the trailers was identical. Each one had distinctive markings and characteristics, from paintwork and fittings to damaged bodywork. My idea was to make a detailed note of the description of each trailer and name them separately. I decided on bird names as a shorthand way to identify each one: 'Red Robin' for one with red markings, 'Blue Tit' for a bluish one, 'Yellowhammer' for the same reason, and so on. The task of the surveillance team was to ensure that they could recognise each one, especially during the hours of darkness when they were purported to be crossing the border. Sandridge also came up with PAWS, a portable axle-weighing machine. I gave John the unenviable task of transporting the heavy machine to Warrenpoint.

We had been operating for only about a week when we were taken by the first big surprise. The trucks were leaving Warrenpoint during the day and were not breaking their journeys at the suspect farms and switching tractor units. There were no visits to border farms and no night-time subterfuge. While this did not accord with our information, they may well have begun their operations that way but then discovered that it wasn't really necessary to go to all that trouble, as the authorities did not appear to be taking a blind bit of notice.

That was understandable. For export declarations, Newry Customs Station was quite near the town. It had been blown up several times and was surrounded by high security fences. For the past twenty years of its existence it had not been able to cope with the high volume of vehicles in the yard and most of them parked on the road outside, causing endless problems with local residents. On most days the staff were overwhelmed and stamped the documents on face value, with only a very limited number of highly selective examinations either in the yard or on the roadside. So it was not difficult to bypass them. The related customs post, Killen, was very close to the border and was the best place to challenge vehicles. Drivers would always stop at both the station and this post if it was in their interests to do so; for example, to obtain stamped documents. But there was no need for that in this case since they were evading export MCAs, so the drivers had to use unapproved roads to cross the border. Either that or they simply crossed on the main road having 'bought the border', a suspicion we were unable to verify.

This was highly significant for us now, since we could enlist the aid of our Irish colleagues to try to ascertain, surreptitiously, the final destinations of the trucks. Dublin appointed a liaison office to assist us. Impressively they did this remarkably quickly and we soon had the names and locations of all the Irish mills that were receiving the maize. And we no longer needed the bird names. The birds had flown!

That was the upside. The downside was that it did not provide us with direct evidence of the involvement of the border 'farmers'. And in the short time we were using PAWS, the team discovered that the drivers were overloading their trailers. The first lorry that was put on it was overweight and the driver was shocked rigid; the second lorry was also overweight but the driver was rather more tricky, 'accidentally' running over the more sensitive bits of PAWS that he was not supposed to put his wheels on. He apologised profusely for his clumsiness, offered to buy the boys a beer and left. Some of us were impressed with how quickly they had worked it out and the simplicity of the counter-move, which left us without a useful tool.

I TURNED ON THE BBC *Six O'clock News* and froze. It was 27 August 1979, a Bank Holiday Monday. That morning, said the newsreader, Lord Louis Mountbatten, the Queen's cousin, had been blown apart by an IRA bomb planted on a boat near his family castle in Sligo, Northern Ireland. Two teenage boys, one of them his grandson, had also died. Just a few hours later, at about 4.40pm, two more hellish explosions killed eighteen British Army soldiers, sixteen of them from the Parachute Regiment, in a carefully planned ambush. The location for the second atrocity was Warrenpoint, County Down. I was due to go back there in the morning, after the Bank Holiday.

'Warrenpoint?' my wife said, with a startled look on her face. 'Isn't that where you're working?'

'Yes, my dear.'

'You're not thinking of going back there, are you?' she said, staring at me with that all too familiar look.

'I'm afraid so. I have to. I have no other option right in the middle of a vital operation with all my guys out there. Anyway they've done their bloody damnedest and we're not their targets.' I almost convinced myself.

Aurea did not say any more and we didn't mention it again that evening. When I left the house on that Tuesday morning, the look on her face, however, told me all I needed to know. The mother of three teenage schoolchildren, with a full-time job of her own in an Epsom travel agency, kissed her husband goodbye as he flew off to a war zone. What an incredible support she was.

I spent all of the journey reading the various accounts in the newspapers I bought on the way to Heathrow and the continuing story over the following weeks:

> Lord Mountbatten, aged 79, and his family had traditionally spent their summer holiday at their castle in County Sligo, north west of Ireland. They were aboard his boat, *Shadow V*, which had just set off from the fishing village of Mullaghmore, when the bomb detonated around 11.30am. A witness said the blast blew the boat 'to smithereens' and hurled all seven occupants into the water. Nearby fishermen raced to the rescue and pulled Lord Mountbatten out of the water.
>
> But his legs had been almost severed by the explosion and he died shortly afterwards. Other survivors were pulled out of the water and rushed to hospital. At least one person is believed to be in a critical condition.
>
> The attack has called into question the security arrangements surrounding the Mountbatten party. Lord Mountbatten never had a bodyguard. The local police kept watch on Classiebawn castle for the one month a year Lord Mountbatten spent there. But his boat was left unguarded in the public dock in Mullaghmore where it was moored. The village is only 12 miles from the Northern Ireland border and near an area known to be used by IRA members as a refuge.

Sinn Féin vice-president, Gerry Adams, said of Mountbatten's death:

The IRA gave clear reasons for the execution. I think it is unfortunate that anyone has to be killed, but the furore created by Mountbatten's death showed up the hypocritical attitude of the media establishment. As a member of the House of Lords, Mountbatten was an emotional figure in both British and Irish politics. What the IRA did to him is what Mountbatten had been doing all his life to other people; and with his war record I don't think he could have objected to dying in what was clearly a war situation. He knew the danger involved in coming to this country. In my opinion, the IRA achieved its objective: people started paying attention to what was happening in Ireland.

Much later, in the press:

Thomas McMahon had been arrested two hours before the bomb detonated in what became known later as the Warrenpoint Ambush, at a Garda checkpoint between Longford and Granard, on suspicion of driving a stolen vehicle. He was tried for the assassinations in the Republic of Ireland, and convicted by forensic evidence that showed flecks of paint from the boat and traces of nitro-glycerine on his clothes. He spent 18 years in prison before being released as part of the Good Friday Agreement in 1998.

When I arrived at Belfast Airport, heavy security was in evidence with armed police officers all over the building. Cases were being opened by Customs officers even for domestic flights. The tension was palpable. I went straight to the Unit office in central Belfast for a 'council of war'. We all agreed that there was little we should do to change our approach or methods. They were already as low key as we could possibly devise to obtain the information and evidence we needed. We were, as far as we could discern at the time, well undercover. Little did we know.

Actually I thought we probably had enough already to mount an operation to interview the principal suspects and present them with irrefutable evidence, hopefully, from the southern mill owners. It would take quite some time to organise the final raids and there was also a need to let the tensions die down and life return to some kind of normality. In addition, we did not want to be seen as mounting a retaliatory operation in response to the horrors of 27 August. We would continue to monitor the truck movements and I would return to London to identify suitable officers for the case and to plan the knock.

The operation was both a great success and a monumental failure. I put together a force of over twenty officers, all on a voluntary basis given the nature of the case, to raid premises on both sides of the border with the aid of the Belfast Unit and our Dublin colleagues. Early on in the raids we obtained a large amount of information from one of the lorry drivers, John McNulty, who confessed to his part in the smuggling and named several of the Northern Irish people involved, including 'mastermind' Thomas Murphy and Bartley Fearon. He also told us that 'they', or more importantly 'he', knew who we were, where we lived, what family we had, when we travelled, where we stayed and exactly what we were about. I never did find out whom he meant by 'he'. The mill owners provided the evidence of the maize purchases from their suppliers, implicating Murphy and several others, and gave full witness statements to my 'southern team'. The 'northern team' was successful in uncovering important documents in Bartley Fearon's premises, thanks to the courageous efforts of Hughie Donagher and his Belfast Unit second officer Phil Rogers. A tall, well-built, good-looking man with a great sense of humour – so many of our investigators had that important gift – Hughie, a fellow SIO, was fearless.

Hughie told me that when he drove up to Fearon's farm, near Meigh in South Armagh, with Phil they had difficulty finding the place. They were in an unmarked official car and stopped to ask, politely, three locals sitting on a bridge for directions. One duly obliged, but when they were about to pull away the man said chillingly in his thick Irish brogue, 'Sure you're a brave effing man driving up here in a car like that!' Undeterred, they proceeded to Fearon's premises. During the interview with the unhelpful suspect, Hughie noticed a pile of cheques on the floor of his office and began to pick them up. Fearon shouted, 'Put those effing cheques down. If you don't, I'm going out of here, lock the door and make a phone call.' Hughie turned to Phil, whose role was to advise him of the local politics, and asked, 'Would that be to his solicitor?' Phil, with an anxious look on his face, shook his head vigorously. Nevertheless the interview continued, with a slightly less belligerent attitude on Fearon's part, and they managed to obtain some documents of interest before leaving.

The Investigator

Hughie has told me since that he had conducted enquiries all over the world on drugs trafficking and had been asked what in his opinion was the most dangerous. His immediate reply was always 'Warrenpoint'. It was, he said, virtually impossible to identify friend from foe.

The only person for whom we only had no more than oral evidence was 'Slab'. I was left with the unenviable task of interviewing him. Not at his home in the south, nor at a police station or a Customs office in the north, but somewhere neutral, as I was advised strongly to do by my Northern Irish colleagues. It was decided to call him in for a formal interview in Banbridge, the historic small town on the main N1 route north of Newry, significantly halfway between Warrenpoint and Belfast. We arranged for him to be interviewed in the large room of the Old Town Hall, more suitable for council or Women's Institute meetings than interviews under caution.

He duly arrived as requested, with one of his brothers in support. And some support he was. I don't think I have ever met a more menacing individual, standing behind his seated brother throughout the interview in this unconventional interview hall, glaring at me and interrupting aggressively at some of my direct and unsubtle questions, while Murphy himself was a model of composure. Looking older than his thirty years, with a lived-in countenance, Murphy exuded self-confidence. He was completely unfazed by the evidence that I put to him, over the course of an hour, of his involvement in the grain smuggling activities that we had obtained from the Irish mill owners and McNulty. Needless to say, he said absolutely nothing of value to the investigation. He denied any involvement throughout and, without any direct observation evidence to confront him with and with no search of his premises, I realised I was just going through the motions. The case would have to be proved in court. And he knew it.

We all returned to base. It took several months to prepare the case for court, during which I received the unbelievable news that I had been promoted to Assistant Chief Investigation Officer and appointed to head the Licensing and EEC Branch. In retrospect, the timing may well have been fortuitous. After several weeks of legal representations, preparation of documentation, negotiations with witnesses, and consultation with senior lawyers and my Chief, it was decided to drop the case or, in the parlance, leave it on the file. The reason? None of the key prosecution witnesses was prepared to give evidence in court. Not one of the mill owners was prepared to come north and give evidence in a Northern Ireland court of law. Without their evidence we had virtually nothing. I wondered why they had changed their minds after the witness statements they had given so willingly to our officers. Fear? Well that was one thought. The other was that they were up to their necks in tax evasion themselves; both evading the MCAs and receiving 'stolen' grain from overloaded lorries.

Thomas 'Slab' Murphy was later identified in many press reports as being involved with the South Armagh Brigade of the IRA, before being elected Chief of Staff by the IRA Council. He was named in the media as planning the Warrenpoint Ambush and as being implicated in the Mountbatten murder. Murphy was said to be involved in smuggling huge stockpiles of weapons from Libya in the 1980s and was part of the Army Council that decided to end its first ceasefire with the London Canary Wharf Docklands bomb in 1996, which killed two men and caused an estimated £150 million-worth of damage. Accused by the *Sunday Times* of directing an IRA bombing campaign in Britain, Murphy unsuccessfully sued the paper for libel in Dublin in 1987. The original verdict was overturned by the Court of Appeal because of omissions in the judge's summing up and there was a retrial, which he also lost. Sean O'Callaghan and Eamon Collins, both former members of the IRA, testified against him, as did members of the Gardaí, Republic of Ireland (ROI) customs officials, and the British Army. Collins wrote a book about his experiences, *Killing Rage*, and was later beaten and killed by having a spike driven through his face near his home in Newry. In 1998, a Dublin court dismissed Murphy's case after a high-profile trial during which Murphy stated that he had 'never been a member of the IRA, no way' and claimed not to know where the Maze Prison was. The jury ruled, however, that he was an IRA commander and a smuggler.

In October 2005, officers of the British Assets Recovery Agency and the Irish Criminal Assets Bureau carried out raids on a number of businesses in Manchester and Dundalk. It was extensively reported in the media that the investigation was aimed at damaging the suspected multi-million-pound empire of Murphy, who, according to the

BBC's Underworld Rich List, had accumulated up to £40 million through smuggling arms, oil, cigarettes, grain and pigs, as well as through silent or partial ownership of legitimate businesses and in property.

In his first-ever press release, issued on 12 October 2005, Murphy denied he owned any property and denied that he had any links with a co-accused at the time, a Cheshire businessman. 'I have been a republican all my life and fully support the peace process,' Murphy said. 'I will continue to play whatever role I can, to see it work.' Furthermore, he claimed that he'd had to sell property to cover his legal fees after his failed libel case against the *Sunday Times* and that he made a living from farming. He went on: 'There is absolutely no foundation to the allegations about me which have been carried in the media for some time, and repeated at length in recent weeks. I want to categorically state, for the record, that all of these allegations are totally untrue.'

He apparently acquired the nickname 'Slab' from his father from the slang word 'slabbering', meaning talking too much. He certainly didn't do so much talking these days.

ON 9 MARCH 2006, police, soldiers and customs officials from both sides of the Irish border launched a large dawn raid on Slab Murphy's house and several other buildings in the border region. Three people were arrested by the Gardaí but released three days later. A fleet of tankers, also computers, documents, two shotguns, over 30,000 cigarettes and the equivalent of 800,000 euros in sterling bank notes and cheques were seized. Four laundering facilities attached to a major network of storage tanks, some of which were underground, were also found. The Irish Criminal Assets Bureau later obtained seizure orders to take possession of euro and sterling cash and cheques, together worth around one million euros.

Sinn Féin President Gerry Adams made a public statement in support of Murphy following the March 2006 raids. Under political and media pressure over allegations of the IRA's continued presence in South Armagh, Adams said, 'Tom Murphy is not a criminal. He's a good republican and I read his statement after the Manchester raids and I believe what he says and also and very importantly he is a key supporter of Sinn Féin's peace strategy and has been for a very long time.' He added, 'I want to deal with what is an effort to portray Tom Murphy as a criminal, as a bandit, as a gang boss, as someone who is exploiting the republican struggle for his own ends, as a multimillionaire. There is no evidence to support any of that. He's a good republican. Tom Murphy was one of the supporters of this peace process.'

Murphy was again arrested in Dundalk on 7 November 2007 by detectives from the Criminal Assets Bureau on charges relating to alleged revenue offences. The following day, he was charged with tax evasion under the Tax Consolidation Act. He was later released on his own bail of €20,000 with an independent surety of €50,000. On 17 October 2008, in an agreed legal settlement, Murphy and his brothers paid over £1 million in assets and cash to the authorities in Britain and the Republic in settlement of a global crime and fraud investigation relating to proceeds of crime associated with smuggling and money laundering. After an investigation involving the Irish Criminal Assets Bureau and the UK's Serious Organized Crime Agency, over €625,000 (£487,000) in cash and cheques was confiscated by the Republic's courts, while nine properties in northwest England worth £445,000 were confiscated by British courts. Murphy was still fighting a claim in the Republic's courts relating to tax evasion for the non-completion of tax returns for eight years from 1996. On 26 April 2010, he was further remanded on bail.

In 2011, there were claims that Murphy had become disillusioned with the Northern Ireland peace process and that he had fallen out with Sinn Féin. In March 2013, Gardaí and the (renamed) Police Service of Northern Ireland, along with members of the Irish Customs Authority and the (renamed and restructured) HMRC, raided Murphy's farm again. The search of his property this time uncovered bags with over €250,000 and over £111,000 in cash, along with documents, diaries and ledgers. And On 17 December 2015, Murphy was found guilty on nine charges of tax evasion by a three-judge, non-jury Special Criminal Court in Dublin, after a nine-week trial. It had been convened under anti-terrorist legislation, owing to the belief by the Director of Public Prosecutions that a normal jury trial might be subverted by intimidation of witnesses or jurors. Murphy was found guilty on all charges of failing to furnish tax returns on his income as a 'cattle farmer' between 1996 and 2004. On 26 February 2016, he was sentenced to eighteen months in prison and was immediately transferred from court to Ireland's high-security Portlaoise Prison, reserved for dissident Republican terrorists and serious gangland criminals. You can imagine my interest in hearing, watching and reading about all of this. How minor our investigations seem now in the light of all these developments that followed. And you wonder why no-one was prepared to give evidence against him in the maize case.

WHEN I HEARD THAT Eamon Collins had written a book about his IRA activities and that he had given evidence in court against Murphy, I read his *Killing Rage* from cover to cover. I was simply astounded to learn that Collins had been a customs officer and had worked in the Warrenpoint office at the time of our operation in 1979. It was Collins who arranged for the murder of Ivan Toombs by the 'Iceman', a member of the IRA's so-called Nut Squad, which Collins himself later joined – hence the name *Killing Rage*. Toombs was shot dead in the office we had used at Warrenpoint docks. He was forty-two years old, married with five children. Two men arrived at the Customs office on the morning of 16 January 1981 and gained entry on the pretext that they wished to present export documents. Ivan was singled out and shot several times in the body and head. He died almost immediately. He was a part-time member of the Ulster Defence Regiment (UDR) and it is believed that that was the real reason for the attack. He had survived a previous attempt on his life around 1976 when gunmen fired at him as he drove to work. He was hit a number of times but survived.

When I heard about the killing I spoke to Ray MacAfee, who reassured me that we had nothing to do with it. Toombs had been a target of the IRA well before we arrived in the port. This was borne out by Collins' account of the killing. His book is an extraordinarily frank account of his role in the IRA and most revealing about the way in which the organisation worked. He was arrested eventually and faced a long gaol sentence. Increasingly disillusioned with the 'cause', however, he turned Queen's Evidence and became what was known as a supergrass. He was incarcerated in better accommodation in the Maze prison with a number of other supergrasses from both sides of the divide. He informed on all of his IRA colleagues, giving chapter and verse on their criminal deeds. This led to some of them being sent to gaol for long terms. Just before his own court case, and for those of his IRA associates still imprisoned, he had a change of mind and retracted his evidence. This led to the release of most of those named and he was left to face the full weight of justice. In fact a clever defence counsel managed to convince the judge that Collins had been subjected to inhumane behaviour by being assaulted and forced into admissions by the police over several seven-day interrogations. He walked free. However, the IRA clearly never forgave him, hence his unsavoury end.

What surprised me was that there was no mention throughout his book of our maize case, nor the surveillance we kept in the office where he worked at the time. Unfortunately it is too late to ask him the reason now. It's also too late to ask Mike White, another member of my team who is sadly no longer with us. He reported at the time that he recognised one of the Customs officers in Toombs' office receiving lifts from the very lorries we were watching. We had been warned by the Collector that there could be an informer in the office. The man – I can't actually confirm it was Collins – was therefore moved to another office while our operation was in progress.

Customs, as I was so often reminded, was certainly not sectarian. But having several officers, as it turned out, playing active roles in the IRA as well as the UDR, albeit without the authority of the Department, is understandable in the light of the political divisions obtaining then. This brought home to me even more the dangerous situation we were in. Finally I was further concerned at any role I might have played in the death of the only suspect to make admissions and provide so much information during our investigations, John McNulty. He became another victim of the IRA, found in a ditch in 1989 with the customary, dreadful spike through the head. Once again I was reassured that he was killed by the IRA for having passed information to the RUC and not for anything he had given to us.

20

Major Dunk

IN 1982 I WAS promoted to Assistant Chief Investigation Officer (ACIO) and put in charge of the newly created EEC and Licensing Branch. It was good to put the 'Troubles' behind me and begin to lead a normal, risk-free existence again. I was now one step back from the front line, managing three teams of investigators engaged in a calmer environment – or so I thought. I suppose it's always better to go into a new job with positive expectations than forebodings, but if I'd known what was going to happen to me I would not have been so sanguine and enthusiastic.

The focus of our work was all types of EEC fraud, such as MCA evasion, as in the Warrenpoint case, VAT and excise duty evasion on intra-EC trade, and breaches of the import and export licensing systems then in force, which imposed restrictions on the kind of goods that could be imported or exported, or quantities in excess of prescribed limits, in trade with non-EC nations. These were essentially to protect UK and EC producers and markets or to prevent the wrong kinds of goods getting into the hands of the wrong people. I was fortunate in having three talented SIOs in my new branch and even more so when my friend Terry Byrne transferred from his long and successful spell in the B & C drugs teams to take over the export licensing team. What could go wrong?

In November 1982, Terry received information that one Major Reginald Dunk was exporting armaments to Iraq, in breach of the export licensing embargo imposed at the time to maintain the UK's neutrality during the Iran–Iraq war. This war, started in 1980 by Iraqi strongman Saddam Hussein, would result in half a million casualties and several billion dollars' worth of damage. It was marked by indiscriminate ballistic missile strikes, extensive use of chemical weapons, and attacks on third-country oil tankers in the Persian Gulf. Both sides needed as many weapons as they could procure from any source, usually friendly countries, despite a series of embargoes imposed on Iran in particular by Western powers.

After initial enquiries, Terry being Terry set up a surveillance operation to watch Reginald Dunk and his company, Atlantic Commercial. On 20 December, Arthur Schlesinger, Dunk's London-based representative, was seen visiting the military attaché's office at the Iraqi Embassy and later that day meeting Dunk at the Ritz Hotel in Piccadilly. On 3 January 1983, David Howroyd, a director of Sterling Armament Co. Ltd, submitted an application for an export licence for 200 silenced Sterling Mark V submachine guns to go to the Jordanian Armed Forces in Aqaba. The agent through which the order had been procured was Atlantic Commercial and an end-user certificate (EUC) signed by Major General Hilmi Lozi of the Jordanian Armed Forces accompanied the application. The export licence was granted on 13 January. Terry and his team, however, were firmly of a mind that the ultimate destination for these guns was Iraq.

Twenty-one cases containing the guns were delivered from Sterling Armaments to Victoria Deepwater Terminal at Greenwich on 18 February. That same day, Terry, case officer Phil Matthews, his colleague Chris Hardwick and a number of other customs and police officers went to the premises of Atlantic Commercial in Mansfield, Nottinghamshire. They examined all the documents in the offices and interviewed Dunk. Under caution, he admitted at an early stage that the true destination was Iraq, not Jordan. When Terry challenged him about just what he thought the recipients were going to do with the machine guns, he replied 'Crowd control', by which he meant non-military, civilian use. Terry pointed out that crowd control would surely be best served by maximum noise and minimum lethal damage, whereas the silenced machine guns they had seized would have completely the opposite effect: maximum lethal damage with minimum noise. Dunk soon admitted that he knew it was illegal but said, 'Everybody sends stuff to Jordan if they want it to go to Iraq: Atlantic Commercial, the British government. It's the accepted way of transhipping the weapons because of the licensing controls on Iraq.' He admitted conducting negotiations with the military attaché's office at the Iraqi Embassy, who arranged for the Jordanians to issue the EUC.

In one of the company files, a letter dated 14 June 1982 and signed by Dunk said: 'Because of the difficulty in obtaining an export licence for Iraq, the Jordanian Embassy agreed to purchase the goods on their behalf but there has been some trouble about the size of the reward to be paid by Iraq for the issue of the EUC, and this has delayed matters.' When Terry read out the letter to Dunk, he replied: 'Well that really spells it out, doesn't it?' He went on to admit that an earlier sample export had been sent to Iraq via Lisbon in 1981 and he was hoping for an order of 2,000 guns from Iraq as a result of these two exportations. During the course of the interview, Terry also discovered that Major Reginald Wormald Dunk did not in fact reach the rank of major in his military career: he ended it as a captain. When Terry queried his 'title' – in part, of course, to question his integrity – he said that on retirement, as he understood it, military officers took on the rank one above their service rank. Terry scorned the idea and Dunk 'averted his eyes'.

In a separate interview on the same day, Schlesinger, in answer to the question 'Did you ever discuss (this export) as an Iraqi deal?' said: 'Not really. We joke about these things. My reaction was, yes, a Jordanian transaction but only a smokescreen. We know everything that goes to Jordan ends up in Iraq. Who are we to judge?' Interviews with all those involved at Atlantic Commercial and a wealth of incriminating documents reinforced the Dunk admissions and the weapons at Victoria Dock were seized.

A visit to the Iraqi Embassy three days later produced a different story. The ambassador told Terry that the deal was a typical example of the generosity between Arab countries. Seemingly, a senior Jordanian Defence Officer had been to Iraq and had seen the Iraqi forces using Sterlings in November 1982. He expressed an interest in acquiring such weapons for the Jordanian Armed Forces but the Iraqis were unable to supply any from their stock. He maintained that because of the good relations between their two countries, his own government decided to make a gift of the 200 submachine guns to the Jordanians. Dunk had not been made aware of the true destination.

Phil Matthews and the team considered that the oral evidence of Major Dunk and Schlesinger, coupled with documentary evidence, strongly contradicted this line. They did not believe that the Jordanian or Iraqi ambassadors would be prepared to give evidence at any future court proceedings brought by the Commissioners. In their view they would be presenting themselves for fierce cross-examination on their respective countries' involvement in the illegal export of controlled goods to prohibited destinations. And because of their diplomatic position they would not be subject to any critical cross-examination of their statements during the interviews. I explored this point with them. How could we put the strength of our evidence to the military attachés in conventional interviews without diplomatic immunity and clever ambassadors blocking our lines of inquiry. I felt somewhat out of my depth. Diplomatic immunity was quite literally a foreign field for me. It was agreed that we should seek the advice of the Foreign Office for their guidance on how to proceed. I wrote a letter to the Foreign Office on 25 February 1983 and submitted Phil's report to the Board proposing arrest and charge.

Apart from a brief phone call from the Foreign Office with a couple of questions about the case, I heard nothing more from them. I didn't pursue that line of enquiry further and the case went ahead. I left the Investigation Division in January 1984 to go into a new job in HMCE headquarters well before the actual court proceedings.

On 4 November 1985, Dunk, Schlesinger and Atlantic Commercial all pleaded guilty on two charges of the attempted exportation of arms to Iraq with intent to evade the prohibition in force. They had previously indicated they would be pleading not guilty, using the 'gift' line of defence with the support of the testimony of embassy witnesses. However, before the court hearing the embassies claimed diplomatic immunity and withdrew from the proceedings. Dunk et al, having been assured that there would be no custodial sentences and having lost their crucial witnesses, changed their pleas and were sentenced to a number of fines: Dunk £3,000 on Count 1 and £10,000 on Count 2; Schlesinger £3,000 on Count 2; Atlantic Commercial £2,500 on Count 1 and £5,000 on Count 2. Both Dunk and the company were ordered to pay £10,000 towards the costs. So there was no custodial sentence but a total of £33,500 in fines and costs. And there it was left.

21

A Single European Market

I SPENT THE NEXT eleven years of my career, when I wasn't defending my integrity from a scandal-hungry media and the Establishment, as an international negotiator. They were as interesting, if not more so, than my heady days as an investigator – and a darn sight less risky. I learnt my new trade in a branch of International Customs in HQ under my reserved but highly intelligent Assistant Secretary Paul Kent, negotiating the harmonisation of customs legislation in the EC. This was an intended precursor to the full harmonisation of customs, tax and excise procedures within the Community and at the external borders. My remit for the next five years was the Community Customs Code, an amalgam of all the legislation needed to control our borders brought together in a single legal document so that importers and exporters throughout the Community were subject to identical rules and procedures. People would thereby receive the same treatment in every member state. Simplification would be a better word, although legislating for it and agreeing texts was far from simple, and at the end of it all the rules were far from simple for traders to comprehend and apply.

It meant weekly visits to Brussels, staying at the Gascogne Hotel in the Boulevard Adolphe Max well looked after by the proprietor Jean Marc (those delicious curried moules marinière and the Stella Artois). The meetings involved lengthy 'i' dotting and 't' crossing to reach what were quite often cop-out clauses to achieve agreement. The number of times we had to drop the imperative word 'will' and agree instead to 'Member States may…' to allow a degree of choice as to whether a particular article had to be applied or not. The UK was regarded in those days as being particularly difficult over these discretionary clauses – I often kicked up a fuss in meetings – the reason being that we were always punctilious in applying the legislation when it was agreed and enacted, whereas a number of other member states, which shall be nameless, applied them in the breach, effectively only paying lip service to many of the requirements.

Notwithstanding what followed, the Customs Code has stood the test of time and still applies throughout the now enlarged European Union (EU). It is the bedrock for all movements in and out of the EU and well worth all that frustration and effort we had to put in. But change, big change, was on its way. For me too. We were working under the original 1957 Treaty of Rome. Thirty years later, in 1987, one of the most significant changes to the EU was agreed in the form of the Single European Act (SEA). This had caused great concern among the UK political community. Margaret Thatcher was in power and like so many people on the right was an avowed Eurosceptic. The surprise about the 1987 agreement was that Mrs Thatcher of all people signed on the dotted line to remove internal borders and grant the free movement of people, goods, services and capital within the EU.

The founding fathers of the European Community had a vision to create a political entity that would end the possibility of internecine wars in Europe. But it went much further: not just as a Customs Union to create a trading area large and strong enough to compete with the US and Asian economies, but also a Federal Europe with the establishment, in stages, of a monetary union and finally a political union. Of these three stages, only two have so far been partially completed.

Throughout all of these developments, the UK has been something of a part-time player. We did not join in 1951 when the Treaty of Paris was signed, despite Winston Churchill's strong support for the idea. For him, the European concept was to put an end to the possibility of more continental wars essentially through German and French reconciliation. He thought it was a sound objective but not one for us – at least not until 1960, when we applied to join but were seen as an American Trojan horse by the French President, De Gaulle, who vetoed our application. We had to wait until he was replaced by President Pompidou before we were admitted under the Conservative Government of Ted Heath in 1973. All this is well documented but important to recall since it sets the scene for the negotiations which followed over succeeding

A Single European Market

years and helps to explain the difficulties we, as civil servants, had in reaching agreements. It coloured all of our negotiating positions. For us the European project was and in many ways still is first and foremost a free trade area. Our mantra from on high was to 'enlarge' not 'deepen'.

For me the Single European Act had profound ramifications. Its core requirement was the abolition of internal frontiers. Who better to sort that simple one out but Michael Knox, the ace European negotiator with years of experience. Gulp! In 1987 I was called in to see the HMCE deputy chairman, Peter Jefferson-Smith, and given three weeks to come up with a comprehensive plan to prepare for the removal of frontiers by 1 January 1993. What faced me was the removal of the multitude of checks and procedures we carried out on all the movements of people and goods from other member states at ports, airports and inland clearance depots. These included the charging and collection of customs duty, VAT and excise duty, and the control of a vast list of prohibitions and restrictions on drugs, arms, food products, alcohol, embargoed goods, patents, etc., as well as security measures. And all in three weeks.

After a frantic tour of the country and discussions with divisional heads, I came up with a draft plan which included at its core the simplification of customs entry procedures (commercial import declarations), which I agreed with Doug Tweddle, who was at that time responsible for CHIEF, our computer-based entry system (well before he became a real chief: the Chief Investigation Officer of our Investigation Division). It allowed importers to submit their entries or declarations ahead of their arrival in the country and thereby obtain much faster clearance. Until then, lorry drivers arriving in say Dover submitted their entries on arrival at the dock and went off for a cuppa while the entry was being processed. Under my suggested system, documentation could be presented before the goods arrived in the port and could then be cleared as soon as they landed unless, in a tiny minority of cases, we had occasion to inspect them. This would reduce waiting times by hours. I called it the Fast Lane. I should have called it Fast Track and patented it.

As for the remaining controls, it was mainly for other government departments to decide how far they were prepared to go to relax their requirements. We were after all only working on behalf of the main policy departments. Then all I had to do was assemble all the information I had gleaned as well as my simplification proposal for a meeting of divisional heads under the chairmanship of Jefferson-Smith. This was on a Monday. I will never forget that Sunday. I had spent almost a week writing my report and on that day, in our 17th century cottage in Chobham, I laid out all the sheets of paper from one end of the cottage to the other, some seventy feet, the layout in many ways resembling a railway carriage, to place them in the right order for copying and distribution before the meeting the next day. To add to the stress, I was going through at that time a very painful separation and ultimately a divorce from Aurea.

In a morning-long session, every divisional head had something to say. Peter Wilmott was the most coherent and Martin Brown the most determined, both of whom went on to greater things as commissioners and in Peter's case later head of DG21, the Customs and tax policy division in the European Commission. It was decided that there was an enormous task ahead of us to remove all the barriers to free movement to meet our obligations under the SEA. My Fast Lane proposal was accepted for early implementation, while recognising that it was only an interim measure. However, with still six years to go to 1993, it would show firm intention on our part to progress towards complete abolition and would considerably reduce importation costs during that time.

Prohibitions and restrictions, Martin Brown's policy field, raised a whole number of other issues. Martin said it was not necessarily the preserve of the main policy departments to decide on how far to relax our controls. We had policy responsibilities too and we had the benefit, unlike our European neighbours, of being on an island with the opportunity to intercept illegal importations with a minimum of intervention. We should use that geographical advantage in any way we legally could.

After the meeting, Jefferson-Smith and his head of policy, Richard Allen, put their heads together and came up with a high-level strategy paper outlining the steps needed for complete abolition of border controls, with the exception of a number of vital prohibitions and restrictions. To achieve this objective, they proposed setting up a special co-ordination unit to pull all the strands together, represent the Department where necessary at EU meetings, and liaise with the Cabinet Office, other Government departments (OGDs), the press office and the general public. Richard Allen, an assistant secretary, or Grade 5 in Civil Service jargon, was to head this unit which was to be called, unsurprisingly, the Single Market Unit. I was appointed as Richard Allen's deputy and promoted to senior principal, or Grade 6. We recruited some ten staff, including Lance Railton as my deputy (Grade 7). Not long after the SMU's creation, Richard Allen was promoted to the Board as a commissioner and I was appointed to take his place as the assistant secretary, receiving another promotion to Grade 5. The analogy of buses comes to mind: you wait ages for one and then three come along...

This initial stage in the Single Market negotiations was by far the most interesting for me. I had almost a free hand to work out a feasible plan, working with all the main policy people involved both in and outside the Department and attending Cabinet Office meetings with the Great and the Good. During one such meeting, unusually in the bowels of the Cabinet Office, we were discussing a Commission proposal which had come out first in French, as was the custom then. The thorny question of 'will' and 'may' came up – or in this case an additional 'should' – which was so familiar to me. The chairman remarked that the problem was that there was no subjunctive in English. The deputy head of the Home Office looked up and drily commented: 'Would that that were so!' It was almost as priceless as George W. Bush's comment, in his unmistakable Texan accent: 'The trouble with the French is that they don't have a word for entrepenoor.'

IT WAS NOT ALL meetings and thousands of emails. There was research to be done and I was tasked to visit other member states to see how their preparations were going and to garner as many ideas as I could for our own approach. Tough, I know, but somebody has to. So where to begin? Italy, of course. The most congested border in Europe was, reputedly, the Brenner Pass over the Alps between Italy and Austria. What must have been the longest traffic jam in history took place there in 1980 when the Italian authorities began regulating the export of diesel – 13.5 gallons for trucks and 2.5 gallons for cars – and all vehicles leaving Italy were subject to checks at the border by the Dogana, the Italian Customs. I heard about queues of vehicles stretching back over sixty miles.

Congestion is certainly the reason that a tunnel desperately needs to be built even without these incredibly foolish oil checks but a proposed rail tunnel is still a long way off and the congestion, even now with the abolition of Customs controls on one of the principal routes between Germany, Austria and Italy, is a major source of controversy on both sides of the border and beyond.

I enjoyed my trip to Rome. We held interesting discussions in the main Customs HQ in the suburbs, although I can't say that it was all that illuminating. It was fascinating though, given the very different culture where all work stopped for coffee and the afternoons were for resting and tidying up, not serious work. When the clock reached ten the deputy head of Customs got to his feet and asked me if I would like a cup of coffee. My assent led us out of the office on the fifth floor, where we were holding the meeting, to the lift down to the ground floor, to the large exit doors out to the garden, to the path down to the road, then to a little café in the main street some 400 metres down the hill. There we stood at the bar and were served the smallest coffee I had ever seen at that time of my life, which they all downed in ten seconds. Then it was back up the hill, back into the entry hall, back in the lift and back into the meeting room. All of forty-five minutes for something that hardly wet my palate.

It was agreed at the meeting that I should visit two places at the internal border: Brenner on the Austrian border and Brindisi, the port that handled all the sea traffic from Greece. I was assured that I couldn't fail to be impressed at how much progress they had made in reducing delays. Interestingly there was no mention of the record 1980 bottleneck.

When we drove up the motorway to the 1374-metre summit of the Brenner Pass there were no vehicles blocking our passage, although the continuous upward progression of the nose-to-tail heavy trucks was very slow. Cars were able to pass the long line easily on the dual carriageway but there were no jams as such; the traffic was flowing, albeit slowly, on the inside lane. I was quite impressed. These Italians knew a thing or two, I thought. Even if we had been slowed down the views were so magnificent that it would not have been much of a hardship. Driving past cattle pastures and hay fields with snow-capped peaks all around and over the Bridge of Europe, the highest motorway bridge in Europe at that time, was, in American parlance, awesome.

Just over the peak as we began to descend we took a right turn off the road into a large car park, where several hundred vehicles, mainly trucks, were situated around a large office building. My guide explained that after the great jam – he at least mentioned it – they had built this complex to handle the commercial traffic. Here the customs entries could be lodged and any physical examinations could take place. Yes, these Italians really did know a thing or two: if you can't change the rules, change the infrastructure. They were exceptionally good at that. Their tunnels, flyovers, bridges, railways, motorways and docks all bore testimony to this expertise. They were marvellous engineers but hopeless administrators, I concluded. Italians themselves agree with that view.

It got worse. We were shown the system they operated at the customs office where the drivers lodged their declarations. The driver would present the main customs document at one window, then he was directed to another window on the side of the building where he had to hand in the supporting documents (invoices, packing lists, and so on). If there were licences, permits, or health and other certificates involved, that meant a walk to another window at the back. He was then free to go back to his cab and enjoy a panini, a chat, a nap, a read or whatever, while his documents were being processed; and if he was lucky he would be able to pick up his clearance papers in under three hours. I thought my Fast Lane was quick but by these standards it was lightning.

BACK IN ROME MY next trip was by plane on the following day to the small airport four miles outside the town of Brindisi, down in the heel of Italy. I was met at the airport by a charming man in a blue blazer. He drove a black Mercedes and spoke good English and told me he was taking me to meet the local head of Customs, the 'Capo' as he called him, at the port. At the Custom House overlooking the beautiful port, marina and harbour, the driver escorted me up the stairs to a large office, where I was introduced to the Capo and two of his staff plus an interpreter. The driver sat with us as we discussed confidential stuff about customs procedures and the preparations for the Single Market. It was explained to me that Brindisi handled mainly coal, fuel oil, natural gas and chemicals. My interest, however, was in the regular freight and car ferry services plying once or twice a week between there and Igoumenitsa and Patras in Greece. With my Brenner experience behind me, I was able to be a little more penetrating in my questions during our hour-long meeting, although I learned very little of use. The answers to my questions were often vague to the point of incomprehension even with a very accomplished interpreter. I got the impression that there was a degree of flexibility in the handling of the traffic. Regular commercial container loads seemed to benefit from faster clearance but it was difficult to be sure. The odd expression and look suggested there was a way of speeding up clearance; or perhaps I was being too much the investigator.

What I did pick up for certain was the feeling that the sooner they were on their way for lunch, the better. And so I was taken as their guest to the delightful *ristorante* in the harbour, overlooking boats of all sizes and all the frenetic activity of a bustling seaport, for a superb Italian meal. On the way down, walking behind the Capo with the two officers and the interpreter by my side, I could not avoid noticing the Capo and the driver walking arm-in-arm in deep conversation ahead of us. I turned to the interpreter and asked who the man in the smart blue blazer entwined with his boss was.

'Oh, that's Carlo Lorenzo.'

'Is he your driver?' I asked.

The interpreter was taken aback.

'Our driver? No, he owns the port. He is the head of the company that runs and owns the whole complex.'

Now it was my turn to be taken aback. And it got even more bizarre. Carlo paid for all our meals that day and accompanied us to the customs examination sheds and offices, where I was shown their systems and spoke to a number of the staff. On the following day, he paid my hotel bill before running me to the airport and bidding me a cheerful farewell.

Well that is Italy for you, I thought, as I flew back to Rome and then on to London to collect all my thoughts.

A Single European Market

CONSIDERING ALL THE OPTIONS, I decided on the land boundary between Spain and Portugal for my next visit. My Director of Customs, Sandy Russell, had been planning a trip to Spain to discuss a number of policy issues somewhat wider than my project and we agreed to combine our trips. We began in Madrid, where we were entertained, quite literally, by the deputy director general of the Guardia Civil. Our organisations were quite different. The Civil Guard is essentially a military force with police and customs duties. They are similar in many ways to the French Gendarmerie and the Italian Caribinieri but they go much further particularly when it comes to certain enforcement and international cooperation questions. Sandy had a number of border enforcement questions to raise, which is why, I suppose, we were directed to the Civil Guard. The Customs Service itself, the Aduana Española, had a number of arms including the Agencia Tributaria and the Servicio de Vigilancia Aduanera, all concerned in different ways with tax and customs duties. The Vigilancia had a large fleet of coastal craft, similar to our cutters, in their arsenal.

Our morning discussions covered a wide range of enforcement subjects and included an agreement to arrange for me to be shown around the main border post with Portugal on the next day. Quite which of the different arms of the two services I would then be dealing with I never quite knew. At one o'clock, the deputy DG took us to lunch in their exclusive members' club just along the road from his office; a magnificent building with the most amazing baroque interior. Most impressive was an ornate grand staircase rising in a sweeping curve on two sides to the upper floor and the restaurant. Before the meal we were shown the large heritage library which, we were told, was used in the filming of Umberto Ecco's masterpiece, *The Name of the Rose*, which he had set in a mediaeval monastery in the fourteenth century. The staircase, library and rooms would have provided the ideal setting for the film although the casino on the ground floor would have looked somewhat out of place, not quite the mediaeval appearance to appeal to the filmmakers. The casino didn't spoil the occasion for me and didn't prevent me from tucking into some delicious tapas, main courses and desserts, washed down with copious high quality Spanish wine. This took us to almost 5pm. The working day was clearly over but we were then invited to dinner at the deputy's home that evening.

He picked us up from our hotel at eight o'clock and took us to his comfortable apartment near the centre of Madrid, where we met his wife and family and continued our carousing. However by 10.30 Sandy looked over to me quizzically and signalled that we might take our leave. We had clearly misunderstood the invitation about dinner, as no food had been forthcoming. When I nodded, Sandy got to his feet and said, in his most diplomatic and engaging manner, as was his way, that it had been a long and most interesting day and that it would probably be time for us to return to our hotel. The deputy looked up at him with amazement.

'Aren't you staying for dinner?'

I could hardly get out of the car when we were finally dropped at the hotel at 2am. We had both learned a profound lesson about different cultures and lifestyles, one that was reinforced the next day when I was driven down to the land border between Badajoz and Elvas, a three-hour journey that allowed me to experience for the first time the unique atmosphere of the Iberian Peninsula, with its wild, striking landscapes and ancient fortified towns We travelled through the semi-arid landscapes of Castilla La Mancha, through brush and vineyards, to the massive boulders of Extremadura, with the distant Alpine mountains as a beautiful and surprising backdrop. It was obvious my guide loved the country, pointing out the sights on the drive down and even going out of the way to show me some magnificent Roman aqueducts.

One of the first things I noticed on arrival was that the Customs buildings which straddled the border a short drive west of Badajoz had large car parks on both sides. Significant? The procedures were not quite as bizarre as the Brenner, but straightforward they weren't. As this was the main land route between Lisbon and Madrid, traffic was heavy. All the commercial traffic required declarations and inspections on both sides of the border in both directions: import/export; export/import; into/out of Spain; into/out of Portugal. The complexity was such that I tried to get a grip of the overall effect of the Customs procedures by asking what I thought was a simple question: what was the average clearance time for a standard commercial truck entering Spain? How long would it have to wait at the border?

You would have thought I'd asked about the meaning of life. A group of officials went into a huddle in the office and I was kindly given a cup of coffee while a long discussion took place. Thirty minutes later, I was handed a slip of paper on which was written 'twelve hours'. They realised from the look on my face that they would have to explain such an extraordinary time delay. And here it is. As the larger and richer country, the Spanish had built the offices. They therefore owned them and they paid for everything except the personnel costs on the Portuguese side of the border. The Spanish office opening hours were from 8am to 2pm daily. The Portuguese hours were from 9am to 1pm and from 2pm to 5pm. As the responsible owners of the buildings, when the Spanish finished work for the day at 2pm they closed and locked their offices. Therefore any commercial truck arriving on either side of the border after 1pm would have to wait to submit their documents for clearance until 9am at the earliest the next day, when the Portuguese office opened. While the answer to my meaning of life question was an average of twelve hours, some would have to wait over twenty hours.

At this point I decided that the scenic tour of the local area that was on offer was preferable to a detailed inspection of the official infrastructure. I am glad I did, so that I did not miss the extraordinary turrets, moats and historic buildings of the walled town of Elvas, with the kind permission and guidance of Portuguese Customs.

THE SINGLE MARKET COULD not come quickly enough to get rid of these antiquated and hopelessly inefficient border controls. After the absurdities of Brenner and Badajoz in the south, surely, I thought, there must be some rational joined-up thinking in Europe. What about the busiest road systems in Europe criss-crossing the borders in the north? The sheer volumes of traffic in this interconnected area must call for a more sensible approach. That had to be my final destination on the Grand Tour.

I was right of course, although I knew that before I set off for a limited look around. I found that the controls were virtually non-existent. Traffic flowed. The five core countries with mutual land boundaries – France, Belgium, Germany, the Netherlands and Luxembourg – had signed the Schengen Agreement in 1985, proposing the gradual abolition of border checks at the signatories' common borders. Measures proposed included reduced-speed vehicle checks, which allowed vehicles to cross borders without stopping, the facility for residents in border areas the freedom to cross borders away from fixed checkpoints, and the harmonisation of visa policies. At the time of my visit they were already well on the way to implementing the Agreement.

In 1990 the Agreement was supplemented by the Schengen Convention, which proposed the abolition of internal border controls and a common visa policy. The Schengen Area operates very much like a single state for international travel purposes, with external border controls for travellers entering and exiting the area, and common visas, but with no internal border controls. It now consists of twenty-seven European countries, covering a population of over 400 million people and an area of 4,312,099 square kilometres (1,664,911 square miles). But not the UK.

All the Single Market negotiations had to do was follow that fine example.

MY REPORTS OF MY European excursions were received with a mixture of incredulity and amusement. But they were taken very seriously by senior management both within the Department and later in discussions with the Treasury and the Cabinet Office. The mandarins then were signed up and preparing for sweeping changes. But perhaps a little more importantly, what were the views of our political masters? It soon became obvious that we were not going to give up our island advantage for certain prohibitions and restrictions without a fight. The focus for us therefore became one of coping with our tax systems. How could we collect VAT and excise duties on traded goods within the EU without frontiers? And just in case we managed to come up with a sensible scheme, such as the extension of the 'Origin System' – the basic method for VAT within countries – right across the EU, political priorities stood very firmly in the way.

From the signing of the SEA, the Government of the day would only support the creation of a free trading area. Monetary and political unions so dearly loved by the core group were not on the agenda, even though we joined the Exchange Rate Mechanism in 1990. Taxes, like central interest rates, were therefore seen as very much the preserve of individual member states. A Commission proposal to harmonise all internal taxes across the board to facilitate free movement was therefore opposed by the UK and a couple of others from the outset. Only intensive, highest-level negotiations led to a compromise that set minimum rates for VAT to underpin national revenues and prevent cross-border distortions.

Different rates of VAT and excise duty, albeit at minimum levels, meant that we were unable to accept the Origin System. This was because moving VAT-able goods between registered traders under a Community-wide origin system would be far too complicated and costly for the various exchequers to monitor and control. It was perceived as a possible danger for the hard-fought compromise on minimum rates which could allow the advocates to apply pressure to fully harmonise rates. We were therefore charged to come up with an alternative system; and by we, I mean the Treasury and HMCE. A substantial part of my work in the SMU leading up to 1992, then, became a series of consultations and negotiations with our policy divisions and the Treasury.

Now the trail of papers from one end of my cottage to the other for my first Single Market report paled into insignificance to the effort I had to put in to draft a paper for the Chancellor of the Exchequer on our proposed solution for VAT. I did not meet too many obstacles in agreeing with the VAT divisional heads that, if the Origin System was a non-starter, the only alternative was the retention of the Destination System, whereby all goods that leave any national territory are zero-rated. In other words, all goods chargeable with VAT leaving the UK, whether to the EU or elsewhere in the world, would continue to be free of VAT. Equally all imported taxable goods would be liable for UK VAT. But drafting that lengthy report, with the almost unlimited number of annexes needed to describe the systems and set out the legalities, like the terms and conditions of commercial transactions running these days in some extraordinary cases to tens of thousands of words, was an absolute nightmare. The Treasury was so pernickety over my drafting that it took much longer than I ever imagined, but the end result was greatly enhanced. Eventually, after what seemed like months, my advisory paper, with a helpful two-paragraph summary of the main findings and our recommendations on the first page to save a busy minister valuable time, was completed and submitted to the Chancellor, Norman Lamont

After a considerable lapse of time, a meeting with the Chancellor was convened to discuss the advice. This was held in the large conference room in the Treasury building in Whitehall. All the Great and the Good of the two Departments were there. On our side of the huge oval table in this historic meeting room sat the head of the Treasury, his deputy and divisional heads; to their left were Valerie Strachan and our senior team, including the lowly, exhausted scribe Michael Frederick Knox. Facing us on the Chancellor's side were his political and press advisers and secretaries. After a short delay the Chancellor walked into the room and sat down. He opened the meeting looking down at my paper, which had been placed before his arrival on the table in front of him, and exclaimed: 'Is this the paper I haven't read?'

I don't think I need describe my feelings at that point. I imagine all my colleagues felt the same sense of despair after all the work that had gone into it. However, we had an hour or more to put the main findings and recommendations to him and to obtain his blessing for our negotiating line to progress the discussions in Brussels. Valerie outlined the content brilliantly and succinctly and the Treasury concurred. Norman asked a couple of questions during the short discussion that followed after which he stood up, peremptorily announced that he would give his opinion in due course and walked out of the room. The looks Valerie and I exchanged said it all.

Mind you, this may be a little hard on poor Norman. He was after all holding down one of the two most crucial jobs in government with the busiest and most controversial of portfolios. One just had to see the contents of his red boxes which he had to deal with every day and into the night to understand the pressure a Chancellor of the Exchequer was under. And at the time I am describing he did have a few slightly more important matters occupying his mind, not least the Exchange Rate Mechanism (ERM).

When the ERM was set up in 1979 as an important step towards Monetary Union, the United Kingdom declined to join. This was a controversial decision, as the Chancellor of the Exchequer at the time, Geoffrey Howe, was staunchly pro-European. His successor, Nigel

Lawson, a believer in a fixed exchange rate, admired the low inflationary record of West Germany, which he attributed to the strength of the Deutsche Mark and the management of the Bundesbank. Thus, although the UK had not joined the ERM, from early 1987 to March 1988 the Treasury followed a semi-official policy of 'shadowing' the Deutsche Mark. Matters came to a head in a clash between Lawson and Margaret Thatcher's economic adviser, Alan Walters, when Walters claimed that the ERM was 'half baked'. This led to Lawson resigning as Chancellor. He was replaced by his protégé, John Major, who with Douglas Hurd, the then Foreign Secretary, convinced the Cabinet to sign up Britain to the ERM in October 1990, effectively guaranteeing that the British Government would follow an economic and monetary policy that would prevent the exchange rate between the pound and other member currencies from fluctuating by more than six per cent.

The pound entered the mechanism at DM 2.95 to the pound. Hence, if the exchange rate ever neared the bottom of its permitted range, DM 2.773, the government would be obliged to intervene. At this time UK inflation was three times the German rate, interest rates were escalating to fifteen per cent and the period of boom under Nigel Lawson was heading for a bust. The conditions for joining the ERM, then, were not exactly favourable. And then in 1989 the Berlin Wall came down. From the beginning of the 1990s, German interest rates were raised to counteract the inflationary effects of heavy spending on German reunification. This caused enormous stress across the whole of the ERM. The UK had additional difficulties with a large deficit and the rapid depreciation of the US dollar, the currency in which many British exports were priced. As fixing of exchange rates within the ERM was the pathway to a single European currency, exchange rates were left unchanged. In a referendum in the spring of 1992, the Danish electorate rejected the Maastricht Treaty (the creation of the European Union and the pathway to the euro) and France announced that there would be a referendum there as well. All this turbulence meant that those ERM currencies that were trading close to the bottom of their ERM bands came under pressure from foreign exchange traders.

George Soros, the Hungarian-born American investor, had been building a huge short position in pounds sterling that would become immensely profitable if the pound fell below the lower band of the ERM. Soros recognised the unfavourable position at which the United Kingdom had joined the ERM, believing that the rate at which the United Kingdom was brought in was too high. Inflation was also much too high and British interest rates were hurting asset prices.

Norman Lamont had moved up in the Treasury, from Financial Secretary to Chief Secretary before being appointed to the Chancellorship in November 1990 by his predecessor John Major, who had become Prime Minister after the acrimonious ousting of Margaret Thatcher by her own party. On 16 September 1992, on what became known as 'Black Wednesday', it fell to Norman to take the unenviable decision to withdraw the pound from the ERM. George Soros made over £1 billion profit by short-selling sterling. The cost of Black Wednesday was put at £3.3 billion by the Treasury and newspapers reported that the Treasury had spent £27 billion of reserves in propping up the pound. A very Black Day indeed. And all of this as the UK took over the Presidency of the EU in the run-up to the completion of the Single Market in the second half of 1992.

I don't think I have ever had a busier period in my life. We took over the heavy presidential responsibilities of the EU on 1 July and it was literally non-stop right up to the wire just before Christmas, including chairing committees. The most important were chaired by Valerie, which was remarkable given that, in the later stages, she slipped and fell down outside her home and broke a bone in her leg. Her courage was an inspiration to us all, travelling backwards and forwards to Brussels and attending those crucial meetings on crutches with her leg in plaster. She achieved a great deal in the negotiations and I'm quite sure this was not as a result of sympathy voting. I was involved in most of the negotiations, during meetings and in the margins alongside Mike Norgrove, our permanent representative, as we sought to reach agreement on a raft of Commission proposals. We had bilaterals, often in French, and we briefed ministers to modify positions to reach compromises at an official level before supporting those ministers in the Council of Ministers for the final adoption of the Regulations and Directives. A lot of moules frites mayonnaise and îles flottantes were happily consumed during my weekly visits to Brussels. Our team celebrations that December in

Brussels, and in January at 10 Downing Street with the whole multi-departmental UK team addressed impressively and amusingly by John Major standing on a soap box in the large reception rooms on the first floor, were well justified.

We achieved most of our objectives, thanks to the supreme effort applied at all levels, the advantage of having the Presidency but also the requirement for unanimity on tax matters. Qualified majority voting, where a proposal could be adopted by a two-thirds majority of member states, was reserved for less controversial measures. And the EU had only twelve members then, not the later expansion to twenty-eight. Our proposed Destination System for VAT was agreed to be controlled inland at registered traders' premises. Excise duties were protected by intra-Community movements being covered by fiscal bonds, guaranteeing the duty at stake, with controls exercised at bonded warehouses, not at the border. All restrictions on private importations within the EU were lifted subject to certain criteria.

It was not all sweetness and light, or immediate. When travelling within the EU, individuals could now bring in an unlimited amount of most goods bought in another EU country without paying tax or duty, provided the following conditions were met: tax was included in the price when the items were purchased; they were for one's own use; they had been transported by the traveller. This included gifts but did not include any item that was intended to be used as payment or to be resold. Travellers were advised that should they bring in large quantities of goods from other member states, Customs could well ask for proof of tax and/or duty payment. This would most likely happen for quantities exceeding 800 cigarettes, 110 litres of beer, ninety litres of wine, ten litres of spirit or £600-worth of taxable goods. These limits on duty- and tax-free purchases within the EU took until 1999 to be adopted, to allow the duty-free industry to get their act together; for example, to ensure that passengers did not buy on the ground and in the air in excess of the limits. This led to the addition of the Blue channel at ports and airports for EU travellers in addition to the traditional Red and Green which had been introduced in my time.

So it was not completely free movement, especially if you added the continued restrictions on drugs, arms and other banned goods, and the increased security checks over the years; but it was a huge improvement to what had gone before. And although the Single Market objective was to provide free movement of goods, capital, services and people, there is still much to be achieved. The service industry is only one example of restrictive practices still hindering competition, although on the other side of the coin the free movement of people, following the large expansion of the Community, has become a vexed subject which politicians of all shades of opinion are struggling to manage. The burgeoning refugee crisis since the upheavals of the Arab Spring, the wars in Syria and Africa and poverty around the world have put matters even more severely to the test. And the euro, which I was implacably opposed to from the very beginning along with many of my colleagues (and most of our political leaders), is having its problems as a currency, to say the least. How can a system possibly work which yokes together diverse national economies under a single currency and interest rate while leaving budgetary policies in the hands of individual countries? The UK had therefore consistently set its face against a common currency without the other major planks to make it work: full fiscal, monetary and political union.

This was the ideal of the founding fathers and is still the hopelessly unrealistic objective of many, especially in the original six nations. Listen to the President of the Commission Jean-Claude Juncker and you will know what I mean, especially after the British referendum vote in favour of our leaving the EU on 23 June 2016. One of the guiding principles – free movement of goods, services, capital and people – agreed a generation ago in what seems another age, is looking decidedly wobbly in the light of the seismic changes taking place across the Europe of today. However, despite the obvious weaknesses of the EU, the success of the Brexit campaign was a sad day for me. In my view the benefits have always outweighed the losses. Two days before the referendum, I had a letter about it published in *The Times*:

Sir,

As head of the Customs and Excise division responsible for co-ordinating and negotiating the government's policy for the removal of border controls for the single market by 1 January 1993, I visited a number of border crossings throughout Europe. I found that average delays caused by customs procedures on all borders ranged from two hours to two days.

The border between Spain and Portugal was a case in point: the difference in Spanish and Portuguese opening hours meant that if a truck arrived after 2pm it had to wait until 9am the next morning to submit its customs declarations, followed by a further wait of two to three hours.

The UK was not much better: the average waiting time in Dover was three hours. The administration and labour costs were enormous. It all went at a stroke on 1 January 1993, except for UK borders, where our negotiations enabled us to maintain vital intelligence-based and random checks for prohibitions and illegal imports.

Do we seriously want to go back to all that again?

MICHAEL KNOX

Former head of the Single Market Unit, HM Customs and Excise

They edited out my visit to the Brenner Pass for reasons of length. But as you will realise this was clearly as effective as my previous letter to *The Times* on the legalisation of cannabis!

As we head towards the major, unknowable changes in our political system and our relationship with other countries, and the prospect of a protracted negotiation for a new trade deal with the EU, it's now all about having one's cake and eating it for those who voted for Brexit, namely staying in the Single Market and limiting the freedom of movement of labour to control immigration. From the first reactions of existing members, this looks an impossible ask. More likely is a weaker trade deal, eventually, and the return of border tariffs with the necessary submission of Customs declarations and frontier delays. If this were to happen, I only hope they remember the success of my Fast Lane in the three years leading up to 1993. I really should have patented it.

In July 1993, I was awarded the CBE for my services to the public, in particular my contribution to the establishment of the Single European Market. I'd like to think it included all my efforts in the investigation and international fields too. It was a very proud moment for me and one my family enjoyed when we attended the Palace. We really do these events extremely well. The shortly-to-be-honoured gathered in the Picture Gallery watched over by Canaletto and Van Dyke before being formally announced at the door of one of the nineteen state rooms, where Prince Charles was standing in for the Queen on the day. He was impressively on the ball and charming. He had so many honours to hand out to the long queue of recipients and yet he found the time and had clearly remembered his brief to comment on my work with an opening remark to a long and interesting conversation: 'You must have found fighting drug smuggling difficult and risky work.'

My daughter Julie, my son, Paul and my partner, Marlene, watched from seats in the public area of the room which had been designed, we were told, by John Nash for George IV. They were entertained throughout with light classical music played by a small chamber ensemble. My eldest daughter Suzanne could not attend because she was married (rules, dear boy, rules!) so she and her husband, Matthew, joined us for lunch at an Italian restaurant in Soho. Suzanne later accompanied Marlene and me to a splendid garden party in the grounds of Buckingham Palace that summer. What a fitting end to an extraordinary period of my life.

Unbeknown to me on this bright and sunny day, dark thundery clouds were gathering just over the horizon, about to appear and cast an ominous shadow over me.

22

What's In a Word?

M Y FATHER-IN-LAW ONCE GAVE me a valuable piece of advice. 'Mike,'
he said, 'you can believe everything you read in the newspapers,
except on that rare occasion when you have first-hand knowledge of
the facts.' He was in a position to know, having been a sub-editor on the
London *Evening Standard*. It was only when I fell foul of the Press myself
that I realised how true his cynical words were.

On 29 July 1994, the *Guardian* ran the following report, under the
headline 'Appeal Court Broadside at Customs':

> Senior Foreign Office and Customs officials interfered with the course of
> justice by manipulating the conduct of potential witnesses in an arms-to-
> Iraq trial, The Lord Chief Justice, Lord Taylor said yesterday in the Court
> of Appeal. In a damning indictment of 'machinations' within Whitehall,
> Lord Taylor described how the officials – named in court – indulged in
> 'disgraceful behaviour', the term used by Lord Justice Scott who unearthed
> the episode during the arms-to-Iraq inquiry.
>
> Sitting with Mr Justice Ognali and Mr Justice Gage, Lord Taylor was giving
> the reasons for their decision earlier this month to quash the conviction of
> Reginald Dunk and Alexander Schlesinger, fined in 1985 for planning to
> sell 200 Sterling sub machine guns to Iraq, pretending they were destined
> for Jordan. The guns were seized by Customs at Tilbury docks in London.
> The two men pleaded guilty after staff at the Iraqi and Jordanian Embassies
> reneged on promises to appear as witnesses for the defence. The Foreign
> Office and Customs officials had persuaded the staff not to appear in court,
> claiming it would embarrass their countries.
>
> Lord Taylor said the probability that a jury would not have swallowed
> the evidence of the embassy staff was not the point. That was for the

court to decide. The appeal court ordered Customs to pay the costs of the trial and appeal estimated at about £80,000. The Foreign Office officials named – Patrick Nixon, Carsten Pigott and Graham Boyce – have all been promoted since the Dunk affair. Customs officers named are John Cassey and Mike Knox. Mr Knox, who was singled out yesterday by Lord Taylor for his part in the affair, is now an investigating officer in charge of Customs' European and International Division…Mr Dunk indicated yesterday he would sue Customs for compensation…

The *Times* weighed in on the same day under the headline 'Lord Taylor attacks abuse of justice in arms trial':

Lord Taylor said: 'The machinations in this case to prevent witnesses for the defence being available, coupled with the non-disclosure of what had been done, constituted such an interference with the justice process as to amount to an abuse of it', he said, 'it was for the court…not an Assistant Chief Investigation Officer of Customs and Excise to decide whether the defence was, in his words, "neither credible nor supported by the documentary and oral evidence we now possess"…'

As did the *Independent* under the headline 'Whitehall interference in arms trial condemned':

M F Knox, a Customs officer, had written to the Foreign Office saying that the two embassies had 'put their heads together' to produce a story which was not credible. He added that he was worried about the effect on the case if the diplomats were to give evidence. He continued: 'It may be prudent for us to confront the ambassadors with the contradictory evidence in our possession before such an eventuality becomes fact in the hope that this will deter them taking a potentially embarrassing course of action.

The Foreign Office's Middle Eastern Department had 'an informal word' with the Iraqi ambassador, suggesting that it would be better if he did not agree to waive diplomatic immunity. The Jordanian embassy was also approached by the Foreign Office at the suggestion of an official of the Near East and North Africa Department who wrote: 'I confess to an

> innocent reluctance to connive at impeding the course of justice! But
> you might gently enquire …'
>
> When Lord Justice Scott put it to Sir Stephen Egerton (Head of the
> Foreign Office) that it had been a 'disgraceful' affair, he agreed that it
> had been 'a bad show'. Lord Taylor said he preferred the plain adjective
> used by Lord Justice Scott …

So what really happened? These extracts were accurate as far as
they went. However you will not be surprised to learn that, from my
perspective, the story is somewhat different to these heavily conflated
accounts. We need to turn the clock back a few years. Matrix Churchill
was a long-established quality machine tools manufacturer based in
Coventry. In 1987 it was bought by an Iraqi-controlled company, TMG
(and later TDG). Two contracts were placed with the company for the
supply of machine tools to Iraq: the first by a Chilean company for
the manufacture of fuses for shells, the second by an Iraqi company
for the manufacture of parts for multi-launcher rocket systems. Export
licences were granted on the basis that civil, not military, end-use was
stated on the application. Following the receipt of intelligence from the
West German authorities in March and May of 1990, the Investigation
Division – which I had by then left – made low-key enquiries at Matrix
Churchill's premises, having first notified the DTI and ministers of
their intentions. They found indications of potential breaches of export
licensing controls.

There followed a series of consultations with officials, lawyers and the
intelligence services about the possibility of prosecuting the company
and its directors. It was discovered that one of the directors had provided
the original information that led to the enquiries, which complicated
and delayed the decision to prosecute. In addition to the need to protect
intelligence sources, it was further complicated by the involvement of
ministers, in particular Alan Clark, then Minister for Trade at the DTI,
in the decision to grant the licences in 1988. Interdepartmental and
ministerial agreement to prosecute was finally reached in February 1991,
subject to the granting of Public Interest Immunity (PII) certificates for
the protection of sensitive papers. The company and three directors were
finally charged with export licensing offences on 19 February 1991.

The Investigator

On 2 August 1992, a *Sunday Telegraph* article alleged that 'Mr Alan Clark had helped UK companies to get round export licensing guidelines'. A similar article appeared in the *Independent* four days later. In preparing the case for court, counsel advised that a witness statement should be taken from Alan Clark (ministers do not have immunity from appearing as witnesses), who maintained that before granting the licences he had been assured that the dual-use machines were to be used only for civil purposes. However, under cross-examination by the defence during the trial, Clark accepted that the company may well have inferred from their meeting, in January 1988, that a truthful statement of the machines' actual intended use need not be given in their applications: if they had stated 'military use' in their application, they would have been rejected by a 'clerk'. Prosecuting counsel considered that this evidence was wholly inconsistent with Clark's previous written statement and advised that the prosecution should not continue. The judge directed the jury to acquit the defendants on 9 November 1992.

This hugely embarrassing collapse, plus the decision by the judge to overturn some of the PIIs during the trial, which resulted in the release of a number of sensitive and revealing documents, led to the Scott Inquiry in 1992 under Sir Richard Scott, the Lord Justice of Appeal. His wide-ranging, exhaustive and exhausting inquiry left no stone unturned. Lord Scott commented on the difficulty of extracting some 130,000 documents from government departments. If only! One of those hard-to-obtain documents was my 1983 letter in the Dunk case, buried in the huge bundle given to him by the Foreign Office. Our own reports and documents had long since reached the shredding machine or the archives. Scott reported that Customs and Excise was unable to find out what the Ministry of Defence export policy was, and that intelligence reports were not passed on to those who needed to know; or, as *The Economist* put it: 'Sir Richard exposed an excessively secretive government machine, riddled with incompetence, slippery with the truth and willing to mislead Parliament.'

His 1,806-page report was eventually published in 1995 and was then debated in Parliament. During the debate, Alan Clark admitted that he had been 'economical with the actualité', a wonderfully colourful phrase that was grabbed by the world's press, to the extreme embarrassment of the Government. When it came to a vote on the findings, John Major boldly declared it a 'vote of confidence' in his government and survived only by the narrowest of margins, 320–319. It was seen as the finest hour of the Opposition's Robin Cook, the Shadow Foreign Secretary, who had been given only two hours to read the report before the debate; he produced a brilliantly forensic, excoriating response that was one of the first signals of the end of the Major government.

The first I knew of my entanglement in the Scott Inquiry was in July 1994, when a member of his team advised me by telephone that I was the subject of criticism in a section of the report. I then received a letter from Scott asking me about my letter. Scott conducted a large number of interviews with ministers and officials, cross-examining them to elicit comments on relevant documents and to seek explanations for their actions. This he also did with the FCO officials involved in the Dunk case – but not with me! I was told that I would not be called but would be asked to give my comments on his draft report in due course. Was this because I was really only a little sideshow in the general scheme of things? If so, it was a sideshow that grew to the proportions of a main event and a veritable nightmare for those directly involved. Scott homed in on it as another example of incompetence and possible corruption at the heart of government.

I decided to seek legal advice through my trade union, the First Division Association (FDA) for senior personnel. This advice was later paid for by the Department as the deputy chairman, Peter Jefferson-Smith, was totally convinced that I had not been involved in any wrongdoing. I was reassured by my lawyer that I had done nothing either illegal or improper, and that the consequences that had allegedly followed much later from my letter to the Foreign Office were not at my instigation, especially as I had left my post not long afterwards. However I was advised to set all this down on paper to prepare for searching questions for the Inquiry. I was not called to give evidence. I was only asked some questions in writing by Lord Justice Scott, to which I replied also in writing.

Over a year later, on 9 November 1995, the draft report eventually arrived on my desk. I was shocked, to say the least. Since my letter was really the centrepiece of the criticisms, I shall quote it in full:

P F M Wogan 25 February 1983
Middle East Department, F&CO
Downing Street West
LONDON SW1

Dear Patrick,

You asked for a copy of my officers' reports concerning their visits to the Iraqi and Jordanian Embassies. These are enclosed.

You will see that, given time, the two Embassies have put their heads together and produced a united front with a story which is neither credible nor supported by the documentary and oral evidence we now possess.

My only concern is the possible effect this story may have in future criminal proceedings should the defence lawyers decide to obtain the agreement of Embassy personnel to appear as witnesses. It may be prudent for us to confront the Ambassadors with the contradictory evidence in our possession before such an eventuality becomes fact in the hope that this will deter them from taking a potentially embarrassing course of action.

I am reviewing the strength of our evidence at the moment and before we take any firm decisions on the diplomatic side I may wish to discuss this aspect of the investigation with you.

May I take this opportunity of thanking you for the advice you have already given us which has proved remarkably accurate.
Yours sincerely
M F Knox, Assistant Chief Investigation Officer

In his draft report Scott described the Dunk case accurately, mentioning the admissions made by the defendants when interviewed by our officers and the subsequent collapse of the case against them in court. But about my involvement he wrote:

> The Inquiry referred Mr Knox to the third paragraph in his letter and asked him whether he considered it to be part of his function, as a Customs Investigation Officer, 'to deter' [Embassy personnel] from giving evidence as defence witnesses?
>
> In his written statement in response Mr Knox said: '...At that time

we did not believe that the embassies would be able to offer any tangible evidence to support the unlikely version of events suggested by some of the diplomatic staff...I was convinced that some way should be explored to bring to the attention of the Ambassadors the inconsistencies in the stories put forward and by so doing, to open up a way for them or their staff to provide supporting evidence or to offer some other explanation. We could have pressed this directly with the embassies but given the sensitive diplomatic factors, thought it better to involve the FCO. I was therefore suggesting to the FCO the prudence of bringing the contradictory evidence to the attention of the Ambassadors to discourage the embassy staff from putting forward inaccurate and unsubstantiated information which could eventually prove embarrassing to the Ambassadors themselves and the Governments of Iraq and Jordan. I do accept that this action could have deterred individuals from giving false evidence.'

The end of paragraph J5.12 of the draft report was the damming bit:

The story that had emerged from the Embassy staff may well have seemed an 'unlikely version of events' that was 'inaccurate and unsubstantiated' and contained 'inconsistencies'. But that was a matter for the jury to decide at the trial. It was not for Mr Knox, nor for any FCO officials, to seek to dissuade the Embassy staff from giving that evidence. Mr Knox 'rejected most strongly the suggestion that (he) was seeking to deter the embassy staff from giving evidence as defence witnesses or that (he) was in any way attempting to impede the course of justice'. But how else can his suggestion to Mr Wogan that the Ambassadors should be 'confronted' with the contradictory evidence in our possession 'in the hope that this will deter them from taking a potentially embarrassing course of action' be interpreted? Mr Knox's suggestion had the clear objective of bringing about a situation in which evidence of an intended 'gift' of 200 sub-machine guns to Jordan could not be given by Embassy personnel because their respective Ambassadors would not permit it. In my opinion, whatever the justification for Mr Knox's view of the proposed evidence, his objective was totally unacceptable.

What a broadside! So much for my persuasive powers on paper. Scott's secretary told me that he still had no intention of interviewing me. My written reply to this excoriating analysis – my final opportunity to explain myself – had to be flawless. Above all, it had to anticipate and answer those questions that might come to his mind on reading my reply, since he would not now be asking me any more before finalising his report. I was drinking in the last chance saloon.

I spent almost three days drafting my reply, which I showed to Terry Byrne. He was most helpful, offering me a number of suggestions, which I gratefully took on board. Here are the most important points I made in the ten pages of comments on 4 December 1995:

> It is clear that you have not taken into account the explanation I gave in my written reply to you of what I meant by some of the words I used in the letter. What you appear to be saying is that I set out on a deliberate course of action to stop witnesses helpful to the defence from giving evidence in court, and that this goal was eventually realised before the matter actually came to court. I can assure you that this was quite decidedly not the case. In the extremely short time I was actively involved in this case, I acted with honourable and proper intent to see justice done. The facts bear this out:
>
> - The letter expressed thoughts not actions and no actions were sought by me either then or subsequently
> - The thoughts were about taking an investigation one stage further by, quite properly, confronting potential witnesses with contradictory evidence in our possession, that is interviewing the Ambassadors
> - The Ambassadors were themselves the potential witnesses at this stage
> - Other Embassy witnesses who came forward after the letter was written remained available long after I left the case
> - I left the case and the Investigation Division 21 months before the case came to court
>
> In stating in the third paragraph of my letter that 'It may be prudent for us to confront the Ambassadors', I was expressing thoughts about

another line of enquiry; another approach during the earliest stage of an investigation to let the representatives of the countries concerned see the weight of evidence contradicting the implausible 'gift' story…In any other similar case where diplomatic immunity was not involved, we would have pursued our investigations with the authors of the gift story to test the evidence and to establish the facts: either that the gift story was true and corroborative evidence could be adduced, or that it was false and consideration had to be given to joining them in a conspiracy with Dunk…we clearly thought at the time that putting all the evidence we had to the Ambassadors might be a way of smoking them out one way or another. However because of the 'diplomatic' complications we did not want to take any action without the advice of the Foreign Office. We had advised them before the first visits to the Embassies and we were therefore considering seeking their advice before deciding whether we (i.e. Customs) should see the Ambassadors again…

I was not asking FCO officials to take any action…in the event no further approach was made…Given the FCO's earlier advice and the diplomatic sensitivities prevailing at the time between the UK and Iraq, we came to the conclusion that no further evidence either corroborating the Ambassador's statement or refuting it would be forthcoming…at the risk of belabouring the point, the only action being contemplated was to let the Ambassadors see the evidence in our possession 'in the hope' that they, of their own volition – not through any coercion or pressure – would drop any ideas they might have had about giving what we believed to be false evidence. The phrase 'taking a potential course of action' was about discouraging them from possibly committing perjury in court, if it came to that – to the embarrassment of the Ambassadors and the countries concerned – and not about stopping them appearing in court. There is a world of difference between the two, since it goes to the heart of the investigator's role. Investigators are dealing with potential defendants or witnesses every day. It is their job to seek to expose the truth, especially by probing more deeply when there are doubts about 'evidence' to hand.

Perhaps an analogy would help: a drug smuggler is caught in the act of importing heroin on a given day at a given time. In the first few days of the investigation an associate gives him an alibi which is clearly known to be a lie. Question: is the investigation frozen at that point so that the associate may be allowed to give that evidence on behalf of the defence; or is he shown the alternative evidence showing the accused's presence at the scene of the crime (a) to avail him of the opportunity to confirm the alibi and confound the evidence, or to discourage him from giving false testimony in due course, whichever is appropriate, and (b) more immediately, to discover his motive and culpability? Is the first course of action, namely stopping the investigation in its tracks, the only acceptable or even the right one? Clearly not since investigators would be unable to carry out their task of assembling and testing evidence for court proceedings; in fact it would be quite impossible to conduct meaningful enquiries.

In this case, if the Ambassadors had not produced corroborative evidence, as a potential prosecuting authority we would have had no difficulty with their appearing in court to give such unconvincing evidence especially with the opportunity to cross-examine them. The question was whether to leave them to decide that, or to bring to their attention, in all fairness, the strength of the evidence we were already holding…returning to the letter, the fourth paragraph advises the Foreign Office that before any action of this sort was taken, I would be reviewing the evidence and speaking to them again for their advice…

My second major concern is the assertion that the objective, wrongly attributed by the Inquiry to my letter as I have made clear above, carried through the entire proceedings as a continuum…any reader [of the report] would form the distinct impression that I was one of the senior officials responsible for the decisions that were subsequently alleged to have been taken:

- First, my letter pre-dates the offers made by the Embassies to provide witnesses for the defence;
- Second, I asked for no action to be taken and none was taken at my instigation. The continued apparent availability of the witnesses over the following two years bears this out;
- Third, the letter had a shelf life of no more than a couple of days. It only expressed possibilities and provided information and was not a letter intended to direct or govern future conduct;
- Fourth, apart from seeing the offence report in September 1983,

> I had no direct involvement in the case up to January 1984 when
> I left the ID; I then moved to completely different work and had
> nothing to do with the case whatsoever until this Inquiry.

The most disturbing feature of all of this is that on the basis of a twelve
year old letter written in a few minutes primarily to let the FCO know
what was happening, but which offered some inchoate thoughts about
the next stage of a difficult investigation a full nine months before any
decision was taken to issue a proceedings order, a letter which has lain
inactive in an FCO file since February 1983, unsubstantiated conclusions are being drawn as to its purpose, my underlying objectives and its
effect. With the benefit of 20/20 hindsight the letter could have been
more clearly expressed. The truth is however that anyone can surmise
about the meaning of words, but only I know what my intentions were.
These, I have made a further attempt to explain with, I trust, more
success this time...

CHRISTOPHER MUTTUKUMARU, THE SECRETARY to the Inquiry, finally sent
me Chapter 5 of the final report, 'The Dunk Case', on 19 December
1995. In Scott's report he repeated some of the possible explanations
for the suggestions in my letter. However he then quoted a few relevant
extracts from my 4 December letter and concluded: 'But, of course, Mr
Knox's current explanation may be the correct one and the letter ineptly
worded. In any event, no action was taken either by Customs ID or by
the FCO pursuant to the suggestions contained in Mr Knox's letter. In
January Mr Knox left Customs ID for another post in Customs and had
no further connection to the case.

At long last; it was quite a Christmas present. While many of the earlier
inferences were still there, although shortened and toned down, his
conclusion effectively closed the case for me – albeit in a rather begrudging
fashion, or so it seemed to me at the time. All that remained was the formal
endorsement by the Department. This came in the shape of a letter from
the Chairman, Valerie Strachan, on 3 April 1996, which said inter alia:

> As you know from the note given to you at the time of the publication
> of the Scott Report, Departments have been considering whether disci-

plinary action should be taken against officials criticised in the report.

I realise that the period since publication has been one of some uncertainty whilst the review was carried out. But I am now pleased to tell you that I have concluded that the criticisms in Scott do not justify taking disciplinary action. Although there are lessons to be learned from the Scott report the review found that Customs and Excise officials acted conscientiously, in good faith and in accordance with Government policy.

I could now get on with the rest of my life.

What's in a word? That single word 'deter' hounded me throughout all of this unfortunate period and effectively branded me in the eyes of the judiciary and the press as a corrupt officer of the Crown. A classic tale of unintended consequences, it left me thinking about the imperfections of a judicial process that could confuse continuing investigations with actual court preparations and could take the wording of a transitory letter exploring the minefield of diplomatic sensitivities out of context, effectively accusing someone of impropriety on the basis of their interpretations of a few words that appeared to have a connection to subsequent events. It was that unreliable indicator circumstantial evidence, on which so many trials come to court and so many people are convicted. The truth is so often secondary to the legal process. I'm so glad that I didn't write 'I could kill that Major Dunk!'

Here is a factual summary of the final outcome: all the charges against the defendants were dropped; Major Reginald Dunk received compensation from the Department of £2.1 million; Dunk and Schlesinger received £120,000 from the FCO for its perceived interference in the course of justice; the ambassador's 'gift' story was a complete fabrication and, as stories go, absurdly unconvincing; the 200 submachine guns were always destined for Iraq for military purposes as were so many other armament exports in those days that escaped detection. The efforts Saddam Hussein put in to arm his military with the assistance of Western countries to become one of the largest military forces in the world are a matter of historical record and eventually led to the critical and heavily criticised invasion of Iraq in 2003.

In 1990 our officers in Middlesbrough seized the barrel of a massive gun on a ship bound for Iraq. The barrel, the main part of what became known as the 'Supergun', invented by the Canadian-born engineer Gerald Bull, measured 40 metres long and would have been the largest gun in the world, with a range of 600 miles. A spokesman for the company Forgemasters in Sheffield said they had been told the parts were for a petrochemicals plant. Sound familiar? I'm surprised they weren't giving it to Jordan!

23

The World is My Oyster

WHILE THE SCOTT INQUIRY was a pain, I knew that both Peter Jefferson-Smith and, more importantly, Valerie Strachan, HMCE deputy chairman and chairman respectively, were convinced that there had been no impropriety on my part. This view was supported by the advice of the FDA-appointed lawyer as well as by my colleagues. I was able to continue with all the international negotiations I had been involved in over the years, and those that came my way after the Single Market, without any loss of enthusiasm or energy; in particular, my chairmanship of MAG 92 (see below). I was also the UK representative to the Customs Cooperation Council – later to become the World Customs Organisation (WCO) – the Caribbean Customs Law Enforcement Committee (CCLEC), EU Heads of Customs annual meetings and the UK Association of Chief Police Officers (ACPO).

I would like to think that substantial progress was made during my time in the late 1980s and 90s in improving cooperation between Customs services throughout the world; although given the nature of the beast, precise quantitative and qualitative assessments are difficult. I do know that it facilitated a large number of inquiries in other countries through visits and communications and made it easier, sometimes overcoming national restrictions, to share intelligence and to obtain evidence for court cases. Often a phone call between respective Customs heads could make all the difference: the importance of networking. Above all it smoothed the way for Customs to act not only as a national body but also as a global enforcement authority, something that was not easy with, for example, the UK's regionally-structured police force, even with ACPO and Interpol assistance. I was particularly proud of the contribution I made to the creation of the Customs Information System (CIS) as chairman of a sub-committee of the Brussels-based Mutual Assistance Group, MAG 92, which was set up for the purpose of improving and increasing cooperation among all the Customs services in the EU. The CIS is an EU-wide computer system for the storage and exchange of information, a type of European Criminal Record Office for purely Customs matters, which continues to pool information to this day.

The work took me to all the countries in the EU. Many of the visits enabled me to establish closer relationships with my opposite numbers by discussing common problems, agreeing negotiating positions for EU legislation, and garnering support for UK candidates for posts in the various international organisations. In this way I was able to influence the appointment of Douglas Tweddle, former Chief Investigation Officer, to a senior post in the WCO.

The visits all had their interesting and lighter sides. In Oslo I discovered how seriously they took alcohol. The price of a pint of beer was six times the cost in the UK and pubs had bouncers on the doors just like late-night discos. It might have had something to do with the long winters and the intense cold I had to suffer on every one of my trips. Hot chocolate became a lot more tempting than my usual social beverage. In Denmark I was left almost speechless by the head of Customs in Padborg, on the border with Schleswig in Germany. He rose to his feet after a lunch with all his staff to thank me 'from the depths of my heart for the help you gave to Denmark to combat the Germans during the Second World War'. He spoke for over half an hour about the UK's contribution to the war effort, our bravery during the Blitz, and Churchill's steadfastness. You realise at times like this that you are not just a representative of your government department but an ambassador for your country. The anti-German feelings in that border area were still very strong and unlikely to fade among those who were there during the invasion and who would take those horrific experiences to the grave.

The heads of EU Customs and Turkey took turns in hosting their annual meetings. Turkey, a non-EU country but one very keen to join, has been constantly rebuffed over the years but did reach agreement on taking an active role in Customs cooperation which has been extremely beneficial, not least with the major refugee exodus from the Middle

East. Each service gave the impression of trying to outdo the others: the French in the five-star Carlton Hotel in Cannes, with a firework display over the harbour to rival Sydney (perhaps not quite that extravagant); the Germans in the immaculate spa town of Bad Reichenhal, where we were treated to tours of the spas (well the spouses were, while we slaved away in the meeting rooms) and the surrounding Bavarian countryside, including a boat trip on the Konigsee and a drive up to Berchtesgaden; the Italians in Florence, where they had planned to hold the meetings in the great art gallery, the Uffizi, only to have to change the venue at the last moment when a Mafia bomb blew up part of the building shortly before our arrival and destroyed many irreplaceable national treasures. We had to put up with the old Town Hall, overseen by Leonardo friezes and a replica of Michelangelo's *David* at the entrance.

Eighteen months after the Berlin Wall came down, German Customs took the unprecedented decision to hold the conference on the east side of Berlin, accommodating us in a hotel where I was kindly allocated a room on the nineteenth floor – and the lift didn't work. The hotel was close to the shattered remains of the Wall and I ventured out to pick up a few fragments of this iconic monument to Stalinist Russia. These were being sold as souvenirs set in plastic on the West side, in the Friedrich Strasse, and at the Brandenburg Gate for fifty marks, but this small piece of broken concrete did not merit a penny spent on it. Tours on this trip included the former Nazi Party headquarters, out of reach behind the Wall before 1989 and now a museum, with visits to SS rooms used to extract confessions from the enemies of the regime and ending in the vast office of Reich Air Marshal Hermann Goering.

So what was the UK choice? Heritage and aristocracy of course, what else? We stayed in Nidd Hall, a nineteenth century country house turned into a luxury hotel in the Yorkshire Dales, and dined in the Gallery of Harewood House courtesy of the Earl of Harewood. In this the largest room in the house, its interior design regarded as a Robert Adams masterpiece, we had to try to concentrate on the food and speeches without being deflected by the priceless works of art, with Rubens, Reynolds, Gainsborough lining the walls all around us and the magnificent Adams ceiling above. All this as well as a tour of the magnificent house designed by John Carr for Edwin Lascelles, the

First Baron Harewood in 1759, and set in the glorious landscape of Capability Brown. We don't do these things by halves, we British.

Some people might see all this as a long ride on a gravy train. In fact it was no different to the hospitality afforded to visiting heads of state, politicians, religious leaders, business directors and so on for bilateral, trilateral, multilateral discussions and conferences at all levels of government and the business community. It was, like all hospitality, the done thing. It is therefore only a question of degree. From the viewpoint of these post-2008 days after the global financial crisis and the long period of austerity that has followed, it could well be seen as extravagant, and may have become the subject of more stringent financial constraints and been scaled back since my days.

However it is difficult to criticise those whose culture demands it. Like the Greeks. On a visit I made with Marlene, who was accompanying me as my partner to Crete at the behest of Greek Customs, I was treated like a VIP. I was taken to every Customs office on the island to meet all the Customs staff and boarded their only cutter, after which a grand lunch was to be held in my honour attended by all those I had met. The extraordinary thing was that I was asked where I would like to have this lunch. I thought that the restaurant Marlene and I had seen on a stroll that morning overlooking the harbour was ideal. Mine host paused briefly then ordered his officers to arrange it. We strolled down to the port in animated conversation and when we arrived mine host asked us whether we would like to eat outside or inside. Marlene, whom I call 'Her Outdoors' for her love of the open air, opted for the tables on the jetty right beside the yachts moored in the beautiful marina. Mine host paused for a split second then nodded and sent an officer in to arrange it.

During the meal, after I had given a speech of thanks which went down well as did the copious quantities of Greek wine, it began to rain. We all quickly decamped and went into the restaurant where a large table was already set for us to finish our delightful meal. The extraordinary thing was that the lunch for over twenty people had originally been arranged in my hotel. The booking had been made, a large table had been set and enough kitchen staff were on hand to prepare our lunch. By asking us where we wanted to eat, all that had to be unscrambled. And, as I realised later, the same thing had happened in the port restaurant where we had been expected to eat inside. But Greek hospitality meant that whatever we, the guests wanted, we got

I found out at the end of our visit that the intention was to persuade me, as chairman of MAG 92, to assist them in convincing the European Commission to site the EU training centre on the island, a totally unrealistic ambition given its location on the outer reaches of the Community. My thoughts about Greek hospitality were thus tempered, although I could have been quite wrong. My main thought was that as hospitable as we British are we would certainly not have asked any guest, however distinguished, where they wanted to eat.

My Caribbean involvement was about the most interesting and productive. CCLEC consisted of all the main Caribbean nation islands plus the US, France and the UK. The meetings were held in places like St Lucia, Martinique, Barbados, Trinidad and Tobago, Bermuda, Jamaica and Miami, but we managed somehow to concentrate on the work at hand at least. During my time on the committee we had two seminal lectures, one from representatives of the US-owned Royal Caribbean Cruise Line and the other from the US Central Intelligence Agency, situated in North Carolina, from where they conducted their surveillance operations over the whole of the Caribbean. The intelligence agents showed us examples of the aerial photos they had taken of all the flights that crossed the region between South America and the US. They had uncovered a large number of unauthorised flights and went on to uncover a huge illegal operation involving the dropping of thirty-kilo waterproof sacks of cocaine into the Caribbean Sea at prearranged coordinates, to be picked up by ships and transported to the US and Europe. The intelligence was invaluable and we were able to set up channels of communication to all the relevant agencies.

The cruise managers had more mundane information to impart but it was important for all that. They explained that at every stop on one of their Caribbean cruises – and they seemed to call in everywhere – a large number of documents covering passenger lists, stores, crew details, medical records, health checks and manifests of any cargo being carried had to be presented to Customs on arrival and departure. They did this for every port on every island and on the US and South American mainlands, with an individual set for every national port of call. It was presented in a most persuasive way. The number of documents they had to load on board at the port of embarkation before each cruise was in the thousands. To bring this home to the representatives of all the customs services in the region listening intently to their very professional presentation, they displayed a picture of a box or crate the same size as the room we were sitting in, which was needed to contain all the required documents. You can imagine how this resonated with the Single Market man. But it also had the desired effect on the others. This single session led to the eventual simplification of Customs procedures for all Caribbean cruise lines, at a considerable saving in time and cost. When I left CCLEC at the end of my term, guess who took my place to the annoyance of another couple of hopefuls? My old oppo Terrence Dennis Byrne. He went on, not too surprisingly given his ability and outstanding service, to become a Commissioner of Customs and Excise; and then, this time quite surprisingly at least to me, the number two in the Department and recipient of the Companion in the Most Honourable Order of the Bath.

Another highlight was visiting Hong Kong just before it was handed back to China, where we were addressed most impressively at our final dinner by Chris Patten, the last Governor of the Crown Colony. During the visit we were also treated to a splendid banquet, all eight courses of it, just over the border in Schenzen, the Chinese trading equivalent of Hong Kong. The Chinese view of hospitality was unique and was heavily influenced by the two principal concepts of *guangue* and *xinzen*. *Guangue* means getting to know who you are dealing with, leading to *xinzen*, trust in those people or organisations. It is said that this powerful combination of familiarity and trust has contributed substantially to the success of the Chinese economy and their international relations over the years. I learned some time later that during our luxurious lunch, provided by our generous Customs hosts, three convicted criminals were shot in the back of the head in a public execution in the main square. It was another example, rather more alarming, of their different culture.

It was a fascinating period with so many highlights. Of course *the* highlight was my marriage to Marlene in 1994.

The World is My Oyster

DURING 1996, THE MAJOR Government introduced a number of cost-saving measures in the public sector which, for our Department, resulted in a requirement to shed a large number of jobs. This was to be on a voluntary basis with full compensation meaning that those who elected to go would receive their full pension as though they had retired at the mandatory age of 60. After careful thought I took advantage of this offer to go early at the tender age of fifty-eight. Unsurprisingly there was a rush for the door and the Department lost many of its most talented officials, only to have to recruit again three years later with the change of government under Tony Blair.

Shortly after my early retirement in July 1996, I was approached by my former Investigation Division colleague Roy Brisley, who was then working for Crown Agents, to see if I was interested in taking over as the Head of Customs in Mozambique. It would mean taking an intensive crash course in Portuguese, as Mozambique was a former Portuguese colony, and exposing myself to a number of high risks from all the infectious diseases Africa was famous for, from cholera to malaria, not to mention the violent criminal activity of smugglers, carjackers, burglars, bag and everything else snatchers in one of the world's poorest countries. I would have to live in a secure gated compound with an integral garage for extra safety. All this made the decision easy. I accepted the challenge! However that is an entirely different story which will have to await my next book, entitled *The Wonderful World of Retirement*.

24

The End of an Era

APPARENTLY AFTER I LEFT the Investigation Division in 1985 I wasn't missed at all. Over the next ten years, while I was enjoying myself in the other world, the ID went from strength to strength in the size and seriousness of the cases and the huge surge in staffing levels. The first big changes came with the appointment of Richard Lawrence as CIO from his Deputy Collector post in London North and West. Richard, or Dick as he was more familiarly known, devoted a lot of time and energy to his first major objective, which was to get the new computer system, CEDRIC, fully operational. Commendably he achieved this in his first year. The system allowed the Collection Investigation Units and the police access to ID data, a significant improvement in the information exchanges so vital to detection work and the direction of operations. Dick was convinced that the key to successful investigation work was intelligence. He was able to create a separate deputy post within the Division with the sole responsibility of processing intelligence across all the areas for which it was responsible and passing it to the operational teams. Intelligence became so important that it became a separate division ten years later.

Contributing to intelligence-led investigations was the role of the drugs liaison officer (DLO), the name for a customs investigator based abroad in a country significant in either drug production or trafficking. Peter Cutting had appointed the first in Pakistan in the early 1980s. His success convinced Dick Lawrence to build on the initiative by appointing, during his now fixed five-year term, a further ten around the world, including India, Peru, Venezuela, Jamaica, Portugal, Cyprus and North America. They soon proved their worth. By the year 2000 the number of DLOs had reached fifty, a major achievement given the many difficulties which had to be overcome. At the time Dick was attempting to increase the number of drugs liaison officers there was a general freeze on departmental numbers imposed by the cost-cutting Thatcher Government, and it was only with the support of the Economic Secretary at a meeting with Mrs Thatcher that permission was given to increase ID staffing by 100 to provide back-up to the officers in the field.

Thanks to a decision to strengthen the already good relationship with the security services, particular with GCHQ, the Special Intelligence Service, or MI6, began training DLOs in counter-surveillance, and much closer cooperation generally placed the ID in a stronger position to combat the ever-increasing drug threat. However, at the same time the dispute over responsibility for drug investigation between the police and Customs resurfaced to threaten these enhanced capabilities. It was the familiar argument that police had the responsibility for dealing with all crime, and drug smuggling was crime. With laudable determination and acumen Dick held out against this pressure, especially when assailed at his first ACPO conference, and later he had the high-level support of David Mellor, then a young Home Office minister, who set up a ministerial drugs group to look at the question. This led to a clear definition of the respective roles of the two services, which allowed Customs to continue in the lead to deal with smuggled drugs. But the problem never went away and provided much unnecessary stress for the officers operating in the field.

For some years there had also been growing concerns about gold fraud. Opportunity was provided by the two different VAT treatments of gold: bullion was taxed at fifteen per cent but coins were tax-free. Margaret Thatcher and others were opposed to taxing money, hence the anomaly, which was easily exploited by melting down gold coins, providing the market with tax-free bullion. Fraudsters also used a variety of methods to avoid all taxes and detection by simply disappearing, a longstanding method known as missing trader fraud. The problem became such a threat to the Exchequer that Mrs Thatcher eventually agreed to an emergency Order in Council which taxed gold coin.

In the eventful year of 1985, the Division carried out a major operation into gold fraud, code-named Fiddler, which eventually led to the arrest and prosecution of eight men for tax evasion of £5 million on three-and-three-quarter tonnes of gold valued at £30 million, resulting in a total of thirty-one years' imprisonment. Thanks to the change in legislation, the gold frauds then faded away. Again in 1985, the Division's developing expertise in computer fraud led to the discovery of the early stages of a major tax fraud in Operation Patchwork. Eighty officers raided twelve companies and found in their computer accounts, a 'patch' which suppressed part of the records of the companies involved. A substantial loss of revenue was essentially nipped in the bud.

Further developments encouraged by Dick Lawrence were the increased involvement and openness in publicity, the problem I had confronted in a more devious way, and a proper role for Customs in new asset confiscation legislation, including money laundering. The role of the Department in this provoked much discussion and the then-chairman, Angus Fraser, needed to be convinced that we should be involved as the work was not strictly the responsibility of HMCE. But the argument that 'targeting the money' was an integral part of an investigation won the day and a new branch of some eighty staff was created to deal with it.

Internal concealments became the latest smuggling method. The amount of drugs these 'stuffers and swallowers', as they were known, could smuggle into the country in rectal, vaginal and gastric conceal-ments was almost unbelievable. The South Americans preferred to swallow small latex balls of cocaine, the largest number ever discovered being an incredible 738. In 1985, eighty-four passengers out of 180 intercepted were found to have internal concealments. Special facilities had to be provided at Heathrow to await the 'arrival' of the contents of stomachs, which could sometimes take days. Smuggling in this manner was an exceedingly dangerous game.

Amphetamine was now the popular drug of choice, with a forty-two per cent increase in seizures in 1985 alone. But cocaine remained the biggest impending threat and in 1987, 358 kilos were seized, including the largest single consignment detected up until then, worth £50 million and hidden in a container ship from Colombia. The next two years saw even more shocking seizure figures: forty-four tonnes of cannabis in 1988 and 50.7 tonnes the year after, including the seizure of ten vessels carrying a total of almost 25,000 kilos of drugs. All of this work resulted in increasing staffing levels in the ID during Lawrence's tenure, with investigator numbers rising from 560 to over 900 and an eventual move, completed in 1993, to occupy the whole of the Custom House on Quayside, London, which was a substantial improvement in accommodation and desperately needed.

When Dick departed in 1989 to become Deputy Director Outfield, the Board decided that the CIO post no longer needed to be filled by a current or former investigator. The Division had grown to such an extent that the Chief needed, above all, to be someone who could manage a large organisation; someone with good inter-personal and presentational skills as well as a clear idea of the future direction of a large, powerful enforcement agency. I believe these were qualities that Dick Lawrence had, and more, but the five-year rule for the incumbency of a CIO, introduced in 1984, took precedence. Step forward Douglas Tweddle, who was appointed CIO for the next five-year term.

A Civil Service fast-streamer, Doug had overseen policy in HQ and had considerable experience in all Customs procedures and computer-based systems. I was pleased to hear of his appointment, given the enormous encouragement, guidance and assistance he had given me in developing the Fast Lane clearance system in preparation for the Single Market. Despite some misgivings in some quarters – the loss of promotion opportunities for certain people being one – I felt he was the right man for the job. And so he proved. He was a good listener. With any decisions he had to take, or presentations to the Board or the media which required specialist investigation knowledge, he would always seek the advice of his senior management team or front-line officers. Under his stewardship, the ID continued to achieve the impressive successes of his predecessor.

One big case followed another. In the drugs field, ambitious targets were set, something we had not done in my time, and they were exceeded again and again. The seizures increased in size beyond anything we had secured in the 1970s. In one year alone, 908 kilos of cocaine and 280 kilos of Ecstasy were seized, and sixty-five drug gangs and their 3,248 members were brought to book. In 1993 over forty per cent of ID staff were working on drugs and that year saw the seizure of one tonne of 'designer' narcotics, worth over £130 million. The total of all drugs seized that year was said to be worth an incredible £519 million at street prices. During my time in the ID, in 1972, there were 579 seizures and 411 arrests; in 1992 there were 8,800 seizures and 2,568 arrests.

As an indication of how seriously the drug threat was being taken, the UN declared the years 1991 to 2000 to be the 'decade against drug use'. The EU backed this call for action by setting up the European Committee to Combat Drugs. The drugs threat was regarded so seriously that a World Ministerial Drugs Summit was held in London in 1991, during which Doug Tweddle addressed the conference. He stressed the need to arrest, convict and punish drugs traffickers to act as the best deterrent to discourage the illegal supply of drugs. These actions could only be achieved, he said, by inter-agency and international cooperation, especially in the sharing of intelligence and controlled deliveries across national borders.

These were not just hollow words for media and public consumption. The anti-drugs work was stepped up a gear – several gears, actually – and by 1993 the number of investigators in the ID had hit the 1,000 mark. But this remarkable increase in drugs work was not due to increased staffing levels, although that helped to find and bring the perpetrators to book. The driving force was the substantial increase in drug use, mainly among the younger generation, and the efforts that the criminal fraternity put into servicing demand. The other major contributor was improved intelligence and analysis. Cooperation at both national and international level took off, via the Customs Cooperation Council, Interpol, the new National Criminal Intelligence Service (successor to the National Drugs Intelligence Unit), and the signing of more and more memoranda of understanding between foreign enforcement agencies. NCIS was set up to deal with serious crime and major criminals. While it covered all serious crime, with the exception of terrorism – murder, kidnapping, abduction, extortion, blackmail, serious sexual offences, robbery, burglary, organised fraud, counterfeiting and drug trafficking – drugs accounted for seventy per cent of all intelligence gathered. So it was not surprising that, with the level of intelligence handled by Customs from a variety of sources especially the network of DLOs around the world, one of our assistant chiefs was appointed to head its drugs branch All departmental intelligence work was co-ordinated through the newly established Intelligence Committee. And the passing of the Criminal Justice Act obliged banks and financial institutions to advise the NCIS of suspicious financial transactions.

However, it wasn't just drugs cases that were burgeoning. VAT frauds of all types were being uncovered and dealt with. These included suppression of transactions, false documents, false repayments, false exports, missing traders, contrived liquidations and straight smuggling. The amounts of evasion were usually in the millions of pounds, with the involvement of hundreds of companies and dozens of arrests. Gold, garments, gaming machines, jewellery, precious metals, construction – almost no trade was unaffected. Again the targets set under the new system were being exceeded regularly. There was also my familiar subject, CAP fraud in Northern Ireland, involving maize and also what became known as 'carousel' frauds, with the same cattle criss-crossing the land boundary to either evade EU payments or pick up repayments.

Throughout his spell as CIO, Doug Tweddle had the unenviable task of overseeing, sometimes on an almost daily basis, the Matrix Churchill, Euromac and Iraqi Supergun cases, which began shortly after he took over. I don't intend to dwell further on this affair, save to say that I'm sure it didn't have the detrimental effect on Doug that it had on me. At least he was not the subject of personal attacks in the media and by Lord Justice Scott, as I was during a period I never want to relive. Fortunately there was no personal criticism of Doug in the final Scott Report and it took nothing away from his successful term in office. He left the ID in 1994 to become the Collector London Airports. Later I was very pleased to have a small role to play with my international contacts in helping to secure his appointment as Director Technique in the World Customs Organisation, for which he was ideally suited.

It was then that the Board reverted to appointing a former investigator, namely Richard Edward Kellaway, as the next Chief. Why the reversal so soon after only one very successful term under the new policy? In my opinion, it was simply because he was the ideal man for the job. The policy certainly wasn't abandoned, as we shall see, with questionable consequences. Richard, or Dick as he preferred to be called, got off to a flying start – perhaps more sailing than flying – with the Investigation

Division's takeover of the Marine Branch, putting it in charge of the Customs cutter fleet, a major beneficial change. It had been a long time in coming; we had felt as long ago as the mid-70s, when we used the cutters to such advantage in the *Cornish Lady* job, that the ID's control of the fleet was essential if we were to tackle smuggling seriously, instead of using the ships for 'ceremonial' visits around the country (a bit of an exaggeration, since the vessels had been involved in many successful cases). The much closer working relationship with the ID was most welcome and of immediate benefit. The fleet was deployed in areas of highest risk and had the advantage of all the intelligence sources available to the much larger organisation. By the end of Dick's first year, the fleet had assisted in eight major drug seizures involving 10,910 kilos of cannabis, 375 kilos of cocaine and forty kilos of amphetamine.

The cutters were invaluable in intercepting small vessels, including inflatables, attempting to land drugs in locations like little-used ports, coves and beaches. In one interception in Plymouth, three tons of cannabis were seized from the vessel *Tinker Die* in a throwback to the 'good old days' of the riding officers – without the fatalities. Well, not quite. Tragically one officer, Alastair Souter, was killed in 1996 when he became trapped between the revenue cutter and one of a drugs gang's vessels, *Ocean Jubilee*, which had been transferring three tons of cannabis to shore and which the crew had set on fire when they realised they had been caught. Eight men were arrested and received a total of 126 years' imprisonment.

Our financial investigators continued to be highly successful in obtaining substantial confiscation orders in the tens of millions of pounds, hitting the traffickers where it hurt most – their pockets – and then hitting them again with the read-across to actual smuggling cases leading to long prison terms. VAT frauds continued apace across the board. Investigation became tougher, however, with new disclosure legislation, under which it became mandatory in all court cases for the prosecution to provide the defence with all the documentary evidence at their disposal, including unused material. Defence lawyers became adept in using this to complicate otherwise straightforward cases. Investigations and prosecutions became much more complex and demanding. This led to delays, higher costs and a significant drop in convictions, especially with the increasingly sophisticated type of frauds being perpetrated: carousel, multi-cell, contrived liquidations ('phoenix' frauds), international repayment frauds and so on. Despite this, or perhaps because of it, compounded settlements in place of prosecution – whereby the suspect settled out of court, as the young Richard Branson had – yielded significant results, including a staggering £33 million in one case. Again intelligence, through the VAT Intelligence and Research Team and the Customs Intelligence Team, played a vital role in unearthing a variety of frauds from misdescription, under-declaration, diversions of declared tax-free exportations to the home market, CAP frauds, export refunds, and the smuggling of arms and nuclear material. This led to the separation of investigation and intelligence duties with the establishment in 1995 of a separate National Intelligence Division (NID), headed by Brian Banks with the same rank as the Chief. The NID had responsibility for strategic intelligence while the NIS retained the operational and secret intelligence.

Before the Single Market changes came into force in 1993, I discussed the agreement we had just reached on the treatment of excise dutiable goods from the EU with my local publican. He was in no doubt that, with the difference in duty rates between the UK and France and many other European countries, it would lead to a huge influx of cheap alcohol and tobacco from across the Channel, which in turn would have a significant impact on his industry. I questioned his judgement and tried to reassure him, but he was having none of it. And so it came to pass. No sooner had the new rules come into force, limiting excise dutiable goods to amounts for personal use only and exacerbated by the opening of the Channel Tunnel in 1994, than a whole new group of traders, or more accurately bootleggers, could not resist such a ripe target and jumped on the bandwagon – or rather, filled their wagons, mainly white vans, with the cheaper baccy and booze and flooded the UK market. My publican friend proved right. This was another headache for Dover Customs and Dick Kellaway's excise duty teams to deal with, but they faced up to the challenge. Officers quickly got wise to fanciful stories: *Twelve dozen bottles of spirits, twenty dozen cans of beer and twenty dozen bottles of wine? In a white van? For your own use?*

'For a family wedding.'

'Okay, park over there and we'll see about that.'

The van detained, checks carried out by the local excise officer, and lo and behold, a man very well known to the off-licence trade in his area. Game, set and match! Such 'profiling' became more and more important and not just for excise duties of course. A young woman on her own in a hire car over in Amsterdam for two nights? Stop, search, twenty kilos of cannabis in the spare wheel compartment. Too easy.

The year 1996 saw the first of a number of big changes which were to take place in the coming years. The ID and the Collection Investigation Units spread around the country were combined to form the National Investigation Service (NIS), the end of the ID as we knew it. Many had misgivings about the change but the figures began to speak for themselves, with £495 million in VAT evasion uncovered in one year, £34 million in one case alone. Frauds of mind-boggling complexity and value were regularly uncovered, while drug quantities of previous unthinkable proportions were routinely seized. Indeed the list seemed almost endless, with targets regularly surpassed year-on-year even when they had been increased to take account of the previous years' figures. The biggest cases detected and intercepted were often abroad since intelligence was now being shared with enforcement agencies around the globe. For example: five tonnes of cocaine located on a sea-going vessel in the Caribbean and sent to the US for investigation and prosecution; and a three-year multi-national investigation resulting in a seizure of twenty-five tonnes of cocaine and the arrest of forty-three people who had already shipped sixty-eight tonnes of cocaine to Europe and the USA.

At an early stage, Dick Kellaway had realised that the way forward lay in partnership and cooperation with others outside the Department. Consequently he built upon the good work of his predecessors and also opened up other areas of cooperation and joint working. He expanded significantly the DLO network and appointed fiscal liaison officers (FLOs) in the important EU countries. He also developed a policy of secondments to important partner organisations. At the end of his tenure, the NIS had staff seconded to SIS, MI5, GCHQ, Interpol and NCIS and colleagues at ACIO level in key posts in Europol, FCO (Drugs and International Crime Directorate), Home Office, CDCU (Central Drugs Coordination Unit – the so-called Drugs Tsar), CCLEC, and a DCIO seconded to NCIS to manage its overseas liaison officers. Relations with the police were never easy but there was good cooperation at the higher levels and joint working on the drugs side was greatly improved by an operational protocol which he and Terry Byrne, as the Departmental head of drugs policy, negotiated with the Regional Crime Squads and the Metropolitan Police.

There were also significant developments within the NIS itself. A section of analysts was formed to assist investigators not only in specific cases but also to identify trends. A forensic team was formed with the ability to recover data from computers and other devices found during investigations. A financial investigation branch was created which in 1998 put before the courts Britain's first stand-alone money laundering case. The defendants were accused of laundering the proceeds of drugs trafficking by other unknown persons, in the absence of any prosecutions for substantive trafficking offences. In this case, cash totalling £3 million was seized and the main defendant was sentenced to fourteen years. The telephone intercept ability was greatly increased when an independent NIS suite was set up, and a team of undercover officers successfully infiltrated many criminal organisations.

On the personnel side the number of female investigators was significantly increased during Dick's time as CIO, and the NIS achieved accreditation under the Investors In People scheme, much to the shock of the Chairman, Valerie Strachan, who was once heard to say that if the NIS achieved this accreditation she would eat her hat. She never did! The NIS also achieved accreditation for the award of national vocational qualifications (NVQs) in investigation, security, management and business administration. This enabled members of staff to achieve a qualification which they could take with them on leaving the NIS.

Naturally not all the cases investigated ran smoothly or were a resounding success. Dick did not have to endure the major preoccupation Doug Tweddle did with his bête noire, Matrix Churchill and the Scott Inquiry because, although a major excise fraud, namely London City Bond, was successfully uncovered and progressed throughout his period in charge, it was only after he left that the cases began to unravel. When I joined the service in the 1960s, excise duties were so tightly controlled that even the distillers, brewers and warehouse keepers had difficulty in getting their hands on the stuff before the duty was paid, sometimes after years maturing in bonded warehouses. Any unexplained losses were made good by heavy charges and penalties. This was relaxed in the 1980s, when the warehouse keepers were given control of movements under bond, using documents instead of handcuffs, with checks carried out to ensure that there were no illegal diversions. This worked well with close monitoring by excise officers. In the 1990s, however, with the introduction of the Single Market, this new system was extended for movements within the EU. For example, spirits being moved from a bonded warehouse in the UK to one in Germany only required an accompanying administrative document (AAD), which was sent back once the goods had arrived in the destination warehouse. The problem with this system was that the receipted document could be returned up to six months after the movement, and so it relied on audit checks involving two or more national authorities a long time after the movement had taken place. It proved wide open to fraud. Consignments often never left the country. Fake stamps were applied to the AADs and the goods diverted to the home market, free of duty.

The NIS set up EXCIRT (Excise and Customs Intelligence and Research) to deal with the possibility of wrongdoing and very quickly uncovered the fraud in a warehouse called London City Bond. The problem was then how to deal with it. Large sums of excise duties were being lost and any long-term surveillance operation would be very costly to the Exchequer. However it was considered that hitting it on the head immediately would only provide enough evidence to charge the minor players in the fraud and allow the main organisers to get off scot-free. A major operation was therefore set up with the aid of an informant on the inside in the Bond. He was known as a 'participating informant', an extremely useful tool to uncover all types of frauds as well as drug smuggling. The danger with the use of these 'insiders' was the risk that they could be drawn into the crime and end up instigating or at the very least encouraging and facilitating the frauds. This would be seen as acting as an agent provocateur, thereby allowing defence lawyers to claim that their clients were being enticed and manipulated and would not have dreamt of committing such illegal acts without the encouragement and control of these dreadful people.

The operation went well, resulting in arrests and court cases involving a large number of hauliers and truck drivers, although in the event there was no actual overall mastermind. Substantial penalties were imposed in a succession of court cases, until one operation was taken to task by defence lawyers, who accused the Department of abuse of process. The very defence about participating informants was used to considerable effect, not just in this case but eventually in all the cases brought to court by the NIS. This resulted in convictions being reversed on appeal, some being withdrawn when the prosecution offered no evidence and others being simply dropped. This occurred in respect of the first cases in 1995 right up to the last in 2002. It led to an inquiry by Mr Justice Butterfield into current practices and procedures relating to disclosure, investigative techniques and case management in HM Customs and Excise criminal cases – and a lot of harmful publicity.

In July 2003, Butterfield's report found no evidence of entrapment or incitement by either investigators or employees of London City Bond. However, he found that there had been serious deficiencies in the way in which the investigations had been carried out, including poor strategic planning, frequent changes of personnel, excessive secrecy on a need-to-know basis, inadequate handling of informants and failure to comply with disclosure obligations. Crucially though he found no lack of integrity on the part of investigating officers and the Department had already put in hand the necessary changes he had identified. He recommended that prosecutions should be taken away from our Solicitor's Office and handled by a separate prosecution authority. On the other side, Butterfield felt that the then system of disclosure was unsatisfactory, with excessive attacks by defences on process. He recommended that judges be given greater powers to control proceedings. From a departmental standpoint, these unfortunate outcomes represented a very small fraction of the otherwise excellent work of the NIS, despite their disproportionate negative impact.

When Dick Kellaway left his post in October 1999 to become the Director General of the Commonwealth War Graves Commission, NIS staff numbers had reached 1,813. The last three CIOs had had a number of qualities in common. They were all dedicated, highly competent and personable. They all presided over major expansions in the role and activities of their organisation. It is not surprising therefore that the astonishing speed of the changes and the increasing size of the service under their control meant that it was virtually impossible to keep as tight a grip on all investigations as they may have liked. But it was that very freedom for innovation, intelligent detective work, personal initiative and fearlessness that was the hallmark of the Customs and Excise investigation service and contributed so much to its success. As Doug Tweddle told me: 'It is certainly true that the ID had a remarkable period of success from the late Eighties to the late Nineties. The bulk of the credit, however, should go to the staff who achieved this, particularly the SIOs, who were crucial in delivering results and in taking the organisation forward.' However, it was the end of an era.

I WAS FORTUNATE. I joined the Investigation Branch in late 1968, was at its heart when it became a Division in 1973, and left in 1985. It has often been said that those years and those which followed towards the turn of the century were the halcyon days of the service. During that time its level of professionalism increased to the very highest standards without losing the imperative of integrity as the organisation expanded to cope with the explosion of criminal and fraudulent activities in all fields, especially drugs. It became a world-class organisation respected by other law enforcement agencies in this country and around the world, not to mention by the wider population.

I was also fortunate in that, while I was engaged in combating European Union fraud, Margaret Thatcher signed the Single European Act and I was chosen to assess its effect on the Department, opening up whole avenues of enquiry and a new role as a negotiator. And throughout all of these stimulating and challenging activities and events, I was encouraged, supported, assisted, advised, indeed guided by some exceptional colleagues, most of whom have become life-long friends. I could not have wished for anything more.

I don't feel knowledgeable enough to make informed comments on the huge changes that have taken place since my retirement, but I have a view based on the knowledge I have acquired over the years. I can say that I was disappointed when it was eventually decided to amalgamate HM Customs and Excise with the Inland Revenue in 2005, a merger resisted for many years in my time by successive chairmen. I could see the logic, given the degree of overlapping and the amount of common information held by each department, constrained so often by a cumbersome system of co-operation for exchanges of information and investigations. But to lose that strong sense of identity, that unique culture developed over so many years by Customs and Excise was a greater loss than the gains achieved. Worse still, the opprobrium the larger department has attracted tarnishes the incredible work that so many branches of it do so well. We may not have been the most popular organisation in the country in my day but we did not attract the criticism for delays and excessive bureaucracy that Revenue and Customs does today; and we never lost those most treasured of reputational qualities: integrity and efficiency.

I have spoken to a number of former colleagues in investigation who moved to the new organisations. Almost all said that morale was low and that the changes were very much regretted. When the Investigation Division became the National Investigation Service (NIS) in 1996, merging the ID and the individual Collection Investigation Units (CIUs) as well as creating a separate National Customs Intelligence Service, the numbers reached over 2,000. The decision to separate intelligence from frontline enforcement has been described by many of my interlocutors as a complete and utter failure. It was said to have gobbled up money and achieved precisely nothing. It was alleged to have been done because the ID was getting too powerful.

Our methods had become more sophisticated during the 1990s, with the great increase in the number of drugs liaison officers and in the use of participating informants. Unfortunately a number of officers strayed from the strict agent provocateur rule. While they were allowed to take part and assist in smuggling operations and encouraged to do so – one of the reasons for their existence – they were expressly forbidden from setting up operations themselves to suck in their vulnerable drug-smuggling buddies so that they could be easily caught. This was at the heart of the series of scandals that occurred towards the end of the 1990s. This report in The *Guardian* on 2 November 2002, under the heading 'CUSTOMS LOSE CONTROL' , told a chilling story:

The End of an Era

A customs officer killed himself because he feared he was going to be made the fall guy by police for important heroin cases that went wrong, The *Guardian* has discovered. Amjad Bashir, 37, was found hanged by his wife, Farida, in the garage of his Middlesbrough home in April. His family say he was a 'lowly officer' who killed himself over an inquiry into a drugs operation later called into question.

Customs and Excise – whose elite enforcement arm, the National Investigation Service, is facing two major police inquiries, disclosed by the *Guardian* yesterday – has been battered by the collapse of prosecutions and a series of damning government reports into its competence.

Defence lawyers have described the agency as 'out of control'. NIS tactics have been criticised by judges, who are steadily quashing convictions or ordering retrials – sometimes even where defendants had been persuaded to plead guilty. One in 10 NIS staff in Leeds is currently suspended. A four-year police investigation, Operation Brandfield, into drug smuggling cases is due to report to the crown prosecution service at the end of the year. But a second inquiry, by Scotland Yard, into customs' questionable tactics against the black market in untaxed spirits, has only just begun.

These are massive blows to an organisation that traded on a 'whiter-than-white' image during headline-grabbing tales of police corruption in the 1970s and 1980s...Under strict guidelines, customs are only allowed to facilitate the completion of an existing plot. Neither customs, nor an informant, 'should counsel, incite or procure the commission of a crime'. Most importantly, he must on no account act as an agent provocateur.

However, after an earlier drugs case had collapsed, Mr Justice Foley had commented presciently that the NIS had 'a culture, a climate, of carelessness and recklessness - a catalogue of flawed procedures, misleading requests, illegalities and incompetence'.

Paul Evans, a former MI6 head of station in Vienna, was brought in from outside in 1999 to make reforms. Another outsider, merchant banker Richard Broadbent, replaced the retiring customs chairwoman, Valerie Strachan. But cases continue to unravel.

The Serious Organised Crime Agency (SOCA) was formed in 2005 when the now amalgamated department HM Revenue and Customs (HMRC) lost its drugs remit. In the words of an ex-investigator: 'a sad day!' The UK Border Force was then formed in 2008. In the ensuing years, from a number of reports in newspapers and conversations I have had with former colleagues, it became apparent that SOCA was failing. It was said that Customs border staff were frustrated and demoralized by the lack of useful service from SOCA and that there was severe disenchantment among staff. Hundreds of officers were said to want to be transferred back to their former organisations. An unpublished internal MORI survey showed that less than five per cent were satisfied with the way that SOCA was being run. My erstwhile colleague and press combatant, David Raynes, became a member of the international taskforce on strategic drug policy and is quoted as saying: 'The UK is awash with heroin, mainly from Turkish traffickers, yet there has been a drop in effectiveness from when Customs were the lead agency. The whole drugs strategy has been dysfunctional. Smuggling drugs into Britain in 2007 is easier than at any time in 30 years.'

Even the first head of SOCA, Sir Stephen Lander, admitted that while it was a good concept, implementation had been flawed. This was said to be mainly because the Home Office accepted undemanding performance targets. The agency was riven with personnel, pay and budget issues and obsessed with a few, well-known, mainly UK-based key criminals – regardless of whether they were currently supplying the market with drugs. Customs consequently struggled to put together investigation teams from local inadequately resourced, inexperienced and ill-equipped police forces to deal with major traffickers. Sir Stephen Lander again: 'There are some things we did not get right organisationally at the start. We might have had a slightly difficult transfer of people. It was initially bumpy back in 2005. SOCA has a very clear vision – it's just that it isn't shared by absolutely everyone outside the agency. If you start with four different agencies and 360 different IT systems and 37 pay ranges and 60 buildings, many in the wrong place, you have some housekeeping to sort out.'

As drug investigators transferred across to join SOCA, total seizures fell in 2005–06. Between 2003–04 and 2005–06, cocaine seizures dropped from 20,727kg to 5,798kg and cannabis from 57,617kg to 41,611kg.

The End of an Era

The parallel fall in heroin seizures, from 1,626kg to 1,057kg, went against a wider trend, because Afghanistan raised opium production and seizures rose elsewhere in Europe. In 2013 the then-head of SOCA, Sir Ian Andrews, resigned after he admitted failing to declare his directorship in a management consultancy company. The Home Office and SOCA denied that his departure was related to an ongoing controversy over the agency's probe into private investigators. The allegations were that the agency had suppressed a report into the illegal activities of private investigators, the so-called 'blue-chip hacking' list linked to Operation Millipede, a SOCA-led investigation into private investigators acquiring information illegally. The string of failures in the organisation and this latest controversy led to yet another seismic change as the agency was wound up and replaced by the National Crime Agency that year.

IT IS PERFECTLY NATURAL to dislike change. None of us likes to lose the familiar, especially if it is something we love and respect and then have to work out how we do something different. But it is good if the change proves to be for the better. There have been and will continue to be some outstanding successes in the new organisations, the effective actions taken against the notorious Slab Murphy being just one example. And I must not forget the seismic change in the reorganisation of the IB brought about by Douglas Jordan as well as the Single Market changes which were so beneficial for me and for the Department.

Fortunately, the profound changes to the main organisations of which I was a part happened after I left, and looking at them now I know that it is not my world. I recognise, however, that nostalgia has always played a big part in my view of and enjoyment of the world. We are all capable of wearing rose-tinted glasses when we look back at our time and the way we did things. 'It wasn't like that in our day!' Nevertheless, I hold on to the words of Lucius Cary, the Second Viscount Falkland, expressed during a parliamentary debate as long ago as 1641, but as true today as they were then:

'When it is not necessary to change, it is necessary not to change.'

Acknowledgements

I AM INDEBTED FIRST and foremost to Peter Walsh without whom this book, begun so many years ago and lying dormant for years after that, would never have been finished. He came into the picture at just the right moment during research for his own impressive tome and encouraged me to complete my own magnum opus.

I have already dedicated the book to my granddaughter Emily to whom I offer another vote of thanks for awakening me to the reality of life; that however one thinks of oneself and one's life, others, even very close ones, see you differently. They have their own ideas of who you are and what you have done, but often without the detailed knowledge to provide an all-round and balanced picture. This is so often true of one's work, especially if so much of it is confidential or secret.

A great inspiration was my Australian friend Jack Crigan and his wife, Sheilagh; Jack allowed me the privilege of editing his memoirs and encouraged me to write my own. Also in Australia, Ian Herbert painstakingly edited and formatted the draft texts.

A huge thank you goes to all those friends and colleagues who revived a fading memory with their anecdotes, comments, criticisms, corrections and humour. In particular Dave Raynes, Terry Byrne, Nick Baker, Ray MacAfee, Hughie Donagher, George Atkinson, Jim Jarvie, John Chapman, Dave Hewer, Dick Kellaway, Doug Tweddle and Dick Lawrence.

Of course I could not have gone through all of this without the incredible support of first Aurea during the hard investigation days, and then Marlene in the last period of my career.

And last but by no means least my appreciation of HM Customs and Excise. A government department that with all its shortcomings and changes over the years was an inspiration and source of energy for so many dedicated and loyal civil servants providing an outstanding service to the community.